CRAFT SCHOOL

CRAFT SCHOOL

Over 90 step-by-step craft projects

THUNDER BAY
P·R·E·S·S

First published in the United States
by Thunder Bay Press, 1997

Thunder Bay Press
5880 Oberlin Drive, Suite 400, San Diego, CA 92121

First published in 1997 by Hamlyn
an imprint of Reed International Books Limited
Michelin House, 81 Fulham Road
London, SW3 6RB
and Auckland, Melbourne, Singapore and Toronto

TEXT AND PHOTOGRAPHS
COPYRIGHT ©1994, 1995
REED INTERNATIONAL BOOKS

VOLUME COPYRIGHT ©1997
REED INTERNATIONAL BOOKS

CROSS-STITCH DESIGNS COPYRIGHT ©1994
STEVEN JENKINS

Library of Congress Cataloging-in-Publication Data
Craft school : over 90 step-by-step craft projects.
    p. cm.
    "The material in this volume is taken from the
following volumes in the Hamlyn discover craft series:
découpage, doughcraft, papier mâché, cross stitch,
patchwork, dried flowers"—T.p. verso.
    Includes index.
    ISBN 1-57145-041-6
    1. Handicraft.
TT157.C655 1997   97–169
745.5—dc21   CIP

The publishers have made every effort to ensure that all
instructions given in this book are accurate and safe, but they
cannot accept liability for any resulting injury, damage, or loss
to either person or property, whether direct or consequential
and howsoever arising. The author and publishers will be
grateful for any information which will assist them in
keeping future editions up to date.

The material in this volume is taken from the
following titles in
the Hamlyn Discover Craft Series:
Découpage, Doughcraft, Papier Mâché, Cross Stitch,
Patchwork, Dried Flowers

This volume compiled by Prima Creative Services

Produced by Mandarin Offset
Printed and Bound in China

CONTENTS

INTRODUCTION		7

DECOUPAGE MATERIALS AND TECHNIQUES

Priming and preparing different surfaces		10-11
Paper resources		12-13
Tinting and coloring prints		14
Sealing the paper		15
Choosing a color		15
Cutting paper		16
Arranging and gluing		16
Varnishing and finishing		18
Waxing		19

DECOUPAGE PROJECTS

Key fobs	EASY LEVEL	22-23
Shaker box	EASY LEVEL	24-25
Flower pot	EASY LEVEL	26-27
Gypsy style jug	EASY LEVEL	28-29
Hat and coat rack	EASY LEVEL	30-31
Child's chair	EASY LEVEL	32-33
Pencil holder	INTERMEDIATE LEVEL	34-35
Coat hangers	INTERMEDIATE LEVEL	36-37
Small hinged tin box	INTERMEDIATE LEVEL	38-39
Wall sconce	INTERMEDIATE LEVEL	40-41
Table mats	INTERMEDIATE LEVEL	42-43
Working on glass	INTERMEDIATE LEVEL	44-45
Headboard	INTERMEDIATE LEVEL	46-47
Crackle varnish box	ADVANCED LEVEL	48-49
Watering can	ADVANCED LEVEL	50-51
Enamel jug	ADVANCED LEVEL	52-53
Blanket box	ADVANCED LEVEL	54-57

DOUGHCRAFT MATERIALS AND TECHNIQUES

Making the dough	60
The basic recipe	60
The basic tools	61
Modeling by hand	62-63
Baking	64
Air-drying	65

Filling and repairing		65
Painting		66
Varnishing		67
Finishing your work		67
Preserving your work		67
Project templates		68–71

DOUGHCRAFT PROJECTS

Frowning sun	EASY LEVEL	74-75
Mother goose	EASY LEVEL	76-77
The cow jumped over the moon	EASY LEVEL	78-79
Scallop-edged bowl	EASY LEVEL	80-81
Dough-coil mirror	EASY LEVEL	82-83
Fish tile	INTERMEDIATE LEVEL	84-85
Star pot and lid	INTERMEDIATE LEVEL	86-87
Fish dish	INTERMEDIATE LEVEL	88-89
Candlesticks	INTERMEDIATE LEVEL	90-93
Metal-coil mirror	INTERMEDIATE LEVEL	94-95
Heart container	ADVANCED LEVEL	96-97
White rabbit	ADVANCED LEVEL	98-101
Moon mirror	ADVANCED LEVEL	102-103

PAPIER MACHE MATERIALS AND TECHNIQUES

Equipment	106
Making papier mâché	106
The layered method	107
The pulped method	107-108
Choosing a mold	109
Layering papier mâché onto a mold	110
Pulping papier mâché onto a mold	111
Decorating and finishing	112
Varnishing	113

PAPIER MACHE PROJECTS

Summer bowl	EASY LEVEL	116-117
Spiral plate	EASY LEVEL	118-119
Diamond earrings	EASY LEVEL	120-121
Christmas star	EASY LEVEL	122-123
Flower greeting card	EASY LEVEL	124-125

Plaid tray	EASY LEVEL	126-127
Leaf mobile	EASY LEVEL	128-129
Coil pot	INTERMEDIATE LEVEL	130-131
Large dinner plate	INTERMEDIATE LEVEL	132-133
String-layered brooch	INTERMEDIATE LEVEL	134-135
Chunky earrings	INTERMEDIATE LEVEL	136-137
African bangle	INTERMEDIATE LEVEL	138-139
Letter rack	INTERMEDIATE LEVEL	140-141
Seashell storage box	INTERMEDIATE LEVEL	142-143
Fish dish	ADVANCED LEVEL	144-147
African bead necklace	ADVANCED LEVEL	148-149
Snake fridge magnet	ADVANCED LEVEL	150-151

CROSS-STITCH MATERIALS AND TECHNIQUES

Fabrics	154
Canvas	155
Plainweaves	155
Knitted fabrics	155
Threads	156
Beading	156
Different types of stitch	158
Fixing beads	159
Starting and finishing	159
Sizes	159
Hoops and frames	160
Preparing fabric	160
Using threads	160
Finishing	161
Using a flexi-hoop	161
Lacing and framing	161
Making up cushions	162
Using the charts	163
Displaying your work	163

CROSS-STITCH PROJECTS

Numbers and letters samplers	EASY LEVEL	166-169
Tile cushion	EASY LEVEL	170-171
Starry throw	EASY LEVEL	172-173
Key ring fobs	EASY LEVEL	174-175
Child's wristbands	EASY LEVEL	176-177

Cactus bag	EASY LEVEL	178-179
Baby's towel	EASY LEVEL	180-181
Ethnic frame	INTERMEDIATE LEVEL	182-183
Kitchen sampler	INTERMEDIATE LEVEL	184-185
Fruit bowl picture	INTERMEDIATE LEVEL	186-187
Playing card cushion	INTERMEDIATE LEVEL	188-189
Tea cozy	INTERMEDIATE LEVEL	190-191
Oven glove	INTERMEDIATE LEVEL	192-193
Wedding and birth cards	INTERMEDIATE LEVEL	194-195
Festival sampler	ADVANCED LEVEL	196-197
Sun and moon clock	ADVANCED LEVEL	198-199
Fair Isle billfold	ADVANCED LEVEL	200-201
Dinosaur T-shirt	ADVANCED LEVEL	202-203
Alphabet examples	EXTRAS	204-205
DMC/Anchor conversion chart		206-207

PATCHWORK MATERIALS AND TECHNIQUES

Buying patchwork fabric	210
Using your sewing machine	211
Using a rotary cutter	212-213
Machine patchwork with R.I.T. squares	214-215
Foundation piecing	216-217
Crazy patchwork	216
Quilting	218-219
Pressing and "blocking" patchwork	220
Putting together the layers of a quilt	220-221
Binding a quilt	222
Finishing cushions	223
Project templates	224-225

PATCHWORK PROJECTS

Baby changing mat	EASY LEVEL	228-229
Flying geese throw	EASY LEVEL	230-231
Quilt-as-you-go cushion	EASY LEVEL	232-233
Amish cushions	EASY LEVEL	234-235
Strippy silk vest	EASY LEVEL	236-237
Strippy silk clutch bag	EASY LEVEL	238-239
Jacob's ladder crib quilt	INTERMEDIATE LEVEL	240-241
Trip-around-the-world throw	INTERMEDIATE LEVEL	242-245
Man's wool vest	INTERMEDIATE LEVEL	246-247
Marmalade cat	INTERMEDIATE LEVEL	248-249
Walled garden hanging	ADVANCED LEVEL	250-253
Seminole cushion	INTERMEDIATE LEVEL	254-255

Water lily foundation cushions	ADVANCED LEVEL	256-257
Crazy patchwork vest	ADVANCED LEVEL	258-259
Dorothy bag	ADVANCED LEVEL	260-261
Cottage tea cozy	ADVANCED LEVEL	262-263

DRIED FLOWERS MATERIALS AND TECHNIQUES

Wiring lotus seed heads	266
General equipment	266
Color harmony and contrast	267
Materials for texture and structure	267
Preparing a twig wreath	268
Wire and moss wreaths or shapes	269
Preparing a wire frame wreath	270
Preparing a foam block for a wall-mounted arrangement	271
Preparing a trunk and container	272
Preparing a basket	272
Making a bow	273

DRIED FLOWERS PROJECTS

Twig wreath	EASY LEVEL	276-277
Wall vase	EASY LEVEL	278-279
Hydrangea mirror	EASY LEVEL	280-281
Container for fresh flowers	EASY LEVEL	282-283
Amaryllis bulb holder	EASY LEVEL	284-285
Valentine basket	EASY LEVEL	286-287
Grouped basket	INTERMEDIATE LEVEL	288-289
Rustico wreath	INTERMEDIATE LEVEL	290-291
Freestyle spray	INTERMEDIATE LEVEL	292-293
Mossed tree and topiary tree	INTERMEDIATE LEVEL	294-299
Twig-caged ball	INTERMEDIATE LEVEL	300-303
Wheat and alchemilla	ADVANCED LEVEL	304-307
Flowerpot man	ADVANCED LEVEL	308-311
Harvest sheaf	ADVANCED LEVEL	312-313

INDEX

INDEX	314-19

ACKNOWLEDGMENTS

ACKNOWLEDGMENTS	320

INTRODUCTION

Learning a new craft can be a source of endless pleasure and satisfaction. **CRAFT SCHOOL** explores six very different craft media—découpage, doughcraft, papier mâché, cross-stitch, patchwork, and dried flower arranging—presenting a wealth of ideas, information, and inspirational projects that anyone can attempt. Beginners can specialize in a particular technique, try out each medium until they find the one they like best, or work through all six sections and watch their skills develop. More advanced craft practitioners will find a wealth of new ideas to sharpen their expertise and enliven their handicraft.

DECOUPAGE In essence découpage could not be easier to do, since it consists of using nothing more than scissors, varnish, and paper cutouts to decorate any type of smooth surface—from box lids and tableware to table tops and chairs. Découpage sources are everywhere around you—in books, magazines, gift wrapping paper, catalogs, postcards, and prints.

DOUGHCRAFT The skill of doughcraft lies in combining the simple ingredients of flour, salt, and water with a few basic kitchen utensils such as a rolling pin, kitchen knife, scissors, and pastry cutters. With the imagination you can bring to the subject, it is possible to create attractive figures, animals, flower, wreaths, bowls, and picture frames.

PAPIER MACHE Papier Mâché is another inexpensive craft that can produce exciting results using pulped newspaper strips combined with different molds and decorative techniques to make interesting gifts and items for the home. Ideas range from simple plate and bowl designs to much more elaborate projects such as a tray, colorful jewelry, and containers.

CROSS-STITCH Cross-stitch embroidery has a long tradition and has been known and practiced for hundreds of years in many cultures throughout the world. **CRAFT SCHOOL** includes a complete guide to the various techniques involved in the application of different forms of cross-stitch and shows you how to create objects ranging from kitchen samplers and pin cushions to tea cozies and table linen.

PATCHWORK The ancient craft of patchwork was originally born from thrift, with people making colorful textiles from spare scraps of material as far back as the 16th century. Learn how to re-create traditional designs, particularly for the featured quilts and throws, but also for use in a modern way, with new ideas for old patterns, such as the crazy patchwork design on a vest.

DRIED FLOWERS Dried flowers are the perfect solution for anyone with a busy lifestyle. Although we all appreciate fresh flowers around the home, often there simply is neither time, nor money to maintain fresh flowers. **CRAFT SCHOOL** shows how a simple floral arrangement—used as a centerpiece for dinner parties or arranged in a basket as the focal point in an unused fireplace—will give months or even years of maintenance-free pleasure.

Don't follow every instruction in **CRAFT SCHOOL** to the letter; you will get as much enjoyment from adding your own variations as you will from reproducing the crafts exactly as illustrated. You don't need any particular artistic ability to make any of the projects. Aiming for perfection can be inhibiting, so relax. Production-line perfection is not inspiring and it often lacks the charm of a handmade craft!

DECOUPAGE

MATERIALS AND TECHNIQUES

MATERIALS AND TECHNIQUES

One of the most satisfying aspects of découpage is transforming ordinary household items of no real value into stunning works of art. You will probably find that there are many things around your own home that, with the help of découpage, could be given a new lease on life. Old cookie tins, tea containers, and baby formula cans are all excellent items on which to practice and will make pretty storage containers for the kitchen. Second-hand stores provide all sorts of wonderful and interesting objects, too, such as old enameled jugs, bread boxes and even bedpans!

The condition of these things does not really matter all that much, nor whether or not they are practical—it is what you do to them that is important. If you are lucky, you may find interesting old wooden boxes, trays, or small pieces of furniture. Once découpaged, old trunks can look stunning, as can violin cases. These items can often be bought for next to nothing and they can end up looking like treasured antiques. Other sources of small wooden boxes and chests are craft supply stores, and you will sometimes find hat boxes advertised for sale in the back of

women's magazines. Don't forget to look in your local hardware store for galvanized buckets, watering cans; or any low-value antique container you may discover—they will be scarcely recognizable once you have given them a few coats of paint and added some appropriate motifs. As you will see in this chapter, almost any hard surface is suitable for découpage, including glass, smooth terra cotta, and cardboard.

PRIMING AND PREPARING DIFFERENT SURFACES

For most people, this is the least favorite part of the procedure, but it is almost always necessary. The surfaces to which you apply your cut-out motifs must be prepared with fastidious care, especially if there are any signs of rust on metal objects, or holes, cracks, or splits in wooden ones.

NEW WOOD
Either seal new wood with a quick-drying, water-based undercoat or primer or, if you want to maintain the natural color and

● Before starting work on an old piece, thoroughly clean it with detergent and water to remove all traces of dirt and grease.

● Fill cracks, holes, or splits and sand back to leave a smooth, even surface.

● New pieces often need sanding back to provide a key that allows the primer to cover properly.

● Always check that you use the appropriate type of primer for the object being worked on.

grain of the wood, with a coat of shellac sanding sealer. If you wish, use a dark shellac to take away its "new" appearance. When the wood is dry, lightly sand it to provide a grip for the adhesive to stick to.

OLD WOOD

With wood that has been painted or varnished, first wipe it over with detergent and water and then fill any holes, splits, or cracks with wood filler. Next, sand the surface with a medium-grit sandpaper, ensuring that the surface of the filler is flush with the wood. Then use undercoat or primer, or leave it to be painted later.

NEW GALVANIZED METAL

The first step is to wash the object inside and out with detergent and water to remove its greasy surface and then paint it with galvanized metal primer to provide a key for painting. This liquid turns the metal black as it dries. When it is dry, rinse it off with clean water. The object is then ready for painting.

WEATHERED GALVANIZED METAL

Weathered galvanized metal needs no special preparation, apart from cleaning with water. If, however, there are signs of

rust, follow the advice below for dealing with rusting and old metal.

RUSTING AND OLD METAL

Unless treated, the rust on metal will eventually eat through the paint and spoil your work. First, remove flaking and loose metal with a wire brush or coarse sandpaper. Then either treat it with a rustproofing agent and paint it with oil-based primer, or use two coats of an all-in-one rust proofer and primer.

NEW TIN AND ENAMEL

Water-based paints do not adhere well to tin or enamel, so you will first need to paint them with an oil-based metal primer; one coat is usually sufficient.

TERRA COTTA

Terra cotta pots, plaques and other objects can make ideal surfaces on which to work. Preparation is usually not difficult. First, sand the surface of any new terra cotta object lightly and, second, seal it with a single coat of water-based varnish. If you are thinking of using an old or a used terra cotta pot, you will first have to clean it thoroughly to remove any old soil or raised areas of lime scale.

PAPER RESOURCES

The choice of papers from which to take motifs is huge. But you can never have too many designs on hand, so save anything you come across until you find the right object to use it on.

GIFT WRAPPINGS AND BOOKS

There are many gift wrappings suitable for découpage. Good places to look include museums, galleries, book stores, and large department stores. You will not find many modern designs used in this book, however, because of copyright considerations. But there is nothing to stop you from using some of them yourself providing that you do not gain commercially from them.

Images from books can be used with great success and they provide an infinite variety of subjects. If you find the idea of cutting up a book inhibiting—even one bought inexpensively at a discount store—you can always make a photocopy.

VICTORIAN SCRAPS AND PRINTS

The wonderfully evocative Victorian scrap images that were so popular in the last century are still produced today, and they remain virtually unchanged. These scraps are easily obtainable by mail order if you have difficulty finding them locally.

Traditionally, black and white prints, often colored by hand, were used for découpage. Today we can make photocopies from books, prints, and photographs, without spoiling the original. Photocopies can also be enlarged or reduced to fit the piece being worked on.

OTHER SOURCES

You can use images from magazines, but not newspapers, since the print on the back is likely to show through. Postcards can also be used, but you will need to thin the card by putting your thumbnail between the layers of the image and the backing sheet and peeling them apart. If the image layer is in danger of tearing, start again from another corner. Highly glossy cards have a tendency to curl once thinned, which makes gluing a little more tricky, but otherwise they are fine to use.

TINTING AND COLORING PRINTS

The simplest and most effective way of tinting a photocopy is to stain the paper with a wet tea bag. This takes away the harsh whiteness of the paper and gives it more the look of old parchment. Simply put a tea bag in a cup with about ½in (1.5cm) of boiling water to make a fairly strong brew. When this has cooled, wipe the surface of the paper with the tea bag and leave it to dry. You could experiment on a spare piece of paper, perhaps adding a little more water or giving it a second coating with the tea bag after the first has dried, until you get the color required.

If you want a colored print, colored pencils and watercolor paints are the easiest to use. If you have not tried these mediums before, don't be daunted by the thought. Take a few extra copies of your chosen print and practice on these spares first, using perhaps just two or three colors or tones of the same color. You don't even have to worry about smudging the edges because you are going to cut round them later. The black and white prints have shaded and light areas to guide you, and all you need to do is to start with the lightest tones and gradually build up the stronger or darker colors in the darkest areas. If you like, you can leave the very lightest areas white

COLORED PENCILS

When you are using colored pencils, make a series of light strokes next to each other, running in the same direction as those on the print. Gradually build these up to produce the color density you require, rather than randomly filling in an area in the way a child would do. You can then work a beige-colored pencil over the surface to blend the whole together.

WATERCOLORS

If you use watercolors—an inexpensive box of student's colors is all you need—build up layers of color, leaving the paper to dry thoroughly between applications. An effective way of using watercolor is to choose one color, perhaps a blue or sepia, and apply a thin wash of paint and water over the entire surface of the print. When this is dry, you can then paint over the shaded areas using one or two stronger applications of the same color, carefully blending it in with the brush and kitchen paper towel or a tissue. Finally, mix in a

TIPS

● Black and white photo-copies of colored paper designs cannot usually be hand tinted or colored successfully due to the obvious gray tone produced by the photocopier.

● Some color photocopiers will allow you to change the order of the scans and thus produce unusual color versions of your original. You will then need to experiment a little to find a result that is suitable for the piece you are working on.

little black with the color to paint in the very darkest tones present in the print. This is known as monochrome painting.

SEALING THE PAPER

After you have selected and tinted your paper, you now must seal the surface before cutting it out. For this you need a shellac sanding sealer or white French polish. Using a piece of paper towel, apply the shellac gently over the area to be cut. The shellac will make the paper look a little transparent at first, but after a few minutes this will disappear and, when the paper is dry, you can start to cut. You must seal the surface of all paper used for découpage, not just tinted or colored photocopies.

CHOOSING A COLOR

Deciding on the base color of the object being worked on is an exciting step, which you can approach in two ways. First, decide on a color that matches an established color scheme and then choose a design to complement it, or second, choose a motif

and then select the background color that enhances it.

If you are thinking of producing découpage commercially, then you will need to use your judgment as to which colors are generally most popular and fashionable. With the projects in this chapter, it was the designs that came first, and the choice of background colors stemmed from them.

As you will see, the projects illustrated use an enormous range of colors, all of which are water-based emulsion paints. A particular favorite is a rather chalky type of paint that uses natural pigments, and it has a wonderful softness of color. In the projects where this paint has been used, you can see that when it dries it becomes much lighter in tone. However, after a coat of varnish it returns to almost the color it is in the pot.

Some companies produce small test pots of emulsion and hundreds of colors can be mixed. These are very practical when you only want to paint a small item. Whichever paint you choose, you may need more than one coat, depending on the object's condition.

CUTTING PAPER

A pair of sharp manicure scissors is essential—the better their quality the easier will be your task. Whether you use straight-bladed or curved scissors is a matter of preference. You will also need a sharp craft knife or scalpel for cutting delicate, tiny areas, and a mat to cut on. A special cutting mat is worth buying if you are planning several projects, otherwise use a piece of thick cardboard.

The cutting for the early projects is very simple, since you need only to cut around the outer edge of a design. To do this, first roughly cut around the shape to remove excess paper and make the piece easier to handle. Then, start to cut just on or inside the edge or line of your motif, avoiding at all costs leaving a white or colored edge that will spoil the look of your finished work. Move the paper toward the scissors as you cut and keep your hands relaxed.

When working on more complicated projects, such as the watering can (see pp. 50-1) start by cutting out the delicate central areas, since this is tricky to do last when all you have is a flimsy cut-out struc-ture to hold on to. This is where you need to use your craft knife: press firmly on the blade or you will tear the paper rather than slice it cleanly. If using scissors to cut out a central area, pierce the paper with the point of one blade and then enlarge the hole using the scissoring action.

If you are using borders on a curved surface, you will need to make little cuts along the outer or lower edge of the border at intervals so that you can ease the paper into position without it kinking. A large design, like that used on the blanket box (see pp. 54-7), will need dividing into smaller sections and reassembling later—it is almost impossible to paste a large section of paper without it crinkling and trapping air bubbles underneath.

ARRANGING AND GLUING

If your are using a number of different motifs, cut out more than you think you need to increase your choice of design possibilities. Working on a flat surface, it is very easy to try out different arrangements and permutations; on vertical or curved

surfaces, however, this can be tricky. In this type of situation, temporarily stick your motifs into position using either a proprietary brand of adhesive plasticine-type dough (which can be removed without leaving a trace) or the type of non-contact repositioning glue that allows you to take up your work and restick it elsewhere. Non-contact glue tends to be a little more accurate than the dough and you will not have to remove your work completely before pasting it permanently into position.

Some designs call for the paper motifs to be overlapped. If so, it is best to start at the top of the object and gradually work your way down the surface, using non-contact glue to hold each piece in place until you have a design you are happy with. Next, of course, you have to remove the motifs from the bottom so that you can get to the ones underneath and then start over again gluing them permanently down from the top. To achieve this, you will either have to remember approximately where all the elements were originally positioned or, if you cannot bear to lose a carefully worked-out design, you will have to make an accurate sketch, or take an instant picture snapshot to use as reference.

GLUING TECHNIQUES

For sticking the motifs down permanently, use either a polyvinyl adhesive glue or a simple paste of the type available from art supply stores and stationers. All of the motifs in this book were stuck down with paste, which is slower drying than polyvinyl adhesive. This gives you a minute or two to change your mind if you are not quite happy with your first choice of position and more time to smooth out any wrinkles and air bubbles.

Using a brush, paint the surface of the object with the paste, rather than pasting the back of the print. This is always more accurate as well as being a lot less messy. Press the paper firmly down and make sure that you work any bubbles of air out toward the edge of the paper. You may find a linoleum printing roller helpful for this if you have one, but if not, your fingers will do just as well. Work on a small area at a time, pasting and sticking

down as you go. If you have used non-contact glue on a vertical surface, lift up a section of the design, apply the paste, and move on to the next section. When you have finished sticking your design down, leave it to dry for about half an hour, and then remove the excess glue from the surface with a damp sponge. If you have used polyvinyl adhesive, however, you must remove the excess glue straight away or it will dry hard.

It is worth keeping an eye on the piece during this time, so that if an edge starts to lift you can press it firmly down again. If your paper is rather thin, no matter how careful you have been, you may find that after a while it starts to wrinkle slightly, but it will usually shrink back when dry. If you do have an air bubble, make a small incision with the point of your knife to let the air escape, fill the slit in with a little glue, and press the edges of the cut firmly down. Now leave your work to dry thoroughly for at least a further two hours before varnishing. During this time, as long as the paper feels dry, you can cheat a little and disguise any white edges or little blemishes you may have left when cutting-out by going over them with a lead or colored pencil. And if, by way of an accident or impatience, you have snipped off the antennae of a butterfly you can reinstate them with a fine-tipped indelible pen.

TIPS

● Always apply glue to the surface of the object being worked on, not to the back of the motif.

● Paste is slightly slower to dry than a polyvinyl adhesive and so gives you a little time to change your mind about the final position of a motif. Try to handle the paper as little as possible, however, once it is wet with paste.

VARNISHING AND FINISHING

The object you have découpaged will now need between 3 and 20 coats of varnish, depending on the quality of work you wish to achieve and the amount of overlapping, if any, of the motifs. In general, between 10 and 12 coats of varnish is sufficient for most objects. With old-style varnishes you could apply perhaps only a single coat in a day, but with modern water-based products you can speed this up and get on 4 to 5 coats in the same time without difficulty. Make sure you choose a satin varnish, not a matte one. The matting agents used will make the varnish appear cloudy after several coats have been applied.

It is important to work somewhere dust-free when varnishing, and make sure to wear clothing that will not shed hairs or fibers, since these too will settle on the varnish and ruin the overall effect. Make sure that your brush is absolutely clean and free from any paint residue. Apply a thin even layer of varnish and then leave it for at least two hours before applying the next. If, as you start to build up the layers, the varnish does not feel quite dry after two hours, leave it until it does. If you want a professional finish, lightly sand back the next-to-the-last coat with fine-grade sandpaper until you have a smooth finish. Don't do this unless you have applied at least 6 coats of varnish, however, otherwise you could easily damage the outer edges of the print. The final coat of varnish can be either satin or matte, depending on the finish you require.

ANTIQUING

If you decide on an antique finish for your découpage, it is best to apply it after the second coat of varnish has completely dried. At this stage you can still see the texture of the brush marks in the paint, and it is these that help to give the surface finish depth. For the antiqued items in this book, the following recipe was used:

1 part white emulsion paint
3 parts raw umber pigment
8 parts water

As an alternative you could try raw umber acrylic paint, diluted with water to the strength required, or dark-brown emulsion paint diluted with water.

Whichever recipe you choose, the technique is the same. Brush on the antiquing liquid and, with a clean cloth or paper towel, start wiping it off after a minute or so, leaving the color in the cervices and places where dirt would normally collect. If you want a softer look, don't brush the liquid on, but rub a little in with the paper towel instead. If the whole thing looks like a total disaster, don't worry, just wash it off straight away and start again.

CRACKLE VARNISHING

Crackle varnish is applied on top of the final layer of water-based varnish and it produces a finish resembling that of finely crazed porcelain. The technique uses two different varnishes, both available from art supply stores. The first is slow-drying and oil-based, while the second is a quick-drying, water-soluble one. The cracking occurs due to the difference in the drying time between the two. You next have to rub some oil paint over the surface to reveal the cracks. This technique does need a little practice to get right, however, and so it is a good idea to try it out on some cardboard first.

Brush the oil-based varnish on to the surface as thinly and evenly as possible, making sure to cover the entire area. This varnish can be quite yellow in color and so it is easy to see where you have applied it. Leave it for between two and four hours, until it feels dry to the touch when you brush your fingers lightly across the surface but is still just tacky. Next, brush on the water-based varnish in the same way. This time it will be much harder to see where you have applied the varnish and it is even more important that you cover every bit of the surface—hold your work up to the light to check that you have not missed any. When this second coat is dry, after about 30 minutes, you should find that the surface has crazed, although sometimes a little encouragement may be needed by way of some gentle

TIPS

● Always leave at least two hours between applying coats of varnish to allow it to dry properly.

● Use a good-quality brush for varnishing, one that won't shed hairs.

● Work in a well-ventilated dust-free area when varnishing and pot lids tightly after use.

18

heat. The heat from a lamp works well, as does that from a hair dryer, but be careful not to put it too close to your work or results may look unnatural.

The next step is to squeeze a little raw umber artist's oil color on to a saucer and dilute it with a small amount of turpentine to make a more workable consistency. Using a brush or paper towel, work the diluted paint over the surface, making sure that it gets into all the cracks and crevices. Then take a clean piece of paper towel and wipe off the excess paint. If you find that you have some dirty or smudgy areas, this indicates that you have missed this bit with the water-based varnish. A little turpentine applied with paper or a cotton swab will remove the marks and, if you are really unhappy with the way it looks, remove all the raw umber, wash off the second coat of varnish, and start again with the first coat.

You must now leave your work overnight so that the oil paint can dry. Bear in mind that the last coat of varnish used is water soluble, so take care not to get it wet. Finally, varnish your piece with a coat of oil-based varnish, either satin or matte depending on the finish required, to protect the surface.

WAXING

A coat of wax over the varnish adds a mellowness and a professional finish. Use a natural-colored wax or an antique-colored or a staining wax. Colored waxes may alter the color of your work considerably, so be warned. A yellowing antique wax can greatly enhance the spectrum of colors from mid-red through to the yellows and greens, but it is not always successful on blues, tending to make them look a little green. A medium-brown or a natural wax is usually most generally suitable, but you will need to experiment since different brands vary considerably.

A wax finish usually works best on top of matte varnish, so bear this in mind when deciding what the final layer of varnish is to be. If you have used crackle varnish, the sealing coat of oil-based varnish should also be matte, but leave it to harden for at least two days before waxing.

Apply the wax with a soft cloth, working it evenly over the surface. Then leave it to dry for at least 30 minutes before buffing it with a clean cloth. To maintain this finish, a quick coating with aerosol furniture polish every couple of months should do the trick.

Accompanying each project in this book you will find a list of materials required to carry out the work described. Some items of equipment, however, are common to nearly all découpage work, and these are separately listed here.

BASIC MATERIALS KIT

Manicure scissors

Craft knife/scalpel knife

Household scissors

Cutting mat or thick cardboard

Clear shellac

Non-contact glue
or adhesive dough

Paste for final positioning
of motifs

Household sponge

Lead pencil

Satin or matte finish,
water-based varnish

Brushes for gluing, painting
and varnishing

Fine-grit sandpaper

Paper towel

Methanol for cleaning
brushes used with shellac

turpentine for cleaning
brushes used with
oil-based paint

DECOUPAGE

PROJECTS

1

2

1 Start by lightly sanding the key fobs until they feel smooth. If you are making a set, either choose one color of paint for the background that would be appropriate for all of the cut-outs you are using, or paint the fobs in a variety of colors to enhance the individual print you have chosen for each one. For the fobs illustrated here, light blue was selected for the background to give a feeling of the sea and the sky.

2 Seal your motifs with clear shellac applied with a paper towel, wait for the shellac to dry, and then cut them out using a pair of sharp manicure scissors (*see pp. 10-19*). Coat each painted key fob with paste and carefully arrange your prints on top. Press down firmly with your fingers, taking care to ensure that the edges of the paper are well stuck down. Leave the fobs to dry for 30 minutes and then wipe off the excess paste with a damp sponge. Leave the fobs for a further two hours until they have completely dried. Now you are ready to apply the varnish. Take a clean brush and paint a thin coat of varnish on to the fobs. When this has dried, paint the underside of them with a coat of varnish, and continue in this way, alternately painting the tops and bottoms, until you have as many coats on each side as you require. Key fobs are generally pretty roughly handled, so it is a good idea to give both sides at least 8 coats of varnish.

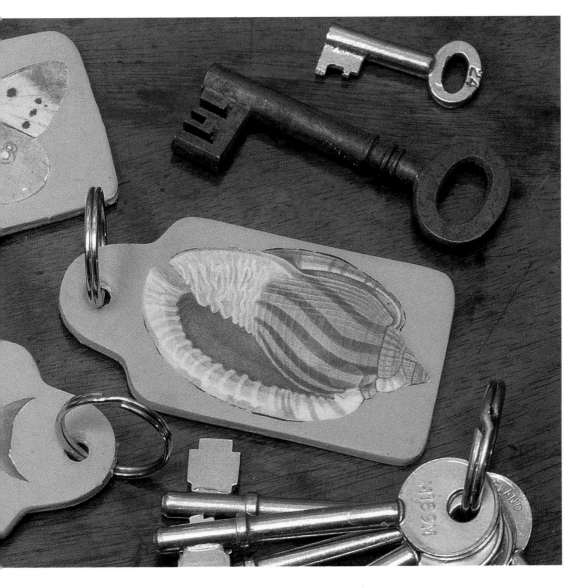

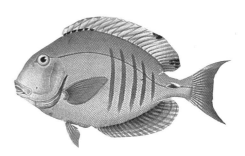

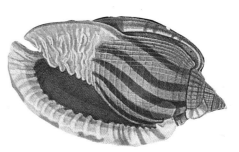

MATERIALS

Wooden key fobs

Natural history prints,
or other source material

Light-blue paint

Basic materials kit (*see p. 19*)

EASY LEVEL

KEY FOBS

With all the keys we seem to accumulate, for the home, auto, suitcases, and so on, an attractive key fob or two is always welcome. The natural history prints used on these chains are very appealing and they are just the right size. It is not always easy to find a design appropriate for something so small, so if you do come across a likely motif, put it away somewhere safe until you find the right object.

Other design ideas for use on a key fob include signs of the zodiac, perhaps cut from the horoscope page of a glossy magazine, and the initials of the recipient's in heavy bold type.

The key fobs designed for this project are intended as a complementary set that could be used for the different rooms of a house. You could either paint them all the same color or give each one a different color code according to its intended use. They would look fantastic hanging all together in a key closet, or lined up dangling from a simple hook rack—especially if either of those items had also been découpaged to match. They would certainly make a very simple, inexpensive and practical gift.

EASY LEVEL

SHAKER BOX

These traditional Shaker-style boxes are lovely to decorate. They come in a large range of sizes, which makes them extremely useful for storing all manner of things around the home, and they make especially good sewing boxes.

They look particularly good when painted with natural-pigment colors, which would have been the only ones available to the 18th-century Shakers themselves. Once the paint has dried, you can decide on the arrangement of motifs you wish to add. Butterflies have been used on the one illustrated here, but Shaker boxes look equally good when decorated with pictures of shells, birds, fish, and flowers.

An aging technique has been introduced on this project, and the color will blend well with most traditional or contemporary interiors. You can often find pictures of butterflies on gift wrapping paper and in books. If you don't want to destroy your book, simply photocopy the relevant parts. If you find black and white motifs to copy, color or tint them in your preferred color scheme (*see pp. 10-19*) before commencing the main work.

1

2

3

4

1 Lightly sand the whole box with a fine-grade sandpaper and seal the inside by painting it with either a clear or a brown-colored shellac. Paint the outside with 2 or 3 coats of a dark cream paint. The number of coats you need to use depends on how well the paint covers.

2 Using a pair of sharp manicure scissors, cut out a number of butterflies of different sizes, leaving a neat, clean edge. Don't worry if you accidentally cut off an antenna or two, you can always draw them in again later. Try out different arrangements on the lid of the box. You might find it easier to position the largest butterflies first, and use the smaller ones to fill in the gaps.

3 When you are happy with the design, brush the paste on to the lid of the box and stick each butterfly firmly down. After about 30 minutes, wipe of the excess paste with a damp sponge and leave the box for a further two hours to dry. During this time, if you have accidentally cut off an antenna, draw it back in again with an indelible pen.

4 Apply 2 coats of varnish to both the lid and the base of the box and when it is completely dry, paint on a coat of the antiquing paint (see pp. 10-19). As soon as you have painted both parts of the box, start to wipe the paint off with a paper towel and leave it to dry. Continue applying several more coats of varnish, finishing off with a matte varnish. Wait a few days until it is completely dry and apply an antique wax to give a deep, mellow sheen.

MATERIALS

Shaker box
Dark cream paint
Dark shellac
Butterfly motifs, or other source material
Antiquing paint
Antique wax
Basic materials kit (see p. 19)

1

2

3

4

1 Choose a flower pot that has a smooth finish, but if it has the odd lump or bump, sand it flush using medium-grade paper. Give the outside a coat of water-based varnish, otherwise your paint will be sucked into the terra cotta.

2 When the varnish is dry, give the outside of the pot 2 coats of blue-gray paint. While the paint is drying, seal the card you intend to use with shellac. You may next

have to thin the card to remove some of the paper's bulk. Place your thumb nail between the layers of backing paper and carefully peel off the print (see p. 12). Next, use a pair or sharp manicure scissors to cut out your design, starting with the tiny internal areas first.

3 Apply paste to the outside of the flower pot and stick your print in place. Use your fingers to smooth it from the center out

toward the edges to remove any air bubbles trapped underneath. After 30 minutes wipe away excess paste with a damp sponge.

4 When the cut-out is thoroughly dry, apply 10 or 12 coats of varnish, leaving at least two hours between coats. Sand back the next-to-the-last coat with fine-grade sandpaper, and use a satin varnish for the final coat.

MATERIALS

Flower pot

Postcard of flower print, or other source material

Blue-gray paint

Medium-grade sandpaper

Basic materials kit (see p. 19)

EASY LEVEL

FLOWER POT

You can transform a flower pot, much like the one pictured above, into a stunning container for either an artificial or a dried flower arrangement. Don't, however, fill the pot with soil to grow a living plant—whenever you refreshed it, the water would seep through the porous terra cotta and eventually lift the pot's decorative finish.

The pot used here was new, but if you want to use one from the backyard, make sure you clean it thoroughly first.

The motifs used came from book of picture postcards, but it would not be difficult to find similar prints in book stores and art museums. You can heighten the decorative effect if you découpage two or three pots, place them in a row on a shelf, fill them with moss-covered foam, and then add an artificial flower to each. With larger pots you could try out even more elaborate floral arrangements.

1 Wash the jug out with detergent and water and leave it to dry thoroughly. Paint only the outside of the jug with a galvanized metal primer. This will turn the metal black. When the primer has dried, rinse it thoroughly in clean water and let it drain until dry.

2 Paint the exterior of the jug with your chosen color of paint—here a shocking pink. You will normally need 3 coats of paint to cover when you are using a color such as this.

3 While the paint is drying, use a pair of sharp manicure scissors to cut out the roses from the sheet of scraps. Spray the back of them with a non-contact adhesive. Begin arranging the motifs around the jug, trying for a design that is balanced but not in any way rigidly symmetrical. Remember that the spaces between your motifs are part of the design, too. When you are happy with the arrangement, remove one motif at a time, apply paste to the jug and stick it firmly back in place. Leave the jug for about 30 minutes and then remove any excess paste with a damp sponge.

4 Wait at least two hours before varnishing. For the jug to look its best, apply at least 12 coats of varnish. Rub the next-to-the-last coat back with a fine-grade paper and give a final coat of satin varnish.

1

2

3

4

GYPSY STYLE JUG

This bright and cheerful jug has a wonderful fresh European gypsy-like quality to it, and it is not dissimilar to the decorative approach of certain types of English bargeware (named after the decorative objects made by the folk who plied Britain's extensive 19th century canal system on longboats, or "barges").

The galvanized jug itself was bought new from a hardware store. It was decided to let it be a container for fresh-cut flowers, and so was left unpainted on the inside. A large bunch of roses in an array of different colors, picked fresh from the garden, would set off the découpage decoration to perfection.

If the deep shocking pink that has been chosen for the background color on the outside of the jug is a little bright for your taste, you could always substitute a deep shade of blue, for example—even a green-blue color would be suitable as a background for the surface decoration.

The flowers used here came from a sheet of scraps and so required very little in the way of cutting out. If you are using other source material, always cut out the tiny internal areas first and then move on to the outside parts.

MATERIALS

Galvanized jug

Galvanized metal primer

Shocking pink paint

Sheet of rose scraps,
or other source material

Basic materials kit (*see p. 19*)

1

2

3

4

MATERIALS

Medium-density fiberboard (MDF) hat and coat rack
Color print of a duck, or other source material
Dark green paint
Medium brown paint
Antique staining wax
Basic materials kit (see p. 19)

1 This rack is made from medium-density fiberboard and therefore needs no special preparation. Before painting, remove the brass hooks, and then apply 2 coats of dark green paint, making sure you cover all of its surface.

2 When the base green color is dry, give the molded edge of the rack 2 coats of medium brown paint, using a small brush for a neat finish. This is not as difficult as it seems, since the molded edge has slightly less depth than the surface of the rack.

3 While the paint is drying, seal the surface of your color print with shellac, applied with paper towel (see p. 15). Wait for the shellac to dry thoroughly and then, using a pair of sharp manicure scissors, start to cut out the duck motif. Start with the tiny area between the duck's legs and then move on to the outside of the print, making sure to leave a neat, clean edge. Brush paste on to the center of the rack and stick the motif firmly in place, smoothing out any bubbles of air trapped beneath from the center toward the edges. Leave it to dry for about 30 minutes and then remove any excess paste with a damp sponge.

4 After two hours you can start to varnish. Apply 10 to 12 coats, leaving at least two hours between coats. Sand back the next-to-the-last coat and finish with a matte varnish. Leave the rack to dry thoroughly, preferably overnight, and then give it a good coat of antique wax. Wait about 30 minutes and then buff it with a soft cloth for a deep, rich shine. Finally, carefully screw the brass hooks back in place.

HAT AND COAT RACK

This is not only a very simple project to make, at the end of the day you will have an extremely attractive and practical hat and coat rack for the entrance of your home. Or it would look equally stylish if screwed to the back of a door.

The colors of both the background paint and the printed motifs give this hat and coat rack a decidedly rustic flavor. If this color scheme does not suit the position you want to use it in, however, then feel free to choose other colors. Why not, for example, think about a light blue color to suggest a watery background for the duck motif? You could then rub some gilt cream on to the border if you want to give it an extra decorative touch, choosing a shade that matches the color of the brass. The choice is yours.

The hat and coat rack used in this project has been finished with an antique staining wax. This is available at hardware and do-it-yourself stores, and it adds an important feeling of age and gives a wonderful depth of color to the completed project.

1 Fill the old screw holes and any other defects in the chair's surface with wood filler. Sand the filler back flush and then sand back all of the wood to achieve a good, smooth finish.

2 Give the chair 2 coats of red paint. Apply the paint in two stages—first the top, then, when it is dry, the underneath parts.

3 Rub the surface of the chair in random areas with a candle, following the grain of the wood. You will need to press fairly firmly to transfer sufficient wax to the chair. Then, using clear wax polish and a cotton swab, add some blobs of wax to the chair, again at random. Leave the wax to dry hard for a few hours.

4 Now paint the chair with 1 coat of blue paint. When it is completely dry, use sandpaper to rub back the surface to reveal random areas of red paint beneath. This will be easiest to do where you have used the wax resist.

5 Cut out the toy motifs with manicure scissors and place them over the seat of the chair. When you have a balanced design, apply paste to the chair and stick down the motifs firmly. Wait 30 minutes and remove excess paste with a damp sponge.

6 Spray the remaining prints with a non-contact adhesive and arrange them on the back of the chair. When you are happy with the design, stick the motifs in place. Apply 3 coats of varnish to all surfaces. Give at least 10 more coats of varnish to the découpaged areas of the chair only. Finish with a coat of matte varnish, followed by an antique wax.

1

2

3

4

5

6

CHILD'S CHAIR

This old school chair is the type you could easily buy very cheaply in a junk store or garage sale, and the transformation that has been brought about is astonishing. The toy motifs used come from a sheet of gift wrapping paper and the chair has been painted in background shades of blue and red to match. A cream-colored paint would also look good and provide more of a contrasting background. The blue paint has been sanded back in places to reveal the red paint beneath and gives a naturally worn appearance.

If you want something a bit brighter for a child's room, try to use some pictures of balloons or cartoon characters against a primary-colored background.

MATERIALS
Wooden chair
Wood filler
Medium-grade sandpaper
Gift wrapping paper of toys, or other source material
Red paint
Blue paint
Cotton swab
Candle
Clear wax
Antique wax
Basic materials kit (see p. 19)

1

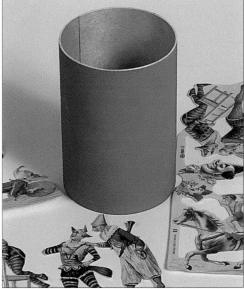

2

3

4

MATERIALS

Pencil holder

Sheets of old-fashioned circus scraps, or other source material

Bright green paint

Basic materials kit (*see p. 19*)

1 Paint the outside of the pencil holder a bright shade of green to pick out and emphasize the colors in the clowns' clothes on the scraps. You will need to give it 2 coats to provide a good surface on which to work. When dry, turn the container upside down to paint its base.

2 Using a pair of sharp manicure scissors, carefully cut away the excess paper from the sheets of scraps, leaving a neat, clean edge. You will have more than you need from one sheet of scraps, so spray the back of the individual figures with a non-contact adhesive and experiment with different arrangements of figures until you find the one you like best.

3 Carefully remove the first scrap, apply some paste to the space left on the side of the container, and then reposition the motif and press it firmly down, making sure that the edges are well stuck and that no air bubbles are trapped beneath. Continue in this way until all the scraps are stuck down in position. Wait 30 minutes and remove excess paste with a damp sponge.

4 When the paste is thoroughly dry, apply at least 10 coats of varnish to give the pencil holder the durability needed to withstand plenty of not-too-careful handling by a child, finishing with a satin coat. This will also give the pencil holder just the right level of gloss to enhance the brightness of the base color and surface motifs.

INTERMEDIATE LEVEL

PENCIL HOLDER

Many people love those colorful old-fashioned circus prints, and they look like great fun used here to decorate the pencil holder that is the subject of this project. Once filled up with multi-colored pencils, crayons, or those decorative pens, it would make a wonderful gift for a child.

Many seemingly throw-away items can be used for découpage and the container here is, in fact, the bottom half of a tall box that originally contained crystallized ginger. It is a good example of the transformation you can bring about with just a little imagination and patience. If you don't have a suitable container, buy any inexpensive one to decorate in this bright and cheerful fashion. Then all you have to do is wait for the smile on your child's face when the gift has been opened.

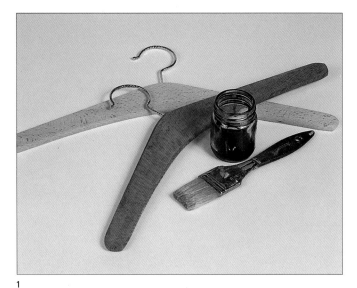

1

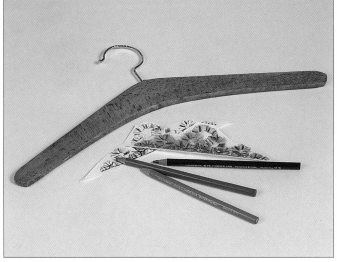

2

3

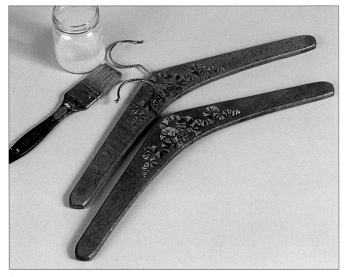

4

MATERIALS

2 coat hangers

photocopies of ribbon
and bow designs,
or other source material

Colored pencils

Dark shellac

Basic materials kit (see p. 19)

1 Start by lightly sanding the hangers until they feel smooth, making sure to remove all traces of any varnish that may be there, and then stain them with a dark shellac. You can mix in a little clear shellac if you wish to give a lighter tone (as was done with one of the hangers opposite).

2 Take black and white photo-copies of the ribbon and bow design from a source book for découpage and choose two different colored pencils—here, dark shades of red and blue were used. Using a series of light strokes next to each other, and following the direction of the lines on the print, gradually build up the color, finishing with the deepest color in the areas of the darkest shading. Then use a beige-colored pencil to blend it all together by coloring across the paper from left to right.

3 Seal the paper with clear shellac applied with a piece of paper towel. Pierce the center of the loops in the bow with one blade of the scissors and cut the middles out first. Once you have finished cutting them all out, divide each ribbon and bow into three sections and reassemble them so that the design fits the curve of the hanger. The easiest way to do this is to overlap the pieces a little where they join. Paste the design in place in the usual way (see pp. 10-19).

4 When the design is thoroughly dry, apply 3 base coats of varnish to both sides of the hanger, and then continue on the front only until you have as many coats of varnish as you require, but use at least 7. Finish with a coat of matte varnish.

COAT HANGERS

Look in any closet you have at home and you are almost certain to find a plentiful supply of those awful metal coat hangers. No matter how many you throw away, next time you look, there they are back again! Where do they come from?

How nice it would be instead, then, to receive some nice, attractive, individually découpaged wooden hangers like the ones illustrated here. No need anymore to hide your hangers away inside the closet.

Instead you could show them off and make a feature of them. Fix a clothes hook to the inside of your bedroom door and hang your nightdress or bathrobe there for all to see. These hangers would also make a lovely gift to give to a child, decorated with favorite or appropriate motifs, such as cartoon characters or animals.

Alternatively, with a little adult supervision and assistance from the father of the household, a decorated hanger or two would make a wonderful Mother's Day present from a child. Looking through magazines and books as a source for ideas, keeping it a secret from Mom, could all be part of the fun.

1

2

3

4

MATERIALS

Hinged tin box
Cream-colored paint
Oil-based metal primer
Pansy and shell motifs from gift wrapping, or other source material
Antiquing paint
Basic materials kit (see p. 19)

1 Prime the outside of the tin with an oil-based metal primer and leave it to dry overnight. Apply 2 or 3 coats of a cream-colored paint and open and close the tin before applying each coat to make sure the hinges are freely working.

2 Using a pair of sharp manicure scissors, cut out the pansy and shell motifs, making sure to leave a clean, neat edge, and arrange a border of pansies around the lid of the tin. Then fill in the middle with a collection of small shells, randomly arranged. When you are happy with the design, take each

motif off in turn, apply paste to the tin and press the paper down firmly, making sure that the edges are well stuck and that no air bubbles are trapped beneath.

3 Using a non-contact adhesive, position more motifs around the base of the tin. Start by centering the pansy design at the front of the tin, leaving enough space for the shell to go beneath. Continue to place the design motifs around each side of the tin until they meet at the back. You may need an extra flower or two to fill a gap or disguise a join. Arrange

the shells below the pansies in a similar way and then use paste applied to the tin to fix them permanently in place. After about 30 minutes, remove excess paste with a damp sponge.

4 With a clean brush, apply 2 coats of varnish to the tin and then rub in the antiquing paint (see pp. 10-18). Keep it fairly light so that you can clearly see the delicate colors of the design. If your motifs overlap, you will need another 10 to 12 coats of varnish, sanding back the next-to-the-last one for a smooth finish.

SMALL HINGED TIN BOX

This unusual and attractive mix of pansies and shells came from a sheet of gift wrapping paper with a cream background. Sources of design material for découpage are abundant if you keep a sharp eye out for them.

The hinged tin box used as the subject of this project has been painted the same cream background color as that of the paper, but consider a pale shade of pink or purple if you are looking for a brighter alternative scheme. This tin box was brand new and so was left plain inside, but if the one you are working on is old and tarnished you could paint the inside, too. Before painting, however, treat any areas of rust (*see pp. 10-19*) or you will find that the paint will soon lift.

When painting and varnishing the outside, take particular care in the areas around the hinges. If they become clogged, the tin box will be awkward to use. When finished, a container such as this would be ideal for a collection of small seashells or, if you wanted to fill it with candies, you might consider changing the decorative motif to something more suitable.

DECOUPAGE

MATERIALS

Wooden wall sconce
Dark shellac
Photocopy of cherub print, or other source material
Blue paint
Tea bag
Basic materials kit (*see p. 19*)

1 Sand back the wood if necessary and then brush a dark shellac over the sconce to take away its new color and give it more of an aged appearance.

2 Paint the sconce with just 1 coat of paint. When it has dried, sand it back with a medium-grade paper to reveal the grain of the wood beneath. Remove more of the paint in those areas where the sconce would naturally receive wear and tear when in use.

3 Photocopy a cherub print, or your own source material, and stain it with a damp tea bag (*see pp. 10-19*). Seal the print with clear shellac applied with a paper towel and, when it is dry, use sharp manicure scissors to cut out the motif carefully, starting with the delicate internal areas. You may find this easier with a scalpel knife rather than scissors.

4 Brush paste on to the sconce and stick down your motif. Apply pressure from the center of the paper out to the edges to remove any air bubbles that may be trapped beneath. Wait about 30 minutes and remove excess paste with a damp sponge. Apply 10 or 12 coats of varnish. Rub back the next-to-the-last coat with a fine-grade paper and give a final coat of matte varnish.

1

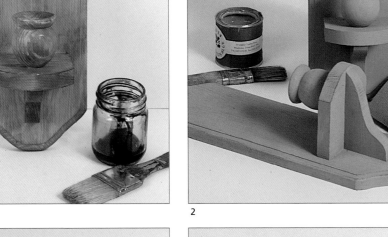

2

3

4

40

WALL SCONCE

The very delicate cherub design selected for this wall sconce looks best on a soft, muted background color, and the extremely attractive shade of blue paint that has been used here comes from an exclusive range of traditionally made historic colors.

The first stage in the preparation of the sconce involved sanding back the wood to reveal and accentuate the grain beneath. Both the wood and the print have been given an aging treatment (*see pp. 10-19*) and this, as well as the patience and skill required for cutting out the motif, make it a more difficult project than some others you have seen so far in the découpage chapter of this book.

Your patience will be more than amply rewarded, however, when you finally hang this elegant sconce on the wall of your dining or sitting room and light your first candle.

1

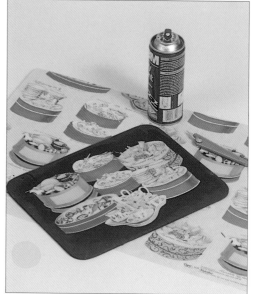

2

3

4

1 Give each table mat 2 coats of paint—here, one mat was painted green and the other blue.

2 While the paint is drying, cut out your motifs using manicure scissors. Arrange the tea set cut-outs on the blue mat, and try different arrangements—start at the top of the mat and work down. It may help to spray the back of the motifs with a non-contact adhesive to keep them in place.

3 Arrange the cups and saucers on the green mat. If you want to keep your designs accurate, outline the arrangement on both mats using light pencil or chalk marks and make a sketch of the final positions of the cut-outs before removing them. Starting with the top-most motif, paste it firmly into position, and continue in this way working down the piece. Apply paste to the overlapping paper as necessary where

one motif sits on top of another. Check carefully that the prints are firmly stuck down where they overlap. Wait about 30 minutes and then remove excess paste with a damp sponge.

4 The overlapping layers of paper will require at least 10 coats of varnish and then 2 coats of an oil-based polyurethane varnish to make the mats resistant to heat and spills.

MATERIALS

Table mats

Prints of china,
or other source material

Dark blue water-based paint

Dark green water-based paint

Oil-based polyurethane varnish

Turpentine for cleaning
varnish brush

Basic materials kit (see p. 19)

TABLE MATS

Table mats would ordinarily make a good choice for a first try at découpage. Their large, flat surfaces lend themselves to almost any decoration. However, the motifs have been arranged in overlapping layers, making this project a little more difficult than those earlier in the chapter. The antique cups and saucers used on the mats above were found in a magazine and those of the toy tea sets came from a sheet of gift wrapping. Together, the designs make a very appropriate theme.

If you want your table mats to be practical as well as decorative, apply 2 top coats of an oil-based polyurethane varnish over between 10 and 12 coats of ordinary water-based varnish. This should be enough to ensure that the mats are both heatproof and spillproof.

43

1

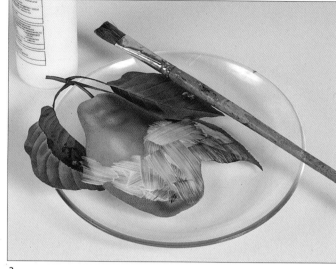

2

3

4

MATERIALS

MATERIALS
Glass plate
Print of fruit, or other source material
Polyvinyl adhesive
Light green paint
Basic materials kit (see p. 19)

1 Choose a fruit design that is an appropriate size to fit under your plate. Using a pair of sharp manicure scissors, carefully cut out the print, starting with the delicate internal areas first, leaving a clean, neat edge all around.

2 Apply an even coating of the polyvinyl adhesive to the surface of the motif, taking particular care that you cover every bit of the print area, and especially the edges.

3 Stick the print firmly to the underside of the plate, squeezing out any air bubbles by applying pressure from the middle of the paper out toward the edges. Because of the curve of the plate, the edges of the paper may tend to lift and you will need to apply pressure with your fingertips until you are confident that the cut-out is securely in place. As soon as it is, remove excess glue from the plate with a damp sponge and leave it to dry for a couple of hours.

4 Before starting to paint your plate, check one final time and make sure that every part of the print is well stuck down. If it is not, the paint will quickly find its way under any area that is loose and ruin all your hard work. When all is well, brush the back of the plate with 2 coats of light-green paint and then apply 2 or 3 coats of varnish to seal the surface and protect the painted surface against knocks and abrasion.

WORKING ON GLASS

You need to employ a slightly different découpage technique when you come to work on transparent glass objects. In this case, you need to apply the adhesive to the front of the paper motif and then stick the print to the underside of, say, a plate or dish, or to the inside of a vase or bowl.

With the glass of the object acting as the surface of your work, you then need only to varnish the back of the print to seal and protect it. Rather than paste, you will have to use a special polyvinyl adhesive because it is both strong and, most importantly, is completely transparent when dry.

The pear design used in this project makes a very attractive fruit plate. If you like the effect, why not make a set of plates using different fruits on either the same or differing backgrounds?

A plate like this would not be suitable for everyday use, however, and it is certainly not dishwasherproof. Don't leave it to soak in water either—carefully sponge it clean, then dry it and use it for special occasions only.

45

1 Prime the headboard with acrylic paint and, when it is dry, smooth it back with a fine-grade sandpaper. Then apply 2 coats of the light-green paint.

2 When the background color is dry, pick out the border with the darker green paint. If you think your technique is not good enough to work freehand, use strips of masking tape to protect the rest of the paintwork.

3 Using manicure scissors and a scalpel, carefully cut out the roses. Start with the internal areas of the wreath first, and then cut around the inside of each and, finally, the outside. Spray the back of each with non-contact adhesive and arrange them on the headboard. When you are happy with the design, remove each, apply paste to the headboard, and stick it firmly back, pressing out any air bubbles with your fingertips. Wait 30 minutes and then remove excess paste with a damp sponge and leave it for a further two hours.

4 Apply 10 coats of satin varnish, leaving two hours between coats. Sand back the next-to-the-last coat to give a smooth finish.

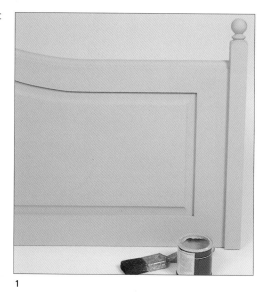

1

2

3

4

MATERIALS

Wooden headboard
Quick-drying acrylic primer
Fine-grade sandpaper
Masking tape
Two shades of green paint
Prints of wreaths of roses, or other source material
Basic materials kit (*see p. 19*)

HEADBOARD

This double headboard has been given a fairly formal découpaged design, one that would make it suitable for a bed in a guest room perhaps. If you are decorating the headboard of your own bed, however, you could make the motifs far more personalized—if you like, using a romantically extravagant theme of cherubs and swags.

A child's headboard would obviously require a completely different design approach. This certainly would be an ideal opportunity to involve the child whose bed it is, getting him or her to choose the motifs to be used together and helping to cut them out and paste them in place. The headboard could be great fun if it were to be decorated with such subjects as cartoon and nursery rhyme characters, dinosaurs, cars, and so on.

The headboard illustrated above has been painted light green, with the inlaid border picked out in a darker shade, and decorated with wreaths of roses. Shades of blue would look equally good with these motifs and you could use a color copier to enlarge or reduce the designs so that they fitted your size headboard.

1

2

3

4

MATERIALS

Oval-shaped wooden box
Green and blue paint
Dark shellac
Prints of fish and shells, or other source material
2 parts of the crackle varnish (*see pp. 10-19*)
Raw umber oil paint
Turpentine
Antique wax
Basic materials kit (*see p. 19*)

1 Seal the inside of the box with dark shellac, and put it aside until it is dry. Paint the lid with 2 coats of a mid-green paint and the base of the box with 2 coats of a mid-blue color of a similar tone.

2 Choose a fish print of the right size for the lid and cut it out carefully using a pair of sharp manicure scissors. When the paint is dry, apply paste to the lid and stick the fish firmly into position, making sure there are no air bubbles trapped beneath. Remove excess glue with a damp sponge after about 30 minutes.

3 Select a number of shell prints in varying shapes and sizes and cut them out. Spray the back with a non-contact adhesive and arrange them around the base of the box. Since this box has no back or front, it is important to position the shell border so that it is even and continuous. An easy way to do this is to choose four of the larger shells of a similar shape (the scallops), and place these at each end and in the middle of both sides. Then arrange more shells in each of the four sections. When you are happy with the design, apply paste to the sides of

the box, stick them in position and remove excess glue with a damp sponge after about 30 minutes.

4 Apply at least 10 coats of varnish. When the last coat is dry, paint on a thin, even coat of oil-based aging varnish and, when it is still just tacky, brush on a coat of the water-based varnish and leave it to dry (*see pp. 10-19*). Rub raw umber oil paint, diluted with a little turpentine, into the cracks and leave this to dry overnight. Seal the box with 1 coat of matte oil-based varnish and, after couple of days, apply antique wax.

CRACKLE VARNISH BOX

This découpaged box looks great fun to make. Although it has been painted in two different colors, the decorative scheme has been carefully chosen so that both colors give a flavor of the sea, which is very much in keeping with the fish and shell prints that have been pasted on top.

Découpage is a multidisciplinary craft, and although the design itself is essentially simple, the crackle varnish finish puts it in the category of a more advanced project. If you have not tried to use a crackle varnish finish before, then it is a good idea to practice it first on a scrap piece of wood or on a piece of thick cardboard. If you cannot find colored prints of fish and shells, you could always photocopy some black and white ones, perhaps from one of the découpage source books that are available in craft stores, and either color them in yourself or stain them with tea (*see pp. 10-19*).

This little box would look charming on a bathroom shelf, perhaps used for storing small tablets of fragrant soap.

MATERIALS
Galvanized watering can
Primer for galvanized metal
Dark blue paint
Prints of flowers, fruit and
vegetables, or other
source material
Basic materials kit (see p. 19)

ADVANCED LEVEL

WATERING CAN

Watering cans are very common, everyday sorts of objects. They are, however, particularly rewarding objects to découpage because of the near total transformation you can bring about. Once filled with flowers, fresh cut or dried, this watering can would look at home in the kitchen, or it would also make a valuable decorative contribution in a sun porch or out on the terrace.

The fruit, flower and vegetable motifs used here were found on different sheets of gift wrapping. They are certainly an appropriate decorative theme, but their colors are a rather unusual mix, however, so take care with your choice of background paint. Dark green would have been a good choice in place of the blue or, for a really vibrant look, you could go for orange.

The motifs are not at all taxing to cut out, apart from the sunflowers, but the overlapping arrangement on a vertical surface makes this project a little tricky. You can leave the inside of the watering can unpainted, if you like, so that it can still be used for watering garden plants or even indoor plants if it is not over large.

1

2

3

4

1 Wash the watering can thoroughly in detergent and warm water to remove any dirt and grease and leave it to drain dry. When dry, paint the outside of the can with primer and, when it has turned black and has dried, wash it carefully again in clean water.

2 Paint the outside of the watering can with 2 coats of dark blue paint and, while it is drying, cut out between 30 and 40 motifs. The finished watering can here has an arrangement of 30 prints, but the additional ones will give you extra design choices.

3 Spray the backs of half the motifs with a non-contact adhesive and arrange them on one side of the watering can, starting from the top and working down. Some of the cut-outs are rather bright so think about the overall color balance of your design. When you have found an arrangement you like, start on the other side of the can. You may be able to use the first design as a guide and paste the second set of motifs permanently down straight away. Always apply the paste to the object, not the motifs. The designs can differ slightly from side to side.

Now turn your attention back to the first side, remove the motifs one at a time, and paste them permanently in position. Finally, paste some of the motifs on to the top of the watering can.

4 Apply between 10 and 12 coats of varnish to all the decorated outside surfaces, leaving about two hours between coats, and sand back the next-to-the-last one for a smooth finish.

1 Clean the jug in detergent and water and allow it to drain dry. Using a sheet of coarse sandpaper, remove all traces of loose and flaking rust, and then paint the outside with 2 coats of a combined rustproofer and metal primer. Leave the handle until last so that you have something to hold while painting. Leave the jug overnight to dry.

2 Apply 2 or 3 coats of the light green background color to the primed surface, again leaving the handle until last.

3 Using a craft knife, cut out the prints of roses, starting with the delicate internal areas. The structure of the roses is very fragile and if you do have a break in a stem, you can reunite it at the pasting stage. Spray the back of the prints with a non-contact adhesive and experiment with different arrangements. If you have one or two gaps, cut out some butterflies and use them as fillers. Lift the top section of one of the roses, apply paste to the jug and stick that section back. Continue down like this until the motif is all stuck down and then turn your attention to the next rose. Finally paste the butterflies in place. Wait 30 minutes before wiping off excess paste with a damp sponge.

4 Paint on 2 base coats of varnish and then apply the antiquing paint (see pp. 10-19). Immediately remove the excess, leaving color in the brush marks and crevices only. Wait for it to dry, and continue to build up another 8 to 10 coats of varnish.

1

2

3

4

ADVANCED LEVEL

ENAMEL JUG

Although it doesn't look like it now, the jug opposite was bought for next to nothing in a second-hand store. It was rusty and at first sight appeared to be beyond repair.

Once découpaged, however, as you can see it makes a marvelous decorative item, one suitable for almost any room in the house. The attractive rose print motifs are difficult to cut out because of the thorns and the serrated leaf edges, but the results make the trouble worthwhile. For subjects like this, you may find a scalpel more convenient than scissors.

The jug has been given a light green background color, but most shades of green and blue would look good with the roses. The inside of the lip has been painted but not the inside proper, since it is hardly visible through the jug's narrow opening.

MATERIALS

Enamel jug

Coarse-grade sandpaper

Combined rustproofer
and primer

Light green paint

Prints of roses and butterflies,
or other source material

Antiquing paint
(see pp.10-19)

Basic materials kit *(see p. 19)*

BLANKET BOX

This blanket box with its découpaged tulip design has been inspired by New England and Dutch folk art. The clever use of color photocopies has created laterally reversed mirror-like images, and the flowers were enlarged to achieve an overall balanced design. The quality and capabilities of photocopiers vary considerably and so you may need to experiment until you achieve the effect you want.

The blanket box has been painted in three different shades of blue and the lines around the panels should not look too regular and perfectly rendered. You could use a *trompe l'oeil* technique if you wish, by painting the top and one side a slightly lighter shade than the other. There is space on the lid of the box for a monogram and you could also decorate the side and the back of the chest if you wished, depending on where it is to be positioned in the room.

MATERIALS

Blanket box
Shellac sanding sealer
Three shades of blue paint
Flower prints, or other source material
Masking tape
Ruler
Template
Antiquing paint (*see pp. 10-19*)
Clear or medium-brown wax
Basic materials kit (*see p. 19*)

1

1 Prime the blanket box with 1 coat of shellac sanding sealer and, when it is dry, apply 2 coats of the medium-blue paint to all surfaces of the box. When the paint is completely dry, lay the box carefully on its side in order to paint its feet (if applicable).

2 Cut a piece of cardboard, or use an appropriate shape such as a table mat, to act as a template, and draw the central panels on the front of the box. Use a ruler to make sure that each panel is evenly placed.

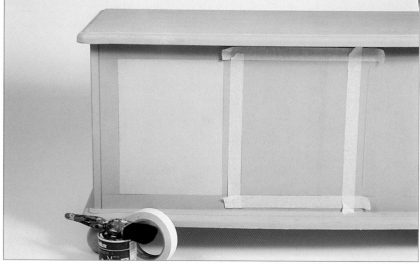

2

3 Place strips of masking tape around the outside edges of the panel and then paint each one in the light-blue color.

4 When the paint is dry, remove the masking tape. Place fresh strips of tape on the inside of the panels and other strips offset by about ¼in (6mm), leaving a thin, even line between the strips of tape. Fill the gap in with the darkest shade of blue paint and, when it is dry, carefully remove the tape. Paint the borders at the top and bottom of the chest in the same color.

5 Using a pair of sharp manicure scissors, carefully cut out all the tulip motifs and arrange the

3

4

5

four smaller ones at each corner of the lid of the box. Apply paste to the lid and stick them down in position. Make sure no air bubbles are trapped beneath.

6 Arrange the flowers on the panels at the front of the box and paste them in position. Wait 30 minutes and then remove any excess paste with a damp sponge. Wait a further two hours before varnishing, and then give the entire chest 2 base coats. Wait for the varnish to dry and then brush the antiquing paint on one surface of the box at a time, wiping off the excess with a clean cloth (*see pp. 10-19*). When this has dried, give the entire chest another coat of varnish. On the lid and front, where the motifs have been positioned, apply at least another 10 coats of varnish, finishing with a matte top coat. Wait at least 24 hours and then rub in a good coat of clear or medium-brown wax and buff to a shine.

6

DOUGHCRAFT

MATERIALS AND TECHNIQUES

MATERIALS AND TECHNIQUES

It goes without saying that you want your dough craft to look as good as possible—but don't be discouraged if any unexpected results should occur. Small flaws can add interesting dimensions to a project, and an "accident" may produce an original texture or unusual surface finish. If you highlight rather than hide these quirks, the object becomes original and unique to you. Nobody is suggesting that you should settle for second best—but think twice before throwing away your mistakes.

MAKING THE DOUGH

The dough used for all the project work in this book is salt dough. Some salt dough experts include a tablespoon of cooking oil for a "smoother, stronger blend," while others would not dream of mixing dough without adding a couple of heaping tablespoons of wallpaper paste, which make the dough more elastic to model and quicker to air-dry (*see p. 65*).

This chapter, however, uses traditional salt dough—not only is it easier to stay with just a single recipe, but when it is made up and handled properly, a simple salt-flour-water mix is very successful, extremely adaptable and behaves with a certain predictability, which is reassuring when you are embarking on new projects!

The recipe given here makes up enough dough for one smallish project and two of the larger ones—a few small, individual decorations, for example, as well as two soup bowl-sized models with relief work. This may seem a lot, but using the oven to bake more than one object at a time makes good economical, and ecological, sense.

If you require less or more dough, then simply halve or double the amounts given accordingly. Bear in mind that, as a general rule, you should always use half the amount of salt to flour.

THE INGREDIENTS
● Flour—Plain white flour has been used throughout this chapter. Use good-quality flour—cheaper brands may be difficult to

handle and they may also vary widely in their degree of absorbency. Whole wheat flours may produce interesting textured effects, but they are heavier to handle and take longer to bake or to air-dry. But this does not rule them out. Self-rising flour puffs up in the oven and therefore should never be used for dough craft modeling.
● Salt—As long as the salt has been finely ground, the cheapest brand available is perfectly adequate to make good dough.

YOU WILL NEED
● Large mixing bowl
● Coffee mug
● Water jug
● Cool surface for kneading

THE BASIC RECIPE

● Two level mugs of plain white flour
● One level mug of finely ground salt
Pour the ingredients into a large mixing bowl and combine them thoroughly.

MIXING
Gradually add sufficient lukewarm water to knead the mixture into a pliable ball. This should take approximately 1½ cups (355ml) of water, but you will need to judge the exact amount by "feel." If the mixture becomes too sticky, add a little more flour; if it crumbles, add more water.

(see p. 65)

DOUGH TIPS

● To make dough paste, take some raw dough and mix it with sufficient water to resemble light cream. If necessary, vary this consistency by adding less or more water.

● The dough reacts best to a warm (but not a hot) working environment. The dough itself is probably the best temperature gauge you have—it will become soft, sticky and moist in an overheated room.

● Always work the dough on a cool surface.

KNEADING

Work the dough for at least ten minutes, slowly and rhythmically, pushing it away from you with the heels of your hands, then folding it back on itself. Turn the dough all the time—the more you knead it, the more pliable it becomes. In the end, its texture should be firm, malleable and elastic enough to stretch into a soft, slightly bouncy "rope" when stretched.

DECORATION

Surface decoration gives vital interest and texture to your model work. Always try to work with the dough directly on the baking sheet itself, otherwise you risk distorting the still-soft model when you come to transfer it.

THE BASIC TOOLS

The tools and materials needed for the individual projects are listed, along with their step-by-step instructions, on the relevant pages, but you may find this checklist of the basic tools useful. You will find most of these modeling tools in your kitchen or around the house; any others will be easily obtainable at your local hardware shop. Some model work requires templates, and these you can cut from any pieces of scrap cardboard.

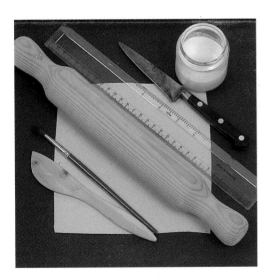

- Cardboard templates (*see pp. 68-71*)
- Non-stick baking sheet—a flat baking sheet without raised edges is best
- Ruler for measuring dough thickness. If it is lightly floured, a ruler also makes a convenient dough cutter
- Rolling pin
- Small kitchen knife
- Small wooden spatula, or any flat, paddle-shaped tool—for patting and smoothing edges and surfaces
- Small lid or jar of home-made dough paste—to stick layers of dough together
- Paintbrush for applying dough paste

YOU WILL ALSO NEED

The following items (*pictured above*) are used for certain projects.
- Pizza cutter—for cutting long strips of dough
- Lids to act as simple dough cutters
- Ovenproof bowls to use as molds
- Pastry cutters of various shapes
- Pastry brush to moisten larger surfaces
- Tweezers for handling small beads
- Cotton swabs for soaking up small areas of moisture, cleaning mirrors, etc
- Wire (½in) for loops and threading
- Thin fuse wire for decoration
- Wire cutters
- Round-ended pliers
- Small mirrors
- Cork tiles for backing
- Self-adhesive or plain felt for backing
- Glue—the stronger, the better
- Aluminum foil for molded objects
- Decorative bits and pieces, such as loose beads from broken brooches, necklaces and earrings, buttons, and so on
- Dried cloves, also for decoration

STORING TIPS

- Take as much dough as you need for the project in hand and then seal the remainder in plastic food wrap (or place it in an air-tight container) and store it in the refrigerator.

- When you are ready to use it, bring the stored dough back to room temperature by kneading it.

- Dough becomes soggy quite quickly and it does not store well for more than a day, or sometimes two, at a time, so only make as much as you can reasonably use.

- When putting dough to one side to use for a project already under way, cover it with a drying cloth.

- Use a damp cover only when the dough has dried out and needs moistening.

MODELING BY HAND

First, make your dough using the basic recipe given on page 60. Make only as much dough as you are likely to use in one baking session. To achieve consistently successful modeling results, make sure that you keep your hands as cool as possible. The dough must be kneaded to make it pliable, but the more you manipulate it while modeling, the stickier and more unmanageable it is likely to become. So always keep some flour handy to dust your hands if the dough becomes difficult to work.

SHELLS

The type of cockle shells and screwshells you see being made below could be used to decorate a photograph frame, for instance. Once you have picked up the basic technique, you could always try improvising by making a wider range of sea creatures. Even complex creatures can be successfully modeled if you reduce the body shape to a series of simple components that give an impression of the subject.

LEAVES

Leaves and petals are popular forms of decoration and are used in many of the dough craft projects in this chapter, but the trick is to make them look as realistic as possible (*see opposite*). Instead of trying to produce precisely the same leaf or petal every time, vary their shapes and sizes and arrange them in a haphazard, natural-looking fashion.

TIPS

● Make smaller shells from small balls of dough, indented in the middle with the handle end of a paintbrush, and then pinched at both ends.

● Starfish are easily made with a pastry cutter, but you could model them by hand.

MAKING COCKLE SHELLS

1 Take an appropriately sized piece of dough, roll it into an even ball and and flatten it to make a fat disc.

2 Pinching one end between the thumb and forefinger of one hand, gently press the opposite end into a shell shape.

3 Use a small kitchen knife to make shallow cuts on the surface of the shell and then score around the edges.

MAKING COCHLEA ("SNAIL" OR "SCREWSHELLS")

1 Take a ball of dough and roll into a short, thin log. The length of the log determines the shell's size.

2 Make sure the log is consistently thick, and then gently turn one end two or three times until it forms a spiral shape.

3 Use your finger to make a hole in the other end of the shell and then turn it upward to make a realistic shell shape.

LOOPING

A piece of wire embedded in a salt-dough base makes an effective hanging loop for lighter objects. Looping is also a good way of securely joining together individual free-standing dough pieces.

THREADING

Threading wire into dough models is a technique used often in the projects in this book. Use ¹⁄₃₂in thick wire to make the holes in the objects to be threaded.

OTHER TECHNIQUES

There are a handful of other techniques, such as scoring, using dough paste, and indenting, that add texture and interest to the surface of your dough models.

Scoring the surface of salt dough is a technique used throughout this book. Not only is it a good way of adding a touch of professionalism to your model, it also provides attractive contrast lines when you come to paint it. Using a small knife, press the blade gently into the surface of the dough. If you are worried about committing yourself to freehand scoring, first draw lines in pencil as a guide.

To attach relief work to a model, mix a small piece of raw dough with some water to make a loose paste (you could use plain water, but this paste gives a firmer finish). Using a small paintbrush, apply the paste sparingly on the underside of the leaf, shell or cut-out shape to be attached. Then paint a little dough paste on the base area and join the two pieces together.

Indenting the dough with a chopstick or the handle end of a small paintbrush produces shallow depressions that can be painted or used as sockets for decorative beads and small balls of salt dough.

Flattening and patting a model's edges and surfaces with a small wooden spatula (wetted slightly) gives a smooth finish. You can also use the paddle of the spatula to transfer small pieces of relief work to the dough base without distorting them.

Cut-outs are simply shapes made with cookie cutters. Over-moist dough will give you soggy results, so make sure that the consistency is right before you start to cut out your shapes.

MAKING LEAVES

1 Flatten a small piece of dough and then cut and trim the basic leaf shape using a small kitchen knife.

2 Smooth the edges of each leaf with a wet knife blade. Add veins by gently pressing the blade into the dough.

LOOPING

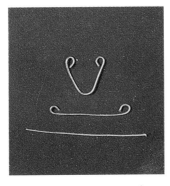 

1 Cut a piece of ¹⁄₃₂in wire about 2in (5cm) long. Using a pair of round-ended pliers, curve the wire and curl each end into an open "O" shape.

2 Using gentle and steady pressure, push the loop of wire into the dough base of the model until both curled ends are hidden from sight.

THREADING

1 Insert a length of wire through the object. As the dough starts to harden, turn the wire to prevent the hole closing up. Repeat this process until the object is cooked.

2 Using pliers, remove the wire, taking great care not to damage the dough, and rethread it according to instructions given on the relevant projects.

BAKING

Salt-dough baking is not an exact science. Ovens differ and cooking times can vary according to the thickness of the dough being baked, the number of objects baked in the oven at the same time and the type of fuel used. By giving a standard ¼in (5mm) thickness for dough bases—additional relief work should be about ⅛in (3mm thick)—it is possible to be a little more specific. The guide given here (*see right*) will give you an idea of approximate baking times.

For best results, preheat your oven at its lowest temperature and put your tray of dough on the middle shelf. Use the oven times given here as a general guide, but don't worry about being too exact—your own judgment should tell you whether an object is done, especially if you use the tap test (*see opposite*). When baking a mirrored object, however, you need to start with a cold oven to prevent the glass cracking.

TOOLS FOR BAKING
- Flat, non-stick baking sheets
- Long, flat-bladed or fish fillet knife
- Oven glove
- Cooling rack

HALF-BAKING
Although this process can be fussy, it is not at all complicated, but you do need to take care when handling half-baked dough. For

example, bake projects that have been molded over crumpled aluminum foil or ovenproof bowls until they are just firm enough to handle without their shapes becoming distorted. Take the objects from the oven, shutting the oven door to retain the heat, gently remove their molds, and return the salt dough models to the oven to harden off. This stage needs careful monitoring since the dough can easily overcook.

APPROXIMATE BAKING TIMES

THINNER OBJECTS

Models ¼in (5mm) thick:

(Cool oven) 3-4 hours
Gas Mark 2—300°F (150°C)

(Warming oven) 7 hours
(Timber/oil-heated oven)—250°F (120°C)

THICKER OBJECTS

Models ¼in (5mm) thick plus ⅛in (3mm) relief:

(Cool oven) 6-7 hours
Gas Mark 2—300°F (150°C)

(Warming oven) 10 hours
(Timber/oil-heated oven)—250°F (120°C)

Faster times are possible with fan-assisted ovens.

TIPS

● Do not flour, grease or wet the baking tray.

● Another way of checking to see if an object is properly baked is to push a pin into the back. If it slips in easily and comes out clean, the dough is done.

● Always allow objects to cool thoroughly before painting and varnishing.

The length of baking gives you a great degree of control over the base color of your model. Here you see examples of unbaked, half-baked and fully browned dough.

BROWNING

This baking technique gives different degrees of color—from a pale gold to a deep brown—and it can be a very effective method for producing a natural finish and as a way of highlighting an object's shape. It can also give a deeper base color, and this effects the appearance of the paint color or the varnish used (*see pp. 66-7*).

After baking, return the salt dough to the oven and allow it to brown. Keep a close eye on this process, since overcooking can make the dough very brittle and prone to cracking.

AIR-DRYING

This method is especially good for mirrors and picture frames (the bases are baked and the frames are attached later and then air-dried). Although it takes longer—days rather than hours—and therefore requires more patience, air-drying saves on fuel bills and doesn't monopolize the oven!

Again, exact drying times largely depend on the thickness of the model being produced and the ambient room temperature. Leave objects somewhere undisturbed on a flat surface in a dry place—a drying closet, for example, is ideal. The temperature should be constant, but you will still need to keep a close eye on the dough since it may start to warp slightly. On warm summer days, you can even dry thinner objects outside in the sunshine.

FILLING AND REPAIRING

Most cracks in dough models can be repaired easily, especially if you are vigilant and brush on some dough paste (diluted with extra water for hairline cracks) while the object is still warm. Heat is an excellent sealant and will aid the repair process.

Where the salt dough has been built up in layers, when using relief work, for example, any gaps and joins should be sealed and smoothed over by brushing on dough paste or water. After repairing, return the model to the oven. If you are still worried about the strength of a join, wait until the model is cool and use a little glue.

PAINTING

If you can't commit yourself to a color scheme straight away, make a rough drawing of the object and experiment on paper first. When you start painting the dough, be decisive. Watercolors dry quickly, so use bold brush strokes on larger areas, and apply the paint evenly. Don't over-fill the brush—the moisture could seep down into the dough.

Forget realism and be as dramatic as you dare. Rich, clashing colors are often far more effective than carefully matched shades. Try restricting yourself to a certain number of colors (the choice is yours), but keep a couple in reserve to create contrast between textures. Some objects lend themselves to groups of colors, but this need not be restricting. A sun plaque can be painted in shades of yellow, sand, brown, rust gold, and burnt orange, for example. Use darker shades of the same color for definition—a deeper green on the veins of leaves, for example.

For a stippled finish, dip a piece of crumpled paper towel or a piece of dry sponge into a small quantity of your chosen paint color, and then dab at parts of the painted surface.

To create slivers of highlights, stroke gold paint onto the edges and rims of objects with a dry paintbrush, and then wipe over quickly with paper towel.

Blend colors with a cotton swab for a soft-edged finish to your work.

TOOLS FOR PAINTING
● Paints—tubes of watercolor are excellent for varying color density and acrylic paints are good, too, but avoid oil-based products
● Paintbrushes—buy the best quality you can afford (four or five, ranging from a wide brush, for stroking on large areas of background color, to a fine-haired brush, useful for small areas of fine detail)
● Paste brushes—cheap brushes are good enough to use for pasting, but ensure that bristles are firmly attached
● Gold paint
● Paper towel—for distressed effect
● Small pieces of sponge—useful to give a distressed paint effect
● Cotton swabs—for blotting, smoothing and blending paint colors

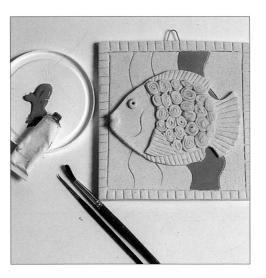

Dough models can be left in their natural, cooked color. Some of them, however, come into their own only when they have been painted.

TOOLS FOR VARNISHING

- Narrow paintbrush—about ½in (1.25cm) for general work
- Smaller brush—for fine detail
- Chopstick or wooden spoon handle, to stir varnish
- Polyurethane varnish (clear matte or gloss)—one small tin of each
- Turpentine—for cleaning brushes

VARNISHING

Not only does varnish help to seal and protect your work, it also adds a veneer of depth and richness to surface colors and brings out the natural tones of baked, but unpainted, salt dough. Careless varnishing, however, can ruin a beautifully painted object, so take your time!

Whether you use matte- or gloss-finish varnish is up to you. Some people prefer a high-definition shine on everything, while others go for a more subtle effect. Generally speaking, surface detail and decoration can be lost under too much shine, while simpler objects often look better with a gloss finish. If you don't intend to finish the back of an object with cork or felt, paint on a coat of varnish to seal it as soon as it is completely cool.

A few rules to bear in mind are: leave each coat to dry thoroughly before applying the next; each object will need five or six coats of varnish; when varnishing more than one object at a time, make a chart to record the number of coats each has received; and

finally, always clean your brushes as soon as you finish working.

Egg white gives a natural-looking glaze for traditional and unpainted salt dough models, such as wreaths. Brush the egg white on before baking. This finish is not as long-lasting as chemical varnish.

FINISHING YOUR WORK

Decorative finishes are largely a matter of taste. You may want to thread hanging plaques with ribbons, for example, or use beads and bells to cover threading wires.

Painting and varnishing the backs of finished pieces will protect your models, but if you are worried about filled cracks, general repairs, or an uneven finish, you may prefer to cover the backs of plaques, frames, mirrors, and some decorations.

- Use (thin) cork tiles as backing. Cut cork to size and glue it into place.
- Felt makes a good backing. Again, cut it to size and stick it in place.
- For a short cut, try sticky-backed felt—simply peel it back and stick it into place.

PRESERVING YOUR WORK

Although it is strong and long-lasting, salt dough is very susceptible to changes in temperature and to atmospheric damp. Varnishing your work will do a lot to improve its appearance as well as sealing and protecting it from harm.

Choose either a matte- or gloss-finish varnish, depending on taste, but don't apply the varnish until the dough is completely cool or the paint thoroughly dry.

Project templates

The templates on the pages that follow relate to the models in the projects section (*pp. 74-103*). Templates are extremely simple to make. Try not to rush the tracing and cutting processes, however, since well-made templates produce better results and can be used time and time again. Enlarge the motifs using a photocopier or squared guide; the motifs here are shown at 100% of the actual size, unless otherwise stated.

● Trace the shapes carefully on to tracing paper.

● Place the tracing paper on the cardboard and, using a sharp pencil, draw over the traced shape, pressing firmly enough to leave an impression of the outline on the cardboard beneath.

● Use a craft knife or scissors to cut around the shapes.

● Alternatively, cut out photocopies of the template shapes, lay them on a piece of cardboard, and carefully cut around them.

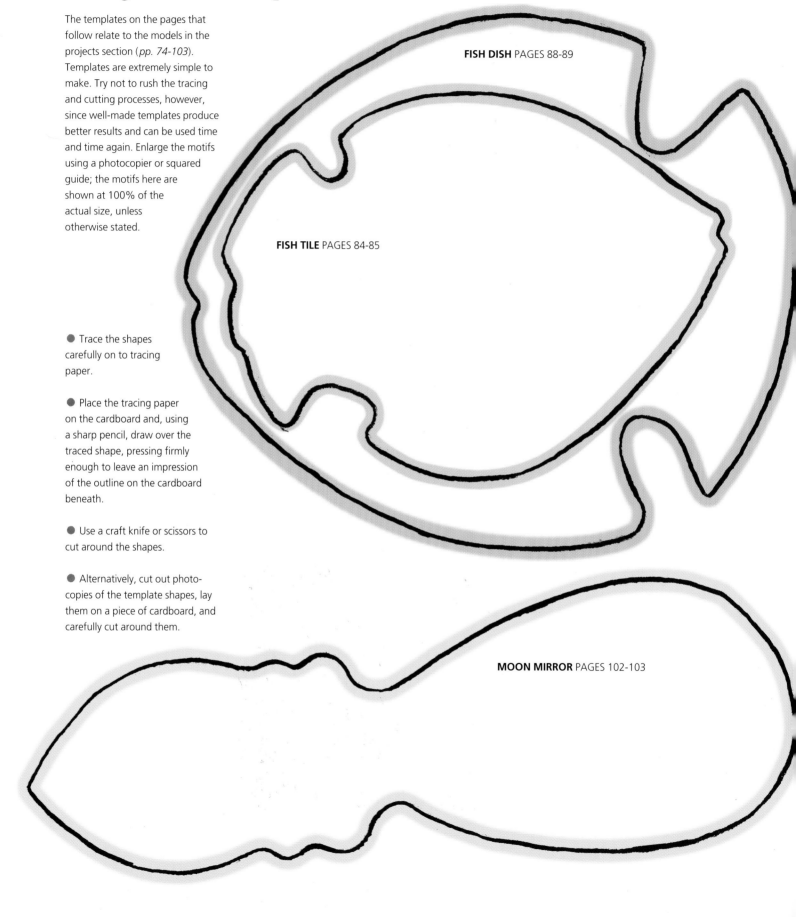

FISH DISH PAGES 88-89

FISH TILE PAGES 84-85

MOON MIRROR PAGES 102-103

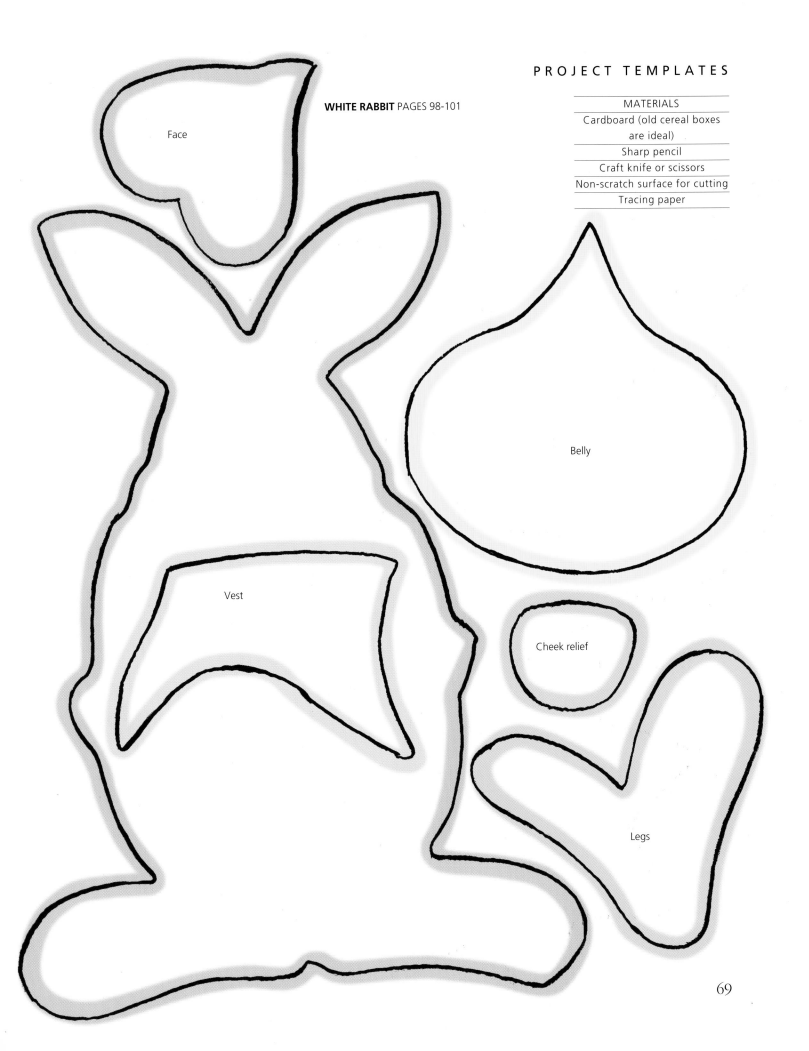

WHITE RABBIT PAGES 98-101

Face

Belly

Vest

Cheek relief

Legs

MATERIALS
Cardboard (old cereal boxes are ideal)
Sharp pencil
Craft knife or scissors
Non-scratch surface for cutting
Tracing paper

DOUGHCRAFT

MOTHER GOOSE PAGES 76-77

Feet

Beak

Wing

Scarf

Apron

Wing

STAR POT AND LID PAGES 86-87
This motif is shown at 80% of actual size

FROWNING SUN PAGES 74-75

70

COW JUMPED OVER THE MOON
PAGES 78-79

Face

Thigh

Moon

HEART CONTAINER PAGES 96-97
This motif is shown at 80% of actual size

DOUGHCRAFT

PROJECTS

1

2

MATERIALS

Non-stick baking sheet

Ruler

Rolling pin

Small kitchen knife

Small wooden spatula

Small jar of dough paste

Paintbrush for dough paste

Plus

Cardboard template
(*see p. 70*)

½2in wire
about 4in (10cm) long

Wire cutters

Round-ended pliers

Small glass (to make central
impression in sun)

Metal beads (or dried cloves)
for eyes

Paintbrush

Varnish brush

3

4

1 Working directly on a baking sheet, roll out the dough to a thickness of approximately ¼in (5mm), place the template on the dough and cut out the basic shape with a sharp kitchen knife. Carefully smooth any rough edges of the dough with a small spatula or barely damp paintbrush.

2 Using a ruler or knife, gently indent the dough diagonally, from point to point of the sun's rays, and outline the face by making a shallow, circular indentation using the rim of a small glass. Don't press down too hard.

3 To make the face, roll out two small, thin log shapes for eyebrows, one and a half for the lips, a slightly thicker log of dough for the nose, and two small balls to represent nostrils. Using the photograph of the finished sun shown opposite as a guide, position and attach all the pieces with dough paste. Press metal beads or cloves into position for the eyes (or use two small dough balls). The cheeks consist of two balls of dough, flattened to about ¾in (2cm) across. Score around the edges of the cheeks and attach them to the sun with a little dough paste.

4 Take a piece of wire and make a single loop at one end. Insert it into the center top of the sun to a depth of about ¾in (2cm). Bend the other end of the wire into a hanging hook. Bake, paint, and varnish.

FROWNING SUN

Although this design is very straightforward, you should not feel that you have to re-create it exactly as it is illustrated above. There is nothing to prevent you using the basic instructions for the sun plaque simply as the starting point for your own ideas.

You could, for example, experiment by adding threaded-dough cut-outs and beads, or any beads and trinkets you may have collected over the years. You could also try using different paint techniques and color schemes to create a more exotic-looking wall-hanging, one tailor-made to fit in with the decoration of your own home. And although this is a stern-looking sun, you could, of course, decide to turn the frowning face into one with a beaming smile. The choice is yours.

The tricks to successful dough craft modeling lie first in thinking the project through thoroughly in advance, and then being prepared—so collect all the tools and materials you will need before starting. For the wire-threading technique used here, see page 63.

MATERIALS

Non-stick baking sheet
Ruler
Rolling pin
Small kitchen knife
Small wooden spatula
Small jar of dough paste
Paintbrush for dough paste
Plus
Cardboard templates (*see p. 70*)
½2in (1mm) wire about 2in (5cm) long
Wire cutters
Round-ended pliers
Paintbrush
Varnish brush

1

2

3

4

1 Working directly on a baking sheet, roll out the dough for the base to a thickness of about ¼in (5mm). With a sharp knife, carefully cut around the template shapes. Roll the dough for the smaller template pieces to a thickness of approximately ⅛in (3mm) and cut them out also. Position the smaller shapes on the base. Using dough paste and a damp brush, carefully stick and seal the shapes to the base. Take care not to press too hard or distort the model's shape when doing this. Tidy and smooth any rough edges.

2 Roll some spare dough into egg-shaped balls and arrange them in the basket. Stick them securely down with some dough paste (or water on a paintbrush). Roll a small ball to form the goose's eye and another, slightly larger, for her cheek. Position and stick them down.

3 Add the feather detailing, the apron frill, and the textured weave on the egg basket by gently indenting the dough with a knife (*see p. 70*). Take care not to cut through the dough or to distort its shape by pressing too hard.

4 To make the hanging loop in the middle of the top wing, curl each end of a piece of wire into an open O shape, using pliers or wire cutters to help bend and shape the wire. Bend the middle of the wire downward and carefully embed the curled ends into the dough until they are completely hidden, leaving just a neat loop or hanging hook on view. Bake, paint, and varnish.

MOTHER GOOSE

Character plaques such as this lovable character make eye-catching details for a child's room. Mother Goose has been a firm favorite with young children for generations—and a hand-made plaque, modeled exclusively with a certain child in mind, adds a very special personal touch.

You will find all the templates for making a Mother Goose on pages 68-71. However, don't be deterred by the number of pieces involved. Once you have cut out all the shapes, the plaque itself is very straightforward to assemble. Take your time when tracing around and cutting out the templates from cardboard, since you can use well-prepared templates again and again. This may be extremely useful if you want to make two geese, perhaps painted in different colors, for a brother and sister, for example. You can also duplicate this plaque to make a series of flying geese to hang at different heights along a wall.

But be warned, this is a decoration, not a toy. Take care to hang it out of the reach of smaller children.

1 To calculate the length of wire, lay out the cow and moon templates with the correct space for the beads, stars, and bell in between. Allow wire for a hook at the top and a bottom loop.

2 Working on a baking sheet, roll the dough for the cow, moon and stars to a thickness of ¼in (5mm). Roll dough for the relief work pieces half this thickness. Cut the template shapes from the dough. Cut the stars with a cookie cutter and thread them with one of the 4in (10cm) lengths of wire.

3 Position the smaller pieces on the cow shape. Roll balls of dough for nostrils, and a thin log in between. Stick them all down. Squash and pierce the nostrils with the handle of a paintbrush. Use the same method for the eyes.

4 Insert wire for the cow's tail. Roll an olive pitt-sized piece of dough and push it (half way) on to the end of the tail. Insert the 5in (13cm) length of wire through the cow's body.

5 Use a small glass or cutter to cut out the moon's cheek. Position it on the base, stick it down and score around the edges. Roll out a sausage and coil it for the eyebrow. Roll a dough ball for the eye (or use a metal bead) and position and stick it down. Insert the 10in (25cm) length of wire through the moon.

6 While baking, turn the wires (except for the cow's tail) regularly to prevent the holes closing. When cooled, withdraw the wires using pliers. After painting, varnishing, and drying, thread the wire with the cow, moon, stars, beads, etc. Shape the upper end of the wire into a hook and make a loop at the other.

1

2

3

4

5

6

THE COW JUMPED OVER THE MOON

The inspiration for this model is the well-known children's nursery rhyme. Since the theme is not realistic, you can be outlandish with your paint, patterns, and textures, or lengthen the wires and add more moons and cut-out shapes.

If you have been working your way through the crafts so far, your confidence and skill should be increasing with each attempt. This plaque is a combination of the relief work you practiced on the Mother Goose project (*see p. 71*).

The small beads and wires could be harmful to young children. Position the plaque high up, well out of reach, if it is hung in a child's room.

MATERIALS
Non-stick baking sheet
Ruler
Rolling pin
Small kitchen knife
Small wooden spatula
Small jar of dough paste
Paintbrush for dough paste
Plus
Cardboard template (*see pp. 68-71*)
Wire cutters
Round-ended pliers
½₂in wire about 10in (25cm) for the moon, 5in (13cm) for the cow, and 4in (10cm) for the tail and stars—if using templates supplied
1mm wire for final threading—see step 1 for length
Beads, bell, etc, for decoration
Star-shaped cookie cutter
Small circular glass or cutter
Paintbrush
Varnish brush

1 Cover an ovenproof bowl with foil, taking care to smooth the surface and to tuck the ends over the edge of the bowl—about 2in (5cm) of the foil should overlap the inside of the bowl.

2 Roll the dough out to a thickness of about ⅓in (1cm). Carefully place the dough over the foil-covered bowl. Trim any excess from the edges with a sharp knife, taking care not to cut into the foil.

3 Now smooth the surface of the dough with a damp (not wet) pastry brush. Trim and smooth the dough, using a spatula to pat and flatten any rough edges. When the edges and surface of the bowl are smooth, turn it over and cut a wavy line around the rim, taking care not to cut into the foil. Smooth any rough edges with a spatula.

4 Add exterior details by scoring lines around the bowl, about ⅛in (3mm) apart, and ½in (1.5cm) down from the rim. Follow the wavy line of the bowl's rim, using the photograph of the finished project as a guide. Score lines around the rim of the pot and between alternate lines. Place the pot upside down on the baking sheet and bake.

5 When the dough is hard to the touch, take it from the oven. Carefully remove the ovenproof bowl, and then peel the foil away from the inside of your dough bowl. Replace the bowl, now the right way up, on the baking sheet and return it to the oven to finish baking.

6 Remove it from the oven when cooked and, when it is completely cool, paint and varnish.

1

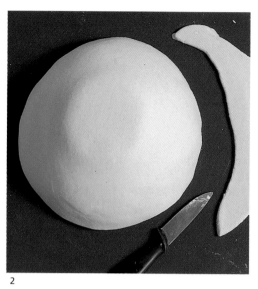
2

3

4

5

6

MATERIALS

Non-stick baking sheet
Rolling pin
Small kitchen knife
Small wooden spatula
Small jar of dough paste
Paintbrush for dough paste
Pastry brush
Plus
Aluminum foil
Ovenproof bowl
Paintbrush
Varnish brush
Sponge or paper towel

SCALLOP-EDGED BOWL

For this project air-drying the dough is an alternative to baking. To do this, you need to dry the dough in its mold until it is hard enough not to distort, and then remove the mold and stand the bowl right side up to finish drying. Rolling out the dough to an even thickness helps to keep the overall shape from distorting.

If this is the first time you have worked with a mold, avoid extremes. The bowls used here are about 5-6in (13-15cm) across. There is no reason why you shouldn't make a larger bowl, but it is better to start on something manageable and fun and which has an excellent chance of success!

Refer to the section on materials and techniques (*see pp. 60-7*) for more ideas on finishes or stick to the colors used here. If you are not absolutely certain about the type of finish you want, then it's a good idea to bake a practice tile of dough with your pot and use it to experiment with colors. If the thought of scoring the bowl worries you, practice on an uncooked piece of dough until you feel confident pressing patterns into the surface.

1 Roll the dough out to a thickness of about ⅓in (1cm). With a sharp knife, cut out a 6in (15cm) square. Smooth the edges of the square with a spatula and make sure that the surface of the dough is flat and even.

2 Position your mirror in the middle of the dough base and press down gently to embed it in the dough. Tap around the edges of the dough with a spatula to even up the square if necessary.

3 Roll out another piece of dough to a thickness of ¼in (5mm) and cut it into exactly the same size square as your base and mirror. Lay the new square on top and neatly seal the two layers of dough together by brushing dough paste around the edges.

4 Making sure that it is centered, place your cookie cutter on the top layer of the dough and press out a square, exposing the mirror underneath.

5 Seal any gaps around the mirror and frame with dough paste. Roll small, thin logs of dough and coil the ends.

6 Arrange the dough coils on your mirror frame and stick them down using dough paste. Clean any smudges of paste off the mirror surface with cotton balls. Bake, or air-dry, the mirror. If using an oven, put the mirror inside *before* turning it on. When it is baked, turn the oven off and allow it to cool down with the mirror still inside. When the dough is cool, paint and varnish it. Add a cork backing if desired.

1

2

3

4

5

6

MATERIALS
Non-stick baking sheet
Ruler
Rolling pin
Small kitchen knife
Small wooden spatula
Small jar of dough paste
Paintbrush for dough paste
Pastry brush
Plus
Mirror—about 5in (12cm) square
Cotton balls for cleaning mirror
Cookie cutters
Cork for backing—slightly larger than size of mirror
Strong adhesive
Paintbrush
Varnish brush

EASY LEVEL

DOUGH-COIL MIRROR

Although it may look complicated to make, this is the simplest of mirror frames. As long as you cook it at the lowest oven setting and avoid extremes of temperature, it can be baked like any other object.

Although the dough for most of the projects in this book is rolled out to a thickness of ¼in (5mm), it is impossible to be this precise with mirrors. Modern, ⅛in (3.5mm) mirrors can be too thick and heavy for ¼in (5mm) dough. Use your judgment and adjust the thickness of the dough according to the size of mirror. As a general rule, use a ⅓in (1cm) dough base for all mirrors of "average" thickness.

As with the previous project, air-drying is a good alternative to baking. Leave your mirror in a warm place—a drying closet is ideal—where it will not be disturbed. Check on it every day, and use the tap test (*see pp. 60-7*) to see if it is ready.

When baking, put the mirror into a cold oven and let it heat up with the mirror inside. When it is baked, leave your model inside the oven as it slowly cools down again to avoid cracking the mirror through sudden heat changes.

MATERIALS

Non-stick baking sheet
Ruler
Rolling pin
Small kitchen knife
Small wooden spatula
Small jar of dough paste
Paintbrush for dough paste
Plus
Cardboard template (*see p. 68*)
½in wire about 2in (5cm) long for hanging loop
Wire cutters
Round-ended pliers
Paintbrush
Varnish brush
Glue for cork or felt backing (if desired)

INTERMEDIATE LEVEL

FISH TILE

You can model this fish tile plaque relatively quickly—the skill lies in applying the surface texture and color. Scoring techniques are used to give the impression of a border, or frame, around the plaque itself, and relief work adds further interest and depth.

In order to make the plaque look as impressive and as professional as possible, cut the dough very carefully and then smooth the edges. It is sometimes tempting to press too hard when you are working on a relatively large and simple shape, so keep an eye out for any distortion and make sure that your scored cuts or indentations are evenly applied to an equal depth.

To convey the feeling of deep, shimmering sea water and slippery fish scales, and to introduce some drama into the decorative scheme, use rich, marine shades and seaweed colors. This plaque uses contrasting colors for the fish. Gold paint was added as a highlight around the border and for the detailing on the fish's scales, eye and lips. For more information on painting techniques, see pages 60-7.

1

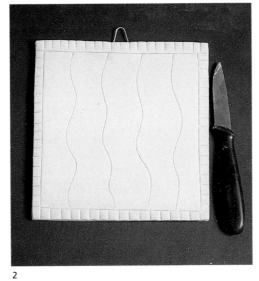

2

1 Working directly on a baking sheet, roll the dough about ⅕in (5mm) thick. Using a ruler and knife, cut a square about 6 x 6in (16 x 16cm). Smooth the edges and surface with a spatula. Make a hanging loop by bending the wire downward and curling both ends into open O shapes. Embed the ends carefully in the middle of the top of the base.

2 Score the border about ⅖in (1cm) in from edge of the tile right around the square. Make the decorative edging using small knife cuts. Now score wavy lines down the tile for the background effect. If you are worried about making these, lightly draw them in pencil first, which can be smoothed away. Cover the work with a dry towel to prevent it drying out.

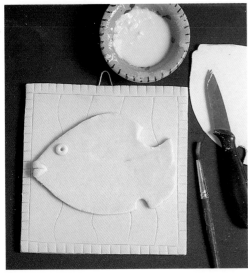

3

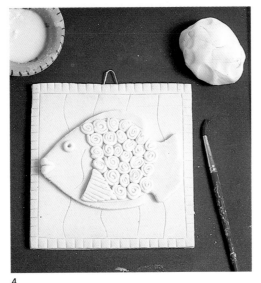

4

3 For the fish, roll the dough out about ⅛in (3mm) thick. Using a template as a guide, cut out the fish and smooth its edges. Attach it to the tile with dough paste. Roll two small dough balls for the mouth and squash them slightly when sticking them down. Roll a tiny ball of dough, stick it down and pierce it with the end of a paintbrush to make the eye.

4 To create the body texture, roll out thin logs of dough. Prepare the fish's body by brushing it with watery dough paste. Don't over-wet the dough. Curl the logs and attach them and cut out a fin shape and attach.

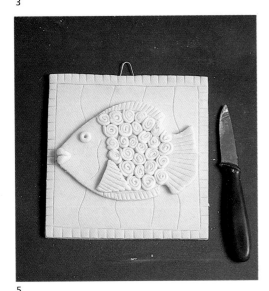

5

6

5 Add texture to the fins and tail by scoring them very carefully. Check that everything is smooth and that gaps between the layers are sealed. Bake and allow to cool.

6 Paint and varnish. Finish the back of your plaque by attaching cork or felt, if desired.

MATERIALS

Non-stick baking sheet
Rolling pin
Small kitchen knife
Small wooden spatula
Small jar of dough paste
Paintbrush for dough paste
Pastry brush
Plus
Cookie cutters
Aluminum foil
Wire about 2in (5cm) long
Ovenproof bowl
Paintbrush
Varnish brush

1

2

STAR POT AND LID

This star pot uses a modeling method similar to that for the previous frowning sun (*see pp. 74-5*) and scallop-edged bowl (*see pp. 80-1*), but includes a lid and cut-outs as decorative relief work.

You can choose any size base by using an appropriate ovenproof bowl as a mold, but note carefully the instructions for cutting the lid to ensure that it is the right size for a good fit!

The shapes here are made with star-shaped cookie cutters, but use other shapes if you wish. If you don't have suitably-shaped cookie cutters, make your own free-hand cut-out moons or geometric shapes, or have a look through the templates for alternatives (see pp. 68-71).

Make sure that the shapes are securely attached. Use dough paste to stick and seal the edges of the shapes and make sure that both the rim of the pot and the edges of the lid are neatly finished by carefully smoothing them before baking.

Rather than bake the pot on its own, it makes good, economical sense to save up a few craft items and then bake them all at the same time, thus making the most of the fuel or power bills.

4

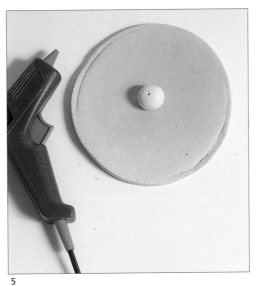

5

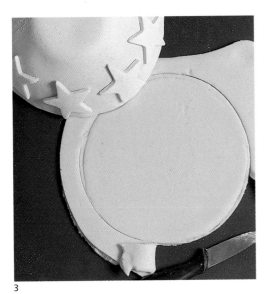

3

6

1 Cover an ovenproof bowl with foil. Smooth the surface and tuck the ends over the edge of the bowl—about 2in (5cm) of the foil should overlap inside the bowl (*see p. 80*). Roll the dough out to a thickness of about ¼in (5mm). Carefully place the dough over the foil-covered bowl. Trim off any excess from the edges with a sharp knife. Smooth the surface of the dough with a damp (not wet) pastry brush, and use a spatula to pat and flatten any rough edges. Now turn it over and start to add exterior details. Roll another piece of dough to a thickness of ⅛in (3mm) and press out as many star shapes as necessary, depending on the size of your pot.

2 Attach cut-outs to the exterior of the bowl with dough paste. if you want to add more texture, score the stars from point to point and add detailing around rim. Place your pot upside down on a baking sheet and bake. When the dough is hard to the touch, carefully remove the ovenproof bowl and peel the foil away from the inside of your dough. Return to the oven to finish baking.

3 To make the lid, roll the dough to thickness of ¼in (5mm). Place the cooled pot upside down on the dough and carefully cut around the rim to make a lid shape. Smooth the edges of the lid before baking.

4 Roll a small bead of dough. Push one end of the length of wire half-way into the bead and embed the other end into a dome-shaped foil base. Bake the lid and bead on the same baking sheet.

5 Attach the bead to the lid with dough paste if it is still warm enough to bond, or use glue.

6 When the bowl is completely cool, paint and varnish both the pot and the lid.

1 Cover an ovenproof bowl with foil, folding and overlapping about 2in (5cm) of the foil over the lip. Flatten the foil until it is absolutely smooth all over. Roll the dough out to a thickness of approximately ¼in (5mm) and cut around your template to make the fish shape.

2 Lift the fish dough shape and carefully lay it over the upside-down, foil-covered bowl.

3 Center the fish shape and smooth it with a damp (not wet) pastry brush, taking care not to stretch the dough out of shape as you do so. Pat and smooth any rough edges with a spatula.

4 Using a small kitchen knife, score the fin and tail details on fish, using even pressure and taking care not to cut too deeply into the dough. Bake it until the surface is dry-looking and hard enough to be moved without distorting.

5 Remove the ovenproof bowl and peel the foil away from the dough. Repair any cracks with plain water while the dough is still warm, or use dough paste. Place your fish-shaped dough dish, the right way up, on the baking sheet and return it to the oven to finish baking.

6 When the dough has cooked, remove it from the oven, wait for it to cool, and then apply paint and a varnish finish to seal it.

FISH DISH

Here is a chance to be as adventurous or conventional as you like. You can either make one dish to use as a table centerpiece, a kitchen decoration or a useful container for bread rolls or party appetizers, or make a whole set of dishes in various sizes simply by altering the sizes of the ovenproof bowls and templates used.

This fish dish uses a combination of the skills and techniques you have already seen in this chapter, such as scoring, cutting, and using molds. But this time, instead of covering your ovenproof mold with an unshaped piece of dough, a template is used for the fish outline. The cut dough is then draped over the mold to give the fish its concave bowl-like shape.

Once you have scored in the surface detail, you can next use baking and browning techniques (*see p. 65*) in order to vary the base color of your dish, leaving a natural-looking surface for a plain varnish finish. Alternatively, you could use a mix of marine colors—anything to highlight the surface texture and emphasize the lavish nature of the dish.

1

2

3

4

5

6

MATERIALS

Non-stick baking sheet

Rolling pin

Small kitchen knife

Small wooden spatula

Small jar of dough paste

Paintbrush for dough paste

Pastry brush

Plus

Cardboard template
(*see p. 68*)

Aluminum foil

Ovenproof bowl

Paintbrush

Varnish brush

Sponge or paper towel

CANDLESTICKS

No matter how exclusive they may be, store-bought candlesticks cannot match the originality and charm of home-made crafts.

Once you have followed the basic modeling instructions on the following pages, you can then proceed to paint and finish your candlestick with some very personal finishing touches. You can choose either to reproduce the colors as shown here, or to decorate your candlestick to match your table linen and tableware, for example.

Making a few candlesticks at a time is a sensible precaution—especially if you are at all nervous about the end result. Spare legs for the stand or an extra bowl could come in

useful as replacement parts for defective pieces, or simply make more than one candlestick to decorate a festive table.

All the proportions for this craft relate to a 3⅓in (8.5cm) ovenproof bowl. You will probably find it easier to follow the instructions if you use a similar-sized bowl. If you want to make bigger or smaller candlesticks, however, then simply adjust the proportions accordingly.

The coiled legs are a very important structural element of this project. They provide a tripod arrangement for the decorative bowl and should make a secure and steady base. For this reason, ensure that you roll out the dough to exactly the same lengths and widths for each leg.

MATERIALS

Non-stick baking sheet
Ruler
Rolling pin
Small kitchen knife
Small wooden spatula
Small jar of dough paste
Paintbrush for dough paste
Pastry brush
Plus
Aluminum foil
½in wire
Wire cutters
Round-ended pliers
Small ovenproof bowl
Paintbrush
Varnish brush

1

2

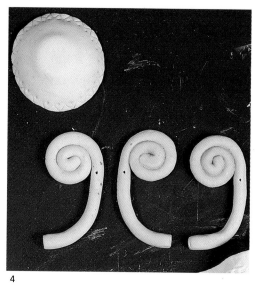

3

5

4

1 Working directly on the baking sheet, roll out three thin logs of dough, each measuring about 10in (25cm) long and ⅓in (1cm) wide.

2 Curl the ends of the dough logs, positioning them in a straight line on the baking sheet. Doing this will make it easier to assess the lengths and ensure that they are equal. Using a piece of ½in-thick wire, make a threading hole just below the coil of each leg. Check that the hole goes right the way through the legs by rotating the wire gently and slowly

6

7

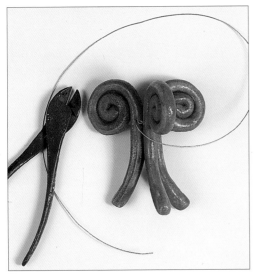

8

9

until you can feel the baking sheet underneath the dough.

3 Cover a small ovenproof dish with aluminum foil, making sure that the foil overlaps the rim of the bowl and tucks inside it by about 2in (5cm). Smooth the foil carefully all over. Roll the dough out to a thickness of ¼in (5mm) and place it over the foil-covered bowl. Trim off any excess dough, taking care not to cut into the foil.

4 Bake the bowl and legs together in the oven. When the dough bowl is hard enough to be

handled without distorting its shape, remove the ovenproof bowl and peel away the foil. Return the bowl to the oven until it is cooked. Whether or not the legs are baked by this time will depend on their thickness as well as the type of oven you are using.

5 Remove the dough from the oven and when it is cool, paint the legs and bowl.

6 When the paint is dry, apply coats of varnish, but take care that you don't clog the threading holes in the legs.

7 When the varnish is completely dry, thread ½in-thick wire through the holes in the coiled legs.

8 Maneuver the legs carefully into position to make a firm and even tripod arrangement.

9 Continue wrapping the wire around the coiled legs until they are firmly and neatly secured.

1 Roll the dough out to a thickness of about ⅜in (1cm). With a knife, cut a base measuring about 6½ x 8in (16.5 x 20cm).

2 Now position your mirror in the center of the base and press it down into the dough.

3 Roll out more dough to a thickness of ¼in (5mm). Cut it to exactly the same size as the base and lay it over the top of the base and mirror so that they are evenly covered. Seal all the edges carefully with dough paste. Cut out an oblong a little more than 1in (3cm) smaller all round than the mirror and carefully peel away the surplus dough to expose the mirror below. Seal the edges with dough paste and clean the mirror with cotton balls.

4 Using wire cutters, cut lengths of ½in wire and bend them into coils with the pliers.

5 Score a line in the dough around the mirror, about ⅛in (3mm) in from the edge.

6 Embed the wire coils in the frame. Place the mirror in a cold oven and then turn the oven on. When baked, turn the oven off and allow the dough and mirror to cool down. This avoids subjecting the glass to sudden temperature changes, which may cause it to crack. When the dough is thoroughly cool, paint and varnish it. Attach cork backing, if desired, using a strong adhesive.

1

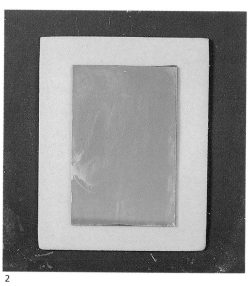

2

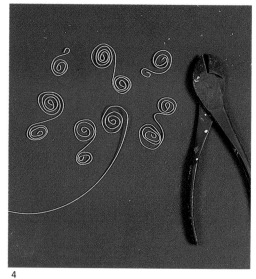

3

4

5

6

MATERIALS
Non-stick baking sheet
Ruler
Rolling pin
Small kitchen knife
Small wooden spatula
Small jar of dough paste
Paintbrush for dough paste
Plus
Mirror—5 x 7in (13 x 18cm)
Cotton balls
½in wire
Wire cutters and pliers
Cork for backing
Strong adhesive
Paintbrush
Varnish brush

METAL-COIL MIRROR

Up until now, wire has been used as a material for hanging and threading crafts, but it has decorative qualities, too. This mirror features coils of ½in wire pressed into the dough to make an unusual finish. The coils themselves are made by curling lengths of wire around the head of a pair of pliers.

To make sure that the decorations are firmly attached to your frame, press them in place and then lever them out carefully and apply a strong adhesive before putting them back.

Bake metal decorations only. If you want to use plastic beads, for example, press them in place, remove them before baking and glue them back when the mirror is cool. Air-drying the dough circumvents this problem.

For a more opulent effect, use beads, sequins and/or colored glass, but try not to press the dough too hard when embedding these decorative finishes.

Keep a close eye on the baking process. A thick base, a mirror, and an extra layer of dough surround will take longer to harden than other projects.

1 Working directly on a baking sheet, roll the dough out about ¼in (5mm) thick. Using the cutter, press out the heart and smooth all over with a spatula. Make a hanging loop by bending the wire downward and curling both ends into open "O" shapes. Embed the curled ends carefully in the middle of the top of the heart, leaving about 2in (5cm) protruding to create a hanging loop. Cover the dough and put it aside.

2 Make a mold by shaping the foil into a hollow pocket about 3 x 3½in (8 x 9cm) and ⅜in (1cm) thick. Roll the dough out to about ¼in (5mm) thick, lay it over mold and trim around the edges.

3 Roll a bead shape from any scraps of left-over dough from the above steps.

4 Bake the heart-shaped, molded dough pocket and bead side by side in the oven. While it is still warm (but not too hot to handle), remove the foil very gently from the pocket and place the pocket on the heart-shaped base.

5 Taking advantage of the fact that both pieces are warm, join them together (using thick dough paste to close any gaps). Use the dough paste to attach the still-warm bead. Return the assembled plaque to the oven and keep a eye on it while the paste hardens and seals the pieces. This should take about 15-20 minutes. Don't allow the dough to become brittle through over cooking.

6 Allow the dough to cool. If you are in any doubt about the pieces sealing firmly, use glue for a stronger finish (*see pp. 60-7*). Paint and varnish the model and fix cork or felt backing, if required.

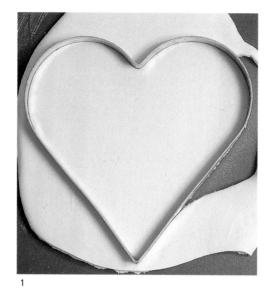

1

2

3

4

5

6

MATERIALS
Non-stick baking sheet
Ruler
Rolling pin
Small kitchen knife
Small wooden spatula
Small jar of dough paste
Paintbrush for dough paste
Plus
Cardboard template (*see pp. 68-71*) or pastry cutter
Aluminum foil
½in wire about 3in (7cm) long for hanging loop
Wire cutters
Round-nosed pliers
Paintbrush
Varnish brush
Glue and cork or felt for backing (if desired)

ADVANCED LEVEL

HEART CONTAINER

Echoes of folk art give an ethnic flavor to this attractive container. The heart plaque is practical, too, since you can use it to hold dried flowers, chopsticks, or lightweight kitchen implements.

The colors are the key to its success, so here's a chance to be daring with your choice of paints. Follow the basic modeling technique which is described here, and then the paint effects are up to you. You could use the ideas illustrated above, or take inspiration from any number of traditional folk art sources.

The "pocket" is made by using a simple molding technique, which you can easily adapt to make containers in many different shapes and sizes. If you would rather make a smaller heart, for example, simply reduce the size of the template, pocket and mold, and then follow the modeling and baking techniques opposite to create your own very individual design.

Because aluminum foil is so pliable, it is an ideal material for molding—just scrunch it into any suitable shape and then cover it with dough.

WHITE RABBIT

When it comes to making children's dough plaques, this classic character is far too well known to ignore, and almost too popular to need any form of introduction. Because he has so much personality (without being at all over-cute or sentimental), the White Rabbit, inspired by the book *Alice in Wonderland*, makes a perfect hanging plaque for children of all ages.

However, don't let the fact that he appears in the advanced section put you off—the rabbit is a combination of a lot of the skills used earlier in this chapter and, apart from some careful paintwork, there are no techniques used here that you have not already come across. The plaque is made up of different templates, placed on a rabbit-shaped base, and built up in relief. Don't forget to cover any pieces of dough that are not in immediate use with a dry towel.

It is the detailing that makes this plaque really special—everything, from the watch and chain to his wire spectacles, contributes to the overall effect. Work steadily and don't be tempted to rush the process or to cut corners, since the end result relies on careful craftwork.

This plaque is not a toy. If you use the rabbit as a hanging in a young child's bedroom, place it high up safely out of reach.

MATERIALS

Non-stick baking sheet
Ruler
Rolling pin
Small kitchen knife
Small wooden spatula
Small jar of dough paste
Paintbrush for dough paste
Plus
Cardboard template (*see p. 68*)
⅟₃₂in wire about 2½in (6cm) long for hanging loop
About 2½in (6cm) of thin, pliable fuse wire (for spectacles)
Toy eyes (from a craft store) or two metal beads
Wire cutters
Round-ended pliers
Paintbrushes (including fine brush for detail)
Varnish brush
Glue for cork or felt backing (if desired)

1 Working directly on a baking sheet, roll the dough to a thickness of about ¼in (5mm). Using a template as a guide, cut out the basic shape and make a hanging loop from ⅟₃₂in wire, bending the wire downward and curling both ends into open "O" shapes. Embed the curled ends carefully in the middle of the top (between the ears). Roll the rest of the dough to a thickness of about ⅛in (3mm) and cut carefully around the other templates.

2 Carefully lay each shape on to the rabbit's base, smoothing rough edges as you go, and use dough paste to stick them neatly into position. Check there are no gaps between the layers and that the rabbit figure is built-up and shaped as neatly as possible. Make the ear indentations and cover the dough to prevent it drying out.

3 To make the bow, roll a long, thin log of dough about 5in (12cm). Flatten it unevenly and shape it into a horizontal "figure-8." Add a blob of dough for the central knot. Roll two more logs, just over 1in (3cm) long, for the bow-tails and cut V's into the ends with a knife.

4 Use a small spatula or flat blade to carefully lift the bow on to the rabbit, and attach it with dough paste.

5 To make the watch, roll a ball of dough and flatten it roughly into the shape and size of a small coin. Stick it on to the rabbit and add two tiny balls of dough to represent the watch's winding mechanism.

6 Roll a thin log about 2in (5cm) long for the watch chain. Attach one end to the watch and drape the rest across the rabbit's

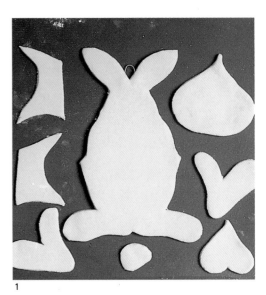
1

2

3

4

5

6

7

8

9

body, sticking it down carefully. Now score a line just inside the circular watch face for the casing. To make the eyes, use either toy eyes or beads. Use the eyes to indent the dough. Put them to one side and stick them on after baking, or they may melt. Metal beads can be positioned and stuck on the model before baking, or you could roll small balls of dough to make the eyes and then paint them later.

7 To make the spectacles, use thin fuse wire. Make a wide, double-loop shape and push the straight ends into position, so that they rest naturally above the rabbit's nose.

8 To make the teeth, roll a small, fat log of dough about ½in (1cm) long. Score down its middle with a sharp knife. The finished result should look like a coffee bean. Stick it into position.

9 To add texture, use a sharp knife to score in whiskers, hair, eyebrows, and paws. Try to make the surface texture look as natural as possible. Bake the model and allow it to cool, and then fill any cracks or gaps with dough paste. Paint it with a fine-haired brush, adding extra details to the watch, jacket, and so on. Finally, varnish the piece and add a backing if desired.

1 Choose a plate, about 1¾in (4cm) larger than the mirror you intend to use. Roll the dough out to a thickness of about ½in (1cm) and carefully cut around the plate with a sharp knife. Smooth any rough edges.

2 Position your mirror in the center of the dough and press down, taking care not to distort the circular shape of the surround.

3 Roll out more dough to a thickness of ¼in (5mm). Cut around the plate to make another circle exactly the same as the first. Drape the circle of dough over a rolling pin and lower it over the dough base and mirror. Seal all the outside edges with dough paste. Position the template in the exact center of dough circle and cut around it with a knife. Smooth and seal the edges around mirror.

4 Taking care not to press right through the dough, score zig-zag details around the edges of the frame, overlapping the moon tail outlines at top and bottom of the mirror and the nostril curls.

5 To make the cheeks, cut circles ⅛in (3mm) thick, using the lid of a spice jar. Attach them with dough paste and score line details around the edges.

6 Roll dough balls for the eyes and indent the centers (insert metal beads if desired). Roll dough pieces and coil them up for the eyelids and brows. Place the mirror into a cold oven, turn on and bake. When it is baked, let the oven cool down with the mirror inside (or air-dry). When it is cool, paint and varnish. Keep a close eye on the baking process. A thicker base, mirror, and an extra layer of dough surround will take longer to harden than some other projects.

1

2

3

4

5

6

MOON MIRROR

The shape of this mirror surround is perfect for a moon theme. Specific measurements are not given, since sizes depend on the size of the mirror used—choose a plate a little larger in size to make the base and surround. This project recycles an old mirror taken from a chipped frame; a dinner plate gives the shape for the base and surround.

The moon employs straightforward techniques, but its success relies on careful joining and a neat finish. If you have the confidence to go for a bold paint effect, the end result is guaranteed to be spectacular.

Although the instructions are given here for baking, you may find air-drying more convenient (and less expensive) than monopolizing the oven and spending money on fuel.

By now you should be experienced enough to put other craft skills to use. Varying the size of the template to fit a smaller or larger mirror and cutting around an appropriately sized bowl, dish, or plate should be no problem, especially if you are keen to reuse a mirror you can't bear to throw away!

MATERIALS

Non-stick baking sheet
Rolling pin
Small kitchen knife
Small wooden spatula
Small jar of dough paste
Paintbrush for dough paste
Plus
Cardboard template (*see p. 68*)
Mirror
Cotton swabs
Cork for backing
Strong adhesive
Paintbrush
Varnish brush

103

PAPIER MACHE

MATERIALS AND TECHNIQUES

MATERIALS AND TECHNIQUES

All the projects in this book use the two basic papier mâché methods: layered or pulped. Before starting any of the projects, it is advisable to read through all the instructions and study the pictures for the whole project. Check that you have all the materials and equipment you will need, particularly the basic ingredients that are outlined here.

Simple household equipment is needed for the layered method (below), while the pulped method (bottom) requires a few more accessories, such as a blender and also a saucepan.

EQUIPMENT

Much of the basic equipment needed to make papier mâché is readily available in most homes. Check that craft knives are sharp before you start cutting card or trimming papier mâché, and ensure that any paintbrushes being used are in good order and won't drop hairs in the varnish. It is best to work on a large, flat surface, one that you can move around if necessary—a square of plastic-coated medium-density fiberboard would be ideal.

YOU WILL NEED
For the layered method
- Bucket for the newspaper strips
- Cotton swabs for bead molds and applying releasing agent
- Paintbrushes to apply PVA (polyvinyl acetate) medium to the strips of newspaper. A flat, square-ended type of paintbrush is best
- Hair dryer to speed up the overall drying process
- Craft knife for cutting card
- Scissors

For the pulped method
- Bowl or bucket for soaking the newspaper
- Saucepan to boil the newspaper in
- Sieve
- Cotton swabs for bead molds and applying releasing agent
- Wooden spoon
- Hand-held blender or whisk to pulp papier mâché
- A roller, rolling pin, or large bottle to roll out the pulp
- Craft knife
- Waxed paper or plastic wrap to hold still-wet projects—they can be left to dry on this
- Baking foil to cover unused pulp and prevent it drying out
- Hair dryer for speeding up the overall drying process

MAKING PAPIER MACHE

Both the methods described here give particularly good results, producing an easily workable papier mâché. The layered method, as it name suggests, is done by building up layer upon layer of newspaper strips; the pulped method is a good medium for modeling and sculpting.

THE LAYERED METHOD

THE INGREDIENTS
● Double sheets of newspaper—torn into strips or squares, according to the type of project to be made
● PVA medium—widely available in craft stores, this makes an excellent glue and easily washes off hands
● Water—to thin the PVA medium a little, and to help saturate the newspaper

● Releasing agent—you will need an oil-based releasing agent—petroleum jelly is ideal—to help remove the dried papier mâché from its mold. Without this it is almost impossible to remove the papier mâché intact.
● Brown paper tape—gummed brown paper tape is very useful to join cardboard and papier mâché together. It is very strong, and can safely be pulped on, or layered over.

1

2

1 Tear strips along the grain of the newspaper. These should generally be about 1in (2.5cm) in width. Some projects, however, require smaller squares to go around awkward shapes, while others, such as the tea tray project (*see pp. 126-7*), need broader 2in (5cm) strips that work better when forming a large, flat surface.

2 Thin the PVA medium with a little water and apply to the strips with the pasting brush. Alternatively, you can soak the strips in the solution.

THE PULPED METHOD

THE INGREDIENTS
(Makes enough pulp for each project unless otherwise detailed)
● Double sheets of newspaper—torn into pieces ready to be soaked.
● Water—to soak and boil the newspaper
● PVA medium—the glue used to hold the pulp together
● Linseed oil—makes the pulp supple and easy to handle
● Oil of cloves—has natural fungicidal properties and prevents mold from forming on papier mâché. It is widely available from drug stores
● Releasing agent—petroleum jelly is ideal to use, but other oil-based substances, such as liquid detergent, can also be used to prevent the pulp from sticking fast in its mold
● Brown paper tape—used to tape cardboard together when forming molds

THE PULPED METHOD

1 Take the double sheets of newspaper and tear into pieces no larger than 1in (2.5cm) square. Soak in water for at least 8 hours, ideally 24 hours.

2 Drain the paper and boil in a pan of water on the stovetop for about 25 minutes to loosen the newspaper fibers.

3 Remove the saucepan from the heat, cool, and pour the contents into a sieve, shaking out any excess water.

4 Tip the paper into a bowl, and use a hand-held blender or whisk to reduce the paper to a pulp. The alternative method is to use a pestle and mortar.

5 Add in 3 tablespoons of PVA medium, 1 tablespoon of linseed oil, and 3 drops of oil of cloves to the pulp and mix thoroughly with a wooden spoon.

6 The pulp can now be shaped into solid lumps, ready for use. It can also be wrapped in baking foil and stored in a refrigerator (for up to a month) until needed.

PULP TIPS

● Use a broadsheet rather than tabloid newspaper as the type of fibers in the former's newsprint make a stronger product.

● Wallpaper paste can be used instead of PVA medium, although it may contain a chemical fungicide, so avoid any direct contact with it.

1

2

3

4

5

6

CHOOSING A MOLD

When deciding on a mold that is suitable for your papier mâché project, one of the main priorities is to make sure that you will be able to release the project cleanly from the mold without causing any tearing or breakage.

For example, when choosing a bowl or dish, avoid one where the main opening is smaller than the bulk of the object, which would make it impossible to release the papier mâché. However, the more experienced craftsperson might feel confident enough to remove the papier mâché by cutting away sections using a craft knife, then refixing them with glue and brown tape and reinforcing the joins with layers of papier mâché. This is a tricky process and is not recommended for a beginner to attempt.

The chances are that you have many plates and bowls around your home that would make suitable molds, but do remember they could be out of action for up to several weeks as the pulp or layers are added and left to dry. A good alternative source would be a second-hand sale or garage sale where all manner of tableware turns up at virtually giveaway prices. It doesn't matter if the mold is made from china, metal, or plastic as long as it is the right shape.

Kitchenware and tableware that are suitable for use as molds include:

- Shallow salad dish—broad with a wide opening
- Soap dish
- Cereal bowl
- Various plates
- Baking sheet
- Spoons

Many different objects, including natural ones, make interesting molds, as do many other items of household and backyard bric-a-brac, including:

- Leaves
- Shells
- Avocado pitts
- Balloons—ideal for making masks
- Cardboard tubes
- String
- Wire
- Modeling clay
- Cotton swabs—pulp "beads" can be neatly formed on them

WIRE SUPPORTS

Larger projects may be made using the layered method of papier mâché over meshed wire, which is a strong but malleable support. Copper wire and fuse wire are ideal to create simple shapes or maquettes. You can mold pulp straight onto these when the wires are "knitted" together (*see p. 138*).

MODELING CLAY

You can use modeling clay for building shapes on which to apply papier mâché, or you can make the necessary mold and fill it with pulp.

USING PAPIER MACHE ON A MOLD

Before you start to layer or pulp your papier mâché onto your chosen mold, check that you have all the necessary equipment and ingredients to hand, and that the mold you are using is clean and thoroughly dry. Work on a clear, clean surface and try to avoid creating any unnecessary clutter.

Always be on the lookout for potential molds for papier mâché, for example,

items that normally get thrown away, such as yogurt cartons, shampoo bottles, and plastic lids, are all suitable.

If you are using modeling clay as your mold to work on, you can leave it to harden in the refrigerator before applying the releasing agent, as it becomes very soft with continual handling.

When you are making wire structures for pulping or layering onto, have some wire cutters on hand, as normal scissors will blunt in seconds if you attempt to cut wire with them.

LAYERING PAPIER MACHE ONTO A MOLD

MATERIALS

1 large dinner plate
Petroleum jelly
PVA medium, thinned half and half with water in a bowl
Flat-ended pasting brush
Newspaper, torn into 1in (2.5cm) strips in a bucket
Paper towels
Scissors

1 Prepare the dinner plate by smearing petroleum jelly (the releasing agent) over the entire surface that will be covered with papier mâché strips, and also onto the rim of the plate.

2 Brush the thinned PVA glue onto the torn strips of newspaper. Lay them horizontally across the mold overlapping each strip slightly. When you have completed this first layer, set aside to dry for several hours. Each layer must be absolutely hard and dry before you apply the next.

3 For the next layer of papier mâché work in exactly the same way, but apply the strips vertically on the plate. This will help to make a stronger and smoother papier mâché. It doesn't matter if the strips extend beyond the edge of the mold, but make sure that the whole of the mold is covered by each layer.

4 When you have built up eight layers of papier mâché and they are all hard and dry, gently release the project from the mold. Remove any residue of petroleum jelly with the paper towels, and then trim with scissors around the edge of the papier mâché mold to make an even and neat shape.

1

2

3

4

PULPING PAPIER MACHE ONTO A MOLD

MATERIALS

1 large dinner plate
Petroleum jelly
Papier mâché pulp (see pp. 107-8)
Paper towels
Scissors or craft knife

1 Take the large dinner plate and cover the entire surface that will be coated with papier mâché pulp with petroleum jelly to act as a releasing agent.

2 Take a quantity of pulped papier mâché and apply a layer about ¼in (6mm) thick over the surface of the upturned plate. Papier mâché pulp has a tendency to shrink in the drying process, and it may be necessary to apply an additional layer to the first layer, while still damp, to increase the thickness. Leave the pulp to dry for about a week, or until it feels hard and dry.

3 When the papier mâché is fully dry, and you are happy that you have the right thickness of pulp, gently ease the shape from the mold. Remove any traces of petroleum jelly with paper towels and trim any uneven edges with scissors or a craft knife.

1

2

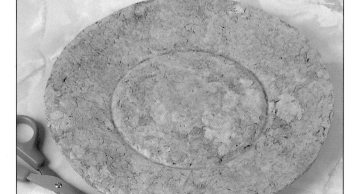

3

TIPS

● The drying process for both pulp and layered papier mâché projects can be accelerated by the use of a hair dryer for about 10 minutes at a time.

● Papier mâché molded on cardboard can be dried and hardened in a microwave oven for up to one minute, but keep a close eye on this process and do not leave the oven unattended.

● The residue from the releasing agent can be removed with lighter fluid, but take great care when using this, as it is flammable, and keep away from children.

● A butter knife may help remove papier mâché that appears to be stuck fast to a mold. Gently ease the knife around the mold and the papier mâché, but avoid using any great force as this might damage both the mold and the papier mâché.

CARDBOARD

Cardboard comes in various thicknesses and is ideal for papier mâché bases and molds. Cartons can be obtained from supermarkets.

You can use many different items other than paints, such as stamps and shells, to decorate your finished papier mâché objects. Ribbons, screw eyes, and jewelry fittings can also be bought to finish other papier mâché projects.

DECORATING AND FINISHING

Once papier mâché objects have reached the gray and hardened stage, they simply need some added color or lacquer finish to bring them to life. After you have trimmed away any excess material from the object, you may want to smooth down the rough edges with a nail file. Pulped papier mâché can look good with a mildly ragged texture. But if this look does not appeal to you, it is possible to smooth over the surface with some wood filler to produce a more even and consistent finish.

USING AN UNDERCOAT

Before you can apply any decoration or paint to the dried papier mâché, it needs to be given an undercoat. Fast-drying acrylic

Apply acrylic gesso onto hardened papier mâché with a paintbrush. Check that any traces of releasing agent have been removed, and that any irregularities have been trimmed as necessary.

gesso is perfect for this job as it gives a thick, extremely smooth layer of paint that provides an ideal surface to take a wide range of paint and ink finishes. Household emulsion is less expensive to use, but is more liable to crack. If you do use it, a matte vinyl finish will give a satisfactory undercoat if it is carefully applied in at least two layers.

PAINTING TECHNIQUES

Each project in this book gives a separate and detailed description on how to apply both paint and decoration, so that you can produce a papier mâché object that is very close to the illustrated project. You may feel confident right from the start to experiment with different types of paints and colors to create your own designs and special effects—the choice is entirely yours. But for the first few projects it is best to follow the guide given.

You can also use a sponge to dab on the paint and create different, subtle, and mottled effects. Make a stencil out of stiff cardboard and then dab a design directly onto your project. By rubbing away some of the paint you can produce a translucent effect.

You can also build up thin coats of inks to produce rich, overlapping colors with a lacquer effect. Try blending colors on top of each other and produce a "distressed" effect by rubbing the surface with an abrasive cloth, revealing the other colors beneath. The possibilities at the painting stage are endless, so enjoy experimenting and be bold with your techniques.

DECORATING TOOLS

● Paintbrushes—it's worth investing in a few good-quality brushes before you start decorating. Use a fine brush for detail, and a larger one for areas of flat color
● Acrylic gesso—to use as an undercoat
● Emulsion paint—ideally a matte vinyl finish to use as an alternative to acrylic gesso
● Drawing inks—these should really be a trade secret as they give such wonderful rich, translucent colors. Inks also mix well with poster and acrylic paints. You can achieve superb effects by building up layers of colors
● Metallic pens and metallic and pearlized acrylic paints—these are are really good for

achieving special effects
● Acrylic paints—offer very good coverage and strong colors
● Poster paints—useful in their own right and effective as a base for paint or ink
● Tissue paper—this can create interesting and delicate textures and subtle colors when glued down in overlapping layers or brushed with inks
● Foil paper—an interesting paper to give bold, rich highlights. It is especially dramatic when used against a solid, dark background, such as black.

Also look out for potential decoration in the form of attractive wrappings and sweet papers. Bus tickets, stamps, and other printed items can provide visual interest when used creatively and are well worth saving.

YOU MAY ALSO NEED
● Ribbons—to thread on masks and plaques
● Shells—to press into a papier mâché pulp to make ornate, whimsical decoration
● Beads, earring posts, and small jewelry-item supports—useful items for making earrings
● Pliers—a small pair is ideal for making jewelry items
● Wire
● Strong glue
● Screw eyes—from do it yourself stores, these are used to hang finished projects

VARNISHING

Varnishing your decorated project will seal the papier mâché and help protect it against damp. It will also enhance the color in your painting, and preserve the detail. Polyurethane varnish is one of the best to use as it is so durable and easy to apply. It is available in both matte and gloss finishes—the choice is yours—but remember the type of varnish you choose will affect the look of the finished project.

Always varnish the entire surface, unless you intend to attach the item to some kind of backing, such as a wooden board. Polyurethane varnish does have a slight yellowing effect, which is not normally very noticeable, but if color control is important you can use clear acrylic craft varnish or undiluted PVA medium.

Take your time when varnishing. Don't rush, just work methodically and evenly, particularly on larger projects—it's worth it in the end. Generally, each object will need five coats of varnish. Allow each layer to dry thoroughly as detailed on the manufacturer's instructions, before applying the next. Take care to wash out your brushes thoroughly in

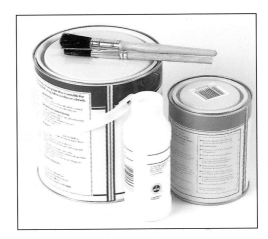

a proprietary brush cleaner between coats of varnish, otherwise they will become rock hard and be completely unusable.

VARNISHING TOOLS
● Paintbrushes—about ½in (1.25cm) for general work
● Smaller paintbrush—for fine detail
● Polyurethane varnish—available in clear, matte or gloss

TIPS FOR PAINTING

● Practice new techniques and designs on some scrap paper first before decorating a papier mâché item

● If you are unhappy with your paint finish, leave for a while and return to it later. You may find you suddenly see the way to resolve a problem after coming back to it after a break. However, if you want to repaint an area, just apply a coat or two of white acrylic paint and start again.

PAPIER MACHE

PROJECTS

1

2

3

4

MATERIALS

1 shallow bowl for mold
Petroleum jelly
Thinned PVA medium (see p. 107)
Flat-ended pastry brush
¾in (2cm) and 1in (2.5cm) newspaper strips (see p. 107)
Hair dryer (optional)
Paper towels
Lighter fluid (optional)
Scissors
Acrylic gesso
Various paintbrushes
Orange, red, yellow, green, and blue drawing inks
Orange, red, green, blue, and yellow poster paints
White acrylic paint
Polyurethane varnish

1 Choose a shallow bowl suitable to be a mold. Check that the bowl is clean and completely dry. Smear the outside of the upturned mold with petroleum jelly to act as a releasing agent.

2 Brush the thinned PVA medium onto the ¾in (2cm) newspaper strips with a flat-ended brush to cover the strips quickly and thoroughly. Apply eight layers of papier mâché—in alternate directions—following the method for layering papier mâché onto a mold (see p. 110). Leave the bowl aside to dry and harden for several hours between each layer. To accelerate the drying time of the

papier mâché you can use a hair dryer for ten minutes at a time.

3 When the final layer of papier mâché is hard and dry, gently ease the bowl from the mold. Tear short chunks of newspaper about 1in (2.5cm) wide and apply two more layers of papier mâché around the rim to form a bold edge, and set aside to dry for several hours between layers.

4 Remove any residue of petroleum jelly with the paper towels. Gesso or any undercoat will not adhere to a greasy surface, and if any petroleum jelly remains it could lead to cracking and a breaking up of

the finished decoration. Use lighter fluid to dissolve stubborn areas, if necessary. Then trim any rough edges with sharp scissors and apply the gesso undercoat evenly over the whole bowl. Decorate the bowl with the fruit pattern using the drawing inks, poster and acrylic paints. Finish the bowl with five coats of polyurethane varnish, leaving to dry between coats as detailed in the manufacturer's instructions.

EASY LEVEL

SUMMER BOWL

This decorative fruit bowl is simple to make, and can be filled with colorful fruit to liven up a side table.

The yellow ink background is painted onto the undercoat and then contrasted with a red rim in poster paint. To make the pattern, you paint summer fruits in orange, red, yellow, blue and green inks and poster paints onto the bowl, or alter the colors to suit your taste. Leaves applied with colorful inks and paints inside the bowl can be muted with thinned white paint. Before this dries, remove some for a veiled effect.

PAPIER MACHE

MATERIALS

1 side plate for mold
Petroleum jelly
Thinned PVA medium (*see p. 107*)
Flat-ended pastry brush
¾in (2cm) newspaper strips
(*see p. 107*)
Paper towels
Lighter fluid (optional)
Scissors
Various paintbrushes
Acrylic gesso
Red and green poster paints
Crimson and yellow
drawing inks
White acrylic paint
Polyurethane varnish

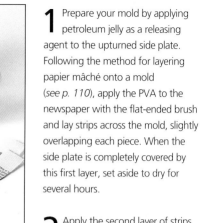

1

2

3

1 Prepare your mold by applying petroleum jelly as a releasing agent to the upturned side plate. Following the method for layering papier mâché onto a mold (*see p. 110*), apply the PVA to the newspaper with the flat-ended brush and lay strips across the mold, slightly overlapping each piece. When the side plate is completely covered by this first layer, set aside to dry for several hours.

2 Apply the second layer of strips across the first layer, but in the opposite direction. Apply eight layers of papier mâché in all, alternating the direction of the strips, and allowing each layer to dry for several hours before applying the next.

3 When the papier mâché is completely hard, carefully release the plate from the mold, and remove any residue of petroleum jelly with the paper towels or some lighter fluid, if necessary. Using sharp scissors trim away any newspaper ends around the rim to leave a neat, even edge. The plate is now ready for an undercoat of gesso over the entire surface. Decorate the plate with the spiral pattern using the poster and acrylic paints and drawing inks. Finally, finish with five coats of polyurethane varnish, leaving to dry between coats as detailed in the manufacturer's instructions .

SPIRAL PLATE

This side order plate is ideal for beginners as it again uses the basic layered method employed on the summer bowl (*see pp. 116-7*). Once you've mastered the painting you can make several plates and use them for afternoon tea.

Take your time when applying the gesso undercoat to give an even surface on which to decorate. The paint technique uses several colored layers. The top layer is partially scraped away to reveal the colors beneath.

The first layer is applied with red poster paint. When it is dry, 'eepen the effect by painting crimson ink over the plate. While this is still wet, use green poster paint to paint a bold spiral pattern from the center of the plate out to the edge. Don't worry if the plate starts to look gaudy as the next stage tones down the color. When the paint is dry, apply some undiluted white paint. Wait briefly, then smear with paper towels to remove some of this paint. Now pour some yellow ink onto the plate and rub in with fresh paper towels, scratching the painted surface through the paper to reveal the color underneath.

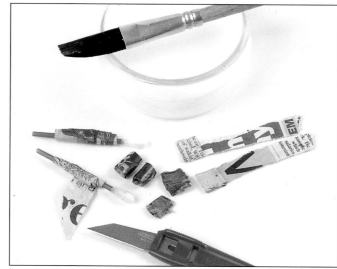

1

2

3

4

1 Smear petroleum jelly over the back of the two dessert spoon molds to act as a releasing agent. Apply eight layers of newspaper squares with the PVA medium onto the spoon backs, following the method for layering papier mâché onto a mold (*see p. 110*). Allow each layer to dry for several hours before adding another. When the papier mâché is hard, lift from molds and remove any releasing agent with paper towels or lighter fluid, if necessary. Using sharp scissors cut a diamond shape from each piece of papier mâché about 2¼in (5.5cm) long by 1⅜ in (3.5 cm) wide.

2 Brush strips of newspaper ½in (1.3cm) wide with PVA medium. Remove one end from two cotton swabs and smear petroleum jelly onto their stems, to act as a releasing agent. Wrap six layers of strips around the molds to form some tubular beads. Fold two other strips into squares to a thickness of about six layers. Leave the beads and squares to dry thoroughly for about four to five days.

3 Using PVA medium attach a relief square of papier mâché to the middle of each diamond shape. Release the beads from the cotton-swab stems when they have completely hardened. Then apply a layer of gesso with a small brush to all four papier mâché earring components as an undercoat

4 Pierce a hole at least ¼in (6 mm) thick at the top of the diamond with the craft knife to insert a jump ring or wire and assemble the earrings. Then use poster paints, pearlized paints, inks, and pens to decorate the diamond shapes and tubular beads. Apply five layers of polyurethane varnish with a fine brush, leaving to dry between coats as detailed in the manufacturer's instructions, or alternatively use PVA medium, leaving to dry for a couple of hours between coats. Assemble the earrings as shown here from top to bottom, with the earring post attached to the jewellery stem at the top. The black and green glass beads and papier mâché beads are threaded onto the stem and the stem is attached to the diamond shapes with jump rings. Use the pliers to bend and trim the stems into shape as necessary.

MATERIALS

Petroleum jelly
2 dessert spoons for molds
Thinned PVA medium (*see p. 107*)
Flat-ended pastry brush
Small newspaper squares and ½in (1.3cm) strips (*see p. 107*)
Paper towels
Lighter fluid (optional)
Scissors
Cotton swabs for molds
Various paintbrushes
Acrylic gesso
Craft knife
Green and red poster paints
Green and gold pearlized acrylic paints
Gold and crimson drawing inks
Silver and gold metallic pens
Polyurethane varnish or undiluted PVA medium
Earring posts for pierced ears, wire jewelry stems and jump rings, pliers
Black and green glass beads (from craft stores)

EASY LEVEL

DIAMOND EARRINGS

With their subtle, but distinctive, decoration, these earrings will really liven up a simple evening dress.

The base color for the earrings is a deep bottle-green poster paint, visible only on the back. A light pearlized green acrylic paint is brushed over the front of the diamond and the beads, and the relief area is highlighted with gold pearlized acrylic paint and ink. When this is dry, rows of gold dots can be added on top with a metallic pen. The beads are decorated with a little gold paint, using quite a dry brush, to achieve the mottled effect.

The diamonds' borders are patterned with silver metallic pen dots with some crimson ink painted on top. Tiny flecks of deep-red poster paint, placed along the diamonds' borders and around the relief areas, help to contrast the green. The areas decorated with metallic pen can blur with normal varnish, so use undiluted PVA medium for a crisper finish.

EASY LEVEL

CHRISTMAS STAR

This bright star decoration is perfect to finish off a Christmas tree. A simple handmade mold and papier mâché pulp is all that is needed to make this easy festive decoration. You can, however, test your painting skills to produce intricate, colorful designs, or alternatively just keep it simple by applying a base coat of metallic silver paint, and highlight with touches of gold as shown here. Because the modeling-clay mold is not absolutely rigid, it will give a lit-

tle when you press in the pulp. This helps to give the star a light, petal-like quality that will look fresh and bright among the Christmas holiday greenery.

For the colored star, paint one side red and one side yellow with poster paints and next apply some white acrylic paint to both sides. Then trace a shape around the edges of the center star in bright green, yellow, blue, pink, and white poster, or acrylic paints working outward. To achieve a richly layered quality, you can add more flecks of the colors used.

You can also use this method to make large stars, which can be hung from the ceiling or fixed to the wall of your home—and they make an ideal festive gift for neighbors.

MATERIALS

Petroleum jelly and plastic wrap
Modeling clay
Papier mâché pulp (see pp. 107-8)
Paper towels
Lighter fluid (optional)
Scissors
Acrylic gesso
Various paintbrushes
Silver and gold metallic acrylic paints
Green, white, yellow, red, blue, and pink poster or acrylic paints
Polyurethane varnish
Craft knife
Screw eyes
Ribbon or hanging thread

1

2

3

4

1 Smear petroleum jelly as a releasing agent onto plastic wrap. Cut five pieces of new modeling clay 4¾in (12cm) in length and ⅜in (1cm) wide. (Use the "ribs" on the modeling clay as a guide, and cut each length two ribs wide.) Form a star shape on the plastic wrap by bending each piece of clay in half and joining it to the adjacent section. Make a simple star shape in the middle with clay one rib high, as shown.

2 Take the papier mâché pulp and press it into the star mold.

3 Leave the pulp to harden for about a week, before removing the modeling clay. Wipe away any residue of petroleum jelly with paper towels and some lighter fluid, if necessary. Trim, and then apply gesso to the star's surface.

4 Decorate the star using the metallic, poster, or acrylic paints. Finish with five coats of polyurethane gloss varnish, leaving to dry between coats as detailed in the manufacturer's instructions. With a craft knife, make a hole in the point at the top of the star and attach a screw eye. Thread a ribbon or thread through the hole so that you can hang it on the tree.

1

2

3

4

1 Take the papier mâché pulp and start to model the flower motifs for your greeting cards. Roll a small ball of pulp in the palm of your hand, and press it flat onto a piece of waxed paper that has been smeared with petroleum jelly as a releasing agent. Form five or six petal shapes with the pulp, and carefully attach them to the center of the flower. Leave the pulp flowers to dry and harden for about a week.

2 Fold the thin card stock in half and start to put the flower shapes onto it. Move them into different positions until you think the design is just right, then trace around the flowers lightly with a pencil to mark their place on the card stock.

3 Remove the pulped flowers from the card stock and apply an undercoat of gesso to all of them. Leave to dry. Then decorate the flowers with the pearlized and poster paints. Finish with five coats of polyurethane varnish, leaving to dry between coats as detailed in the manufacturer's instructions.

4 With the inks and poster and pearlized paints, draw some simple leaves to form the background design on the card. Attach the papier mâché flowers to the card with some PVA medium at the points marked in pencil, pressing firmly into position. Finally, write your special message to suit the occasion on the inside of the card.

FLOWER GREETING CARD

Many occasions, such as birthdays, engagements and moving home, call for a greeting card, so this pretty, personalized card is bound to be well received. It is fun to make and does not take long.

Paint the flower motifs in light-gold, blue, mauve, and white pearlized paints to produce delicate and shimmering colors. By adding yellow and orange centers in poster paints, the flowers become bright

and fresh looking. The leaves are painted in a stylized design using different shades of blue, green, and yellow poster paints and inks, plus some green pearlized paint to provide a little variation. The finished effect is simple, but striking.

Although papier mâché is a durable material, it is best to avoid sending this card through the mail, unless it is inside a padded package.

You can also adapt the greeting card for different occasions—you can make a teddy bear to celebrate a new baby, for example, or mold a horseshoe to say "good luck" to somebody moving to a new job or home.

MATERIALS
Papier mâché pulp (see p. 107-8)
Waxed paper
1 sheet of thin white card stock
Pencil
Acrylic gesso
Various paintbrushes
Light-gold, blue, mauve, white, and green pearlized acrylic paints
Yellow, orange, blue, and green poster paints
Polyurethane varnish
Blue, green, and yellow inks
Acrylic gesso
PVA medium

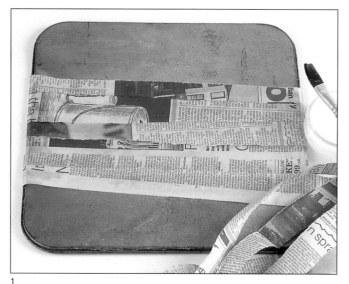

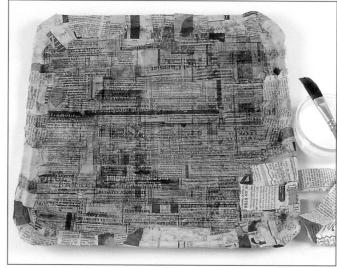

1

2

3

4

1 Smear the top surface and raised edges of the baking sheet with petroleum jelly to act as a releasing agent. Paste PVA medium onto the newspaper strips and apply them to the mold, following the method for layering papier mâché onto a mold (*see p. 110*). Build up the papier mâché to eight layers, working in alternate directions, and covering the raised edges on the mold. Leave to dry for several hours between layers.

2 Remove the papier mâché from the mold when it has fully hardened, and clean away any residue of petroleum jelly with paper towels. Paste the shorter strips of newspaper and apply three layers around the tray's ridge to produce a firm, bold edge. Again, leave the papier mâché to dry for several hours between layers. When dry, trim as necessary with scissors.

3 To make the curved handles, measure and cut two pieces of corrugated paper 3½in (9cm) x 5½in (14cm) with the craft knife. Brush the corrugated side with PVA medium and tightly roll it up until it is only 1in (2.5cm) wide. Secure in place with four pieces of gummed tape that extend from behind the rolled

corrugated paper to the edge. When the handles have completely dried, apply five layers of shorter newspaper strips to cover over the rolled ends of the corrugated paper.

4 Secure the handles onto the tray by first applying PVA medium to the flat edge of the handle and the edge of the curve. Place the handles opposite each other and tape to the back of the tray with the curved part of the handles fitting against the ridge. Use layers of tape to secure the handles in place, placing the tape over the top of the curve onto each side. Then put long strips of tape

horizontally onto both sides of the tray to hold both the taped handles in position. Next, apply an undercoat of gesso to all the surfaces. When dry, apply a blue base coat to the tray and the sides of the handles. Paste the strips of colored tissue paper with some PVA medium and position them on the tray, horizontally and vertically, to form a plaid pattern. Accentuate the colors of the tissue paper with drawing inks, if preferred. Finally, to protect the tray's delicate surface, apply five coats of polyurethane varnish, leaving to dry between coats as detailed in the manufacturer's instructions .

PLAID TRAY

Layers of colored tissue paper have been used here to build up a stylish and fashionable plaid pattern on this tray. It has a bright, cheerful appeal and is perfect for serving appetizers at a cocktail party. It would also look equally good carrying candies or cakes at a children's party.

Paint the base of the tray and the sides of the handles in deep blue poster paint or another color used in the design. You then need to apply the pink, yellow, green, and blue tissue strips (or your chosen colors) in several layers, fixing them to the tray with PVA medium in a criss-cross pattern.

When the tissue paper has dried, the colors can be enhanced by painting on corresponding colors in inks. An alternative is to cut out some shapes—flowers or leaves, for example—and paste them on top of the plaid pattern. You can then also apply this simple method of decoration to many other of the projects in this chapter, such as plates, dishes, or bowls. The varnish will give the tray a glossy finish and protect it against spillages when it is being used.

MATERIALS
1 baking sheet for a mold
Petroleum jelly
2in (5cm) and short newspaper strips (*see p. 107*)
Thinned PVA medium (*see p. 107*)
Flat-ended pastry brush
Paper towels
Scissors, ruler, marker pen, and craft knife
Cardboard and gummed tape
Various paintbrushes
Acrylic gesso
Blue poster paint; pink, yellow, green, white, and blue inks
Colored tissue paper, PVA medium, polyurethane varnish

1

2

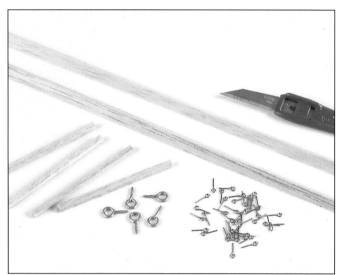

3

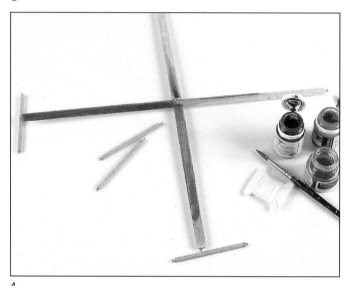

4

1 Take each leaf and lay it face down on a piece of waxed paper. Apply some petroleum jelly as a releasing agent to the back of each leaf. Take some of the papier mâché pulp and press firmly onto the leaves so that each is covered with a thin layer. Leave the leaves to dry for about a week.

2 When the pulp has dried, remove it carefully from the leaves. There will be no residue of petroleum jelly with this method of applying pulp. Paint one side of the leaves with an undercoat of gesso, leave to dry, and then paint a further coat on the reverse side. Later, decorate the leaves with the colored inks and poster paints. Finally, apply five coats of polyurethane varnish to each of the leaves, leaving them to dry between coats as detailed in the manufacturer's instructions.

3 To make a simple hanging structure, you will need two pieces of triangular-ended balsa wood dowel. Each piece should measure about 1ft (30cm) long and ⅜in (1cm) wide. You will also need four finer square-ended rods: 2¾in (7cm) and ⅜in (4cm) wide. Using the tip of a craft knife, make a hole in both ends of each piece of wood and the rods. Insert a small pin eye into each hole and apply some wood glue to each.

4 Join the two longer dowels together to make a crosspiece as shown above. Apply some wood glue to the middle point of one piece of dowel and attach the other piece of dowel, flat side on, to make a cross shape. Use a craft knife to cut a little of the wood away on the middle point of the join so that you can insert a screw eye here. This fixing helps to reinforce the join and thread can be attached to it so that you can hang the mobile. Fix the four small rods to the four sections of the crosspiece by attaching two short pieces of thread from each rod's pin eye to the corresponding one on the crosspiece. Then hang a long thread from each pin eye on the rods. Paint the wood structure with the inks and paints in colors that complement the leaves. Then attach the leaves by piercing each leaf with a needle, feeding the thread through and tying a knot to secure. Add a small piece of modeling clay in a matching color to the stem of each leaf to balance it, if necessary.

MATERIALS

8 different leaves with raised veins
Waxed paper
Petroleum jelly
Papier mâché pulp (*see p. 107-8*)
Acrylic gesso
Various paintbrushes
Green, pink, yellow, and blue drawing inks
Lime-green, purple, and brown poster paints
Polyurethane varnish
Large and small balsa wood dowels
Wood glue
Craft knife
Pin eyes
Screw eyes
Needle
Nylon thread
Modeling clay

EASY LEVEL

LEAF MOBILE

Real leaves have been used as the molds in this project because they give a natural, delicate detail to the papier-mâché foliage. The leaves are so light that they will spin gently in the slightest breeze and conjure up an image of the swirling fall leaves.

Green, pink, yellow, and blue drawing inks are ideal for decorating the leaves, as they collect in the veins and accentuate the natural detail. You can add in some lime-green, purple, and brown poster paint for a more opaque finish.

Balance the leaves against each other when you hang them. Add a tiny amount of modeling clay in a matching color to the stem of each leaf to act as a counterbalance, if needed. Decorate the finished crosspiece with evergreens or dried foliage for a wonderful natural finish.

1

3

2

MATERIALS

| Modeling clay |
| Petroleum jelly |
| Cotton swabs |
| Papier mâché pulp (see pp. 107-8) |
| Paper towels |
| Scissors |
| Acrylic gesso |
| Various paintbrushes |
| Red, yellow, orange, green, and blue drawing inks |
| Brown, orange, green, and blue poster paints |
| Polyurethane varnish |

1 Roll out lengths of modeling clay into logs about ⅝in (1.5cm) thick. Carefully coil the clay in a spiral, evenly bringing up the sides to create the pot shape—narrow at the bottom and wider at the top. Apply petroleum jelly as a releasing agent to the inside, using a cotton swab to get into the difficult, recessed areas of the coils.

2 Following the method for pulping papier mâché onto a mold (see p. 111), press a quantity of pulp inside the mold only to a depth of ¼in (6mm). Overlap the pulp at the rim of the mold to form a lip.

Allow the pulp to dry thoroughly for about a week. Then add another layer and again leave to dry until completely hard.

3 When the papier mâché is completely dry, carefully release it from the mold by unwinding the modeling clay from the outside of the pot. Remove any residue left by the petroleum jelly with paper towels and trim away rough edges around the bowl rim with the scissors.

4 Using a small clean brush, apply a coat of gesso evenly over the entire pot to give a smooth base coat

for decorating. Allow the gesso to dry thoroughly before you begin to decorate the pot in the rich terracotta color. Then add the zig-zag or Aztec design using the drawing inks and poster paints. When the painting is complete, finish by applying five coats of polyurethane varnish, leaving to dry between coats as detailed in the manufacturer's instructions.

130

COIL POT

This simple pot design is based on the centuries-old tradition of coil pot making. It is decorated in a way that enhances its unusual, uneven exterior relief. When it is finished, fill the bowl with fruits or with scented potpourri to add a pleasant fragrance to a room.

The edge of the bowl needs to be trimmed carefully after releasing it from the mold. Don't expect perfect smooth curves as the real charm of the coil pot lies in its quirky simplicity, and the small irregularities that add to its "handmade" character.

To paint the pot, blend a rich terra-cotta brown using brown and orange poster paints plus red and yellow inks. Apply this carefully to the pot.

Take your time to decorate the exterior. It may take several colored layers to produce a rich, earthy effect. Add fine lines for detail after the first layers have dried. Try applying different designs using zig-zag or Aztec patterns in orange, green, and blue paints and inks to complement the relief areas. Practice your designs on paper first, before applying them to the pot.

LARGE DINNER PLATE

This stylish plate is perfect for serving mints or dessert candies to your guests after a dinner party. It can also be placed on a plate stand or in a show cabinet to make a striking home decoration.

To make your papier mâché plate, choose a dinner plate with a bold ridge on its base as a mold. This will make a distinct circular indentation toward the center of the papier mâché plate from which the foil design radiates. Paint the finished plate in blue ink, followed by a coat of black poster paint brushed over the textured surface, to produce a lustrous midnight blue.

The pattern has been created with foil paper—it's worth remembering to save a few different types from chocolate bars and gift wrappings. Some foils are richly embossed and glossy, others have a matte finish and are more subdued. Silver paper will provide a sophisticated finish on the dark blue, background while bright foils lend a cheerful quality. Experiment with your design on scrap paper before committing yourself to the final effect.

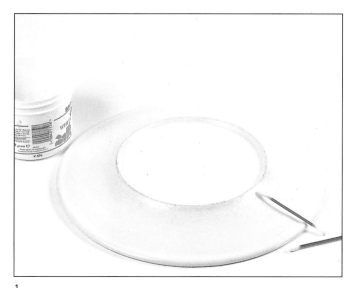

1

2

3

4

MATERIALS
1 dinner plate for mold
Petroleum jelly
Cotton swabs
Papier mâché pulp (see pp. 107-8)
Paper towels
Lighter fluid (optional)
Acrylic gesso
Various paintbrushes
Blue drawing ink
Black poster paint
Torn strips of foil paper
PVA medium
Polyurethane varnish

1 Select a dinner plate to use as a mold and carefully apply petroleum jelly as a releasing agent to the upturned plate. You can use a cotton swab, if necessary, to reach right into the recesses around the ridge of the plate on the base.

2 Apply the newspaper pulp to the plate, following the method for pulping papier mâché onto a mold (see p. 111), to a thickness of around ¼in (6mm). Leave the pulp to dry for about a week, then apply another layer to the same thickness. Again, leave to dry thoroughly for about the same amount of time.

3 The pulp must always be absolutely hard and dry before it can be released from the mold. Even slightly damp pulp will separate and stick to the mold if you attempt to try to release it before it has fully hardened. So gently remove the papier mâché and wipe away any residue of petroleum jelly with paper towels and lighter fluid, if necessary. Then apply the gesso with a paintbrush as an undercoat to the papier mâché plate.

4 Paint the finished plate with the blue ink, followed by a coat of black poster paint. When dry apply the torn strips of foil with PVA medium to the plate in your chosen pattern. Finish decorating the plate by applying five coats of polyurethane varnish, leaving to dry between coats as detailed in the manufacturer's instructions.

133

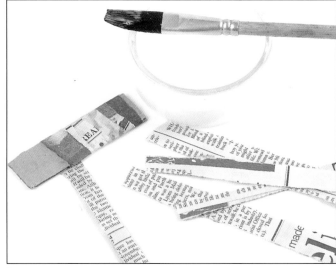

1

2

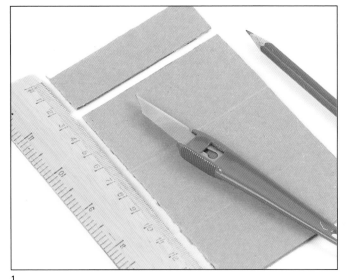

3

4

1 Use a craft knife and ruler to cut out a length of cardboard that is 3in x ¾in (7.5cm x 2cm) to form the base of the brooch.

2 Apply PVA medium to the newspaper strips with a flat-ended brush. Cover the cardboard with five layers of papier mâché by wrapping the strips neatly around the cardboard. Take extra care when applying the papier mâché strips to the ends of the cardboard—this needs to be done evenly to make a neat and tidy finish. Leave the papier mâché strips to dry for several hours between each layer.

3 Brush the PVA medium all over the front surface of the brooch. Then take the string and press it into position on the brooch, curving it in a meandering design along the papier mâché as shown. Adjust the shape to suit your chosen design before the glue dries.

4 Once the PVA medium is dry, check that the string is firmly attached to the papier mâché. Trim away any excess string and then apply gesso to the entire surface with a small paintbrush. Decorate the brooch with poster paint, pearlized paints, metallic drawing inks, and

metallic pen. Then finish with five coats of polyurethane varnish, leaving to dry between coats as detailed in the manufacturer's instructions. To complete this piece of jewelry, attach a brooch fastener to the back of the brooch with strong glue for metal, holding it in place for a minute or two to make sure that you get a strong bonding.

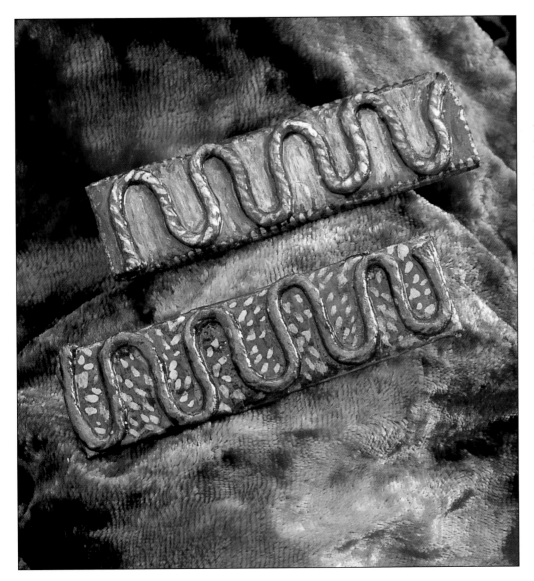

MATERIALS
Craft knife
Ruler
Cardboard
Thinned PVA medium (*see p. 107*)
Flat-ended pastry brush
Thin newspaper strips (*see p. 107*)
String, 7in (17.5cm) long
Scissors
Acrylic gesso
Various paintbrushes
Purple poster paint
Green, blue, purple, pink, and white pearlized paints
Cream, blue, and violet metallic drawing inks
Silver metallic pen
Yellow, pink, and blue drawing inks
Polyurethane varnish
Brooch fastener finding (from art and craft stores)
Strong glue

STRING-LAYERED BROOCH

This brooch has a jewel-like appearance because of the shimmering effect of the painted dots. It looks good worn on both plain and textured fabrics.

The project shows you how to make exciting relief patterns on papier mâché objects. It shows a technique that can also be used very effectively on more ambitious projects, such as small bowls or large boxes.

To decorate the brooch, paint it in purple poster paint or, if preferred, black, navy blue or bottle green. Apply cream, blue, and violet metallic inks, adding purple, green, blue, pink, and white pearlized paints on top. Then use a fine brush to create dots and flashes of shimmering color as seen in the two brooch styles above.

To create some highlights, add some flashes of silver with a metallic pen and then "wash" the brooch with layers of yellow, pink, and blue inks to build up a really luxuriant sheen. Trace the string pattern with threads of the base color and repeat this color along the brooch's edges to finish.

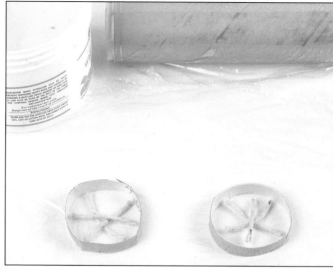

1

3

4

MATERIALS
Cardboard tubes
Ruler, scissors, and string
Petroleum jelly and waxed paper
Papier mâché pulp (see p. 107-8) and cotton swabs
Acrylic gesso
Various paintbrushes
Turquoise, light-gold, pink pearlized acrylic paints
Black Indian drawing ink
Red poster paint
Polyurethane varnish
Craft knife and screw eyes
Wire jewelry stems, red and black glass beads, jump rings, earring posts, pliers

1 Using a cardboard tube, cut two sections measuring ⅜in (1cm) wide. Cut eight pieces of string that will fit snugly across the inside of the two tube discs.

2 Smear a little petroleum jelly onto some waxed paper and place the cardboard molds on it. Make a star design using the pieces of string inside the molds. The petroleum jelly will help keep the string in place.

3 Press the pulp tightly into the molds, filling them right up to the top. Remove one end from two

cotton swabs and apply petroleum jelly to the stems of two cotton swabs, and with the papier mâché pulp mold a bead around each stem. Leave all the papier mâché pieces to dry thoroughly for about a week.

4 When the papier mâché medallions and beads are hard and dry, apply a coat of gesso to form an undercoat on all the surfaces. Then use the tip of the craft knife to make a small hole in the top of each medallion. Decorate the pieces with pearlized and poster paints and inks, and then varnish with five coats of polyurethane

varnish, leaving to dry between coats as detailed in the manufacturer's instructions. To finish the earrings, insert a screw eye into each of the earrings' holes. Then thread the glass and papier mâché beads all along the jewelry stem. Assemble the earrings by attaching the stem to the screw eye with a jump ring. Use pliers to bend the top of the wire stem to hook onto the earring posts, and then trim away excess wire with some sharp scissors.

CHUNKY EARRINGS

These bold, chunky earrings help you make a dress statement and are great fun to make. There's no need to worry about releasing them from the mold, as it forms part of the earring.

Papier mâché is often used to make theatrical props, as it is so lightweight, so heavy-looking jewelry can be produced easily using this technique. The earrings are painted in a light-gold pearlized acrylic paint as a base color, with dabs of pink on top. Black Indian ink is then used to make bold stripes across the beads and on the edge of the earrings. Mix some black ink with the light gold to create a "distressed" effect on the string side of the earrings. You can then highlight the string and each earring's border with a turquoise pearlized paint, adding some spots of red poster paint to contrast with the background color.

Red and black glass beads help to offset the rugged pulp bead on each stem. Alternatively, you can create an antique effect by painting the earrings in bronze and using gold beads.

137

AFRICAN BANGLE

Bright, vibrant and big, this bangle looks striking either worn on its own or with other bracelets. Decorated with bright, spicy colors, it can look good worn with a casual top or a more formal outfit.

The bangle can be finished with a smooth or rugged surface. To make a smooth finish, roll the pulped mold along a flat surface. For a rough effect, just leave the pulp in its natural state. After you have applied the gesso undercoat, paint the bangle in an earthy brown, orange, or yellow base color using poster paints. When this has dried you can add more decoration. Stripes or spots in spicy colors, for instance, give the right look, as is shown in the two styles above. Paint them in gold and crimson ink and black and red paint over the earthy base color to give a vibrant effect to each bangle.

Bear in mind that metallic inks are better finished with undiluted PVA medium to preserve the colors. However, metallic acrylic paint can be varnished normally.

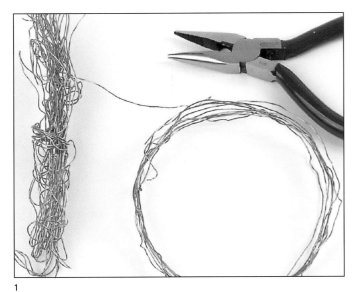

1

2

3

4

MATERIALS

Copper wire
(from hardware stores)

Papier mâché pulp
(see pp. 107-8)

Hair dryer (optional)

Acrylic gesso

Various paintbrushes

Red, black, brown, yellow,
and orange poster paints

Gold and crimson drawing inks
or metallic acrylic paints,
if preferred

Undiluted PVA medium
or polyurethane varnish

1 Copper wire has been used in this project to form a structure for the pulp to be modeled around. Use your own arm as a measure for the size of the wire structure. Form a circle that has at least ⅜in (1cm) spare all round when drawn over your hand and comprises about eight strands of wire. Separate the wire strands slightly, and carefully secure ends together.

2 Using the papier mâché pulp, cover the wire structure until it forms a bangle that is about ¾in (2cm) thick. Roll the bangle along a flat surface, turning it around as you move it along, if you want to make all the sides smooth. If you prefer a bangle with a rough surface, simply let the pulp harden normally in its natural state.

3 Because of the thickness of the pulp, this project may well take up to two weeks to dry at room temperature. You can use a hair dryer to speed up the drying process, but don't attempt to heat the bangle in a microwave as its wire structure makes this method totally unsuitable. When the papier mâché is hard and dry, apply the gesso undercoat to the entire surface.

4 Decorate the bangle in bright colors with the poster paints and metallic inks. Finally, varnish with five coats of undiluted PVA medium, leaving to dry for a couple of hours between coats. Alternatively, if you want to use metallic paints, finish with five coats of the polyurethane varnish as normal, leaving to dry between coats as detailed in the manufacturer's instructions.

139

LETTER RACK

A letter rack is always useful to have in your home as a place to keep letters and bills tidy and easy to find. Making a special one to give as a gift to a friend or a relative will make it a particularly treasured item.

A collage of postage stamps decorates the letter rack, which is then veiled with a thin wash of inks and paint to give an aged look and a slight hint of past foreign adventures.

Use PVA medium to apply old postage stamps over the outside of the box.

Remember to collect all the stamps you receive and keep them safe for this project. Overlap and layer the stamps for a special collage effect, then rub the surface with a little white acrylic paint. Follow this with some pink and yellow ink to achieve a subtle, misty effect. Contrast this subdued style with a bold black and white pattern around the base and along the edges of opening of the letter rack.

The inside is finished with a dark metallic look, which is made by mixing black Indian ink with green and blue pearlized paints, while the base is covered in some red poster paint.

MATERIALS

Cardboard box and cardboard for base, ruler, marker pen,

Craft knife, PVA medium and brown gummed tape

Thinned PVA medium (*see p. 107*)

Flat-ended pastry brush

1in (2.5cm) newspaper strips (*see p. 107*)

Acrylic gesso

Various paintbrushes

Packets of used postage stamps

White acrylic paint

Pink, yellow, and black Indian drawing ink

Green and blue pearlized paints

Red poster paint

Polyurethane varnish

1 Take a 8in x 10in x 3½in (20cm x 25cm x 9cm) box. If you can't find a box, then you can make one out of cardboard. Next, measure halfway up the box and draw a line with a ruler horizontally across the front. Then draw two diagonal lines down both sides of the box from the back, top corners to the line at the front of the box, as shown. Cut a 5in x 10in (13cm x 25cm) cardboard base

2 Use a craft knife to cut away the marked section on the box. Apply PVA medium to the underside of the box and place on the base in the center. Secure with gummed brown paper. Tape over any staples.

3 Paste PVA medium onto the newspaper strips and, following the method for layering papier mâché onto a mold (*see p. 110*), apply five layers over the box and base. Dry for several hours between layers.

4 When dry, trim the papier mâché, and apply a coat of gesso over the letter rack. Then decorate with the stamps, inks, and paints. To finish, apply five coats of polyurethane varnish, leaving to dry between coats as detailed in the manufacturer's instructions.

1

2

3

4

1

2

3

4

5

6

1 Take the cardboard carton or make one to the same dimensions. You will then need to cut a piece of flat cardboard about 7in (17.5cm) square to use as a lid, and two cardboard squares with sides measuring 4in (10cm) to make an insert for the lid.

2 Using brown gummed tape, secure the cardboard inserts together in the center of the lid and cover any staples with tape.

3 Paste PVA medium onto the newspaper strips and, following the method for layering papier mâché onto a mold (*see p. 110*), apply five layers to the box. Leave to dry for several hours between layers.

4 The next stage is to make the shell reliefs for the lid. Use modeling clay to make relief molds from three halves of bivalve shells. Soften a piece of modeling clay and flatten it in your hand. Press the shell firmly into the clay and remove to reveal the details of the shell. Curve the modeling clay edges upward in your hand and place it on waxed paper, smeared with petroleum jelly.

5 Carefully apply petroleum jelly inside the molds to act as a releasing agent. Take some papier mâché pulp and press it into each mold. Leave to dry for about a week.

6 When the pulp has hardened, release from the molds and remove any residue of petroleum jelly with a paper towel and a little lighter fluid, if necessary. Brush PVA medium onto the base of the shell reliefs and arrange on the lid in a simple design. When they have fully bonded, apply a coat of gesso to the box and lid. Decorate with the paints and inks. Finally, finish with five coats of polyurethane varnish, leaving to dry between coats as detailed in the manufacturer's instructions.

MATERIALS

5in (13cm) square cardboard box and cardboard

Ruler, marker pen, scissors and brown gummed tape

Thinned PVA medium (see p. 107)

Flat-ended pastry brush

1in (2.5in) newspaper strips (see p. 107)

Modeling clay and bivalve shells

Waxed paper and petroleum jelly

Paper towels

Lighter fluid (optional)

PVA medium, acrylic gesso

Various paintbrushes

Blue, green, and light-gold pearlized paints

Blue, pink, and yellow drawing inks

White acrylic paint

Polyurethane varnish

INTERMEDIATE LEVEL

SEASHELL STORAGE BOX

If you vacation by the sea, you may also be a collector of seashells, so here is a marvelous box to show off your collection at home. This one is perfect to display with shells and it also makes a very attractive gift for relatives or neighbors. It can be filled with small bottles of perfumed shampoo, bath oil beads, and shell-shaped soaps to make it even more appealing.

The whole of the box and its lid have been decorated with shimmering blue and green and a touch of light-gold pearlized paints, which help to give the shell shapes a delicate feel and a note of realism. If you want to deepen the effect of the marine colors, dapple some blue ink over the first layer of paint, and then highlight with touches of white acrylic paint. To give the box a weathered or slightly distressed appearance, trickle some drawing ink over the wet pearlized paint and then dab gently with a piece of paper towels.

To create the interesting spiral shell design on the front face of the box, use some white acrylic paint. Soften the strength of the background colors a little by applying tiny amounts of blue, pink, and yellow inks before the paint is thoroughly dry.

By varnishing the finished project you will protect the papier mâché from damage and also help to enhance the look of the shimmering and dappled paintwork effects.

FISH DISH

Here's a chance to develop your skills with modeling clay and make this highly individual fish dish. When it has been painted and varnished it makes a delightfully whimsical decoration that is perfect in the bathroom filled with shells, soaps, or other bathroom goodies—although it won't survive submersion in the tub!

As you start to add strips of papier mâché to the tail, you will notice that the finer sculpted edges appear. Try and build on this technique to produce an elaborate, flowing tail. You will also need to apply two coats of gesso to give a really smooth surface to the fish, but be careful not apply any one coat too thickly otherwise the piece may suffer from unsightly cracking.

Dappled, pearlized acrylic paints in marine colors are the best to use to decorate the fish dish. First apply a base color of blue or green poster paint to work on, then add layers of the blue and green pearlized paints and inks on top. When the last coat is dry, add fins, scales, and an eye, using a mixture of red and green inks, white acrylic paint, purple and silver pearlized paints, and red poster paint to give a luxuriant, shimmering effect to the finished dish.

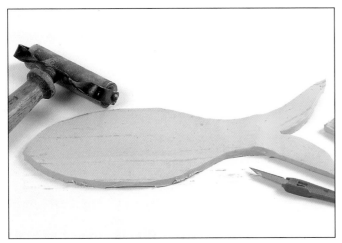

1

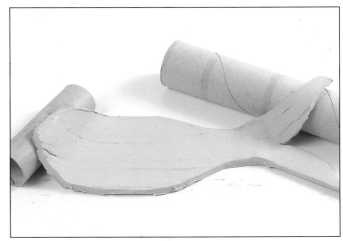

2

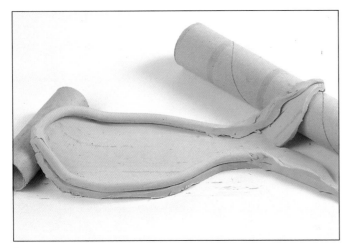

3

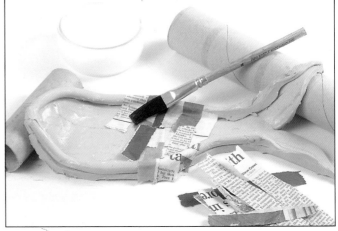

4

MATERIALS

Roller or rolling pin
Modeling clay
Craft knife
1 sheet of letter paper and pen
Cardboard tubes
Petroleum jelly
Thin newspaper strips (*see p. 107*)
Thinned PVA medium (*see p. 107*)
Flat-ended pastry brush
Paper towels
Scissors
Acrylic gesso
Various paintbrushes
Blue or green and red poster paints
Purple, silver, blue, and green pearlized paints; white acrylic paint
Red and green drawing inks
Polyurethane varnish

1 To form the mold for this fish dish roll out some modeling clay onto a suitable work surface. The clay should be about ¼in (6mm) thick, at least 12in (30cm) long and 6in (15cm) wide. Use a craft knife with a blunt blade to cut out a simple fish shape with flowing tail fins. If you are unhappy about cutting the clay freehand, use this photograph as guide to draw a fish shape onto a piece of paper, then blow it up to the required size on a photocopier. When you are satisfied with the result, cut out the template and place it over the modeling clay, so that it lies flat on the surface, then cut around it.

2 Lift the nose end of the fish and one of the tail fins to prop them onto the cardboard tubes. Adjust their angles several times so that they complement one another.

3 Roll out some modeling clay into long, thin logs about ¼in (6mm) thick, and use them to build up a ridge on the outer edge of the fish mold, but leave the inner edges of the fin as they are. Smooth the joins with your finger.

4 Apply petroleum jelly as a releasing agent to the fish mold in readiness for the first layer of papier mâché strips.

5

6

7

8

5 Take the thin strips of newspaper and paste with the PVA medium and then, following the method for layering papier mâché onto a mold (*see p. 110*), apply eight layers to the dish. Remember to alternate the direction of each layer, and allow each one to dry for several hours before applying the next. The newspaper strips will also stick to the cardboard tubes, but this doesn't matter.

6 When the fish dish is completely dry, use a craft knife to help lever it from the mold. Remove any traces of the petroleum jelly with paper towels and trim away excess newspaper with scissors. Then carefully detach the cardboard tubes with scissors.

7 Turn the papier mâché fish over and apply another eight layers of newspaper strips to the underside of the dish, as shown in the picture, alternating them as you proceed. Allow the strips to extend right over the ridge on the front side of the fish, and then neatly blend them in with your fingers. Again let each layer dry for several hours before applying the next.

8 When the papier mâché has completely hardened, trim away any rough pieces of newspaper with the scissors to form an even edge. Then apply two coats of gesso as an undercoat, allowing it to dry thoroughly between coats, for a really smooth surface all over. Decorate the finished fish with the poster and pearlized paints and the drawing inks. Finally, when the paints are dry, apply five coats of polyurethane varnish, allowing to dry between coats as detailed in the manufacturer's instructions.

1

2

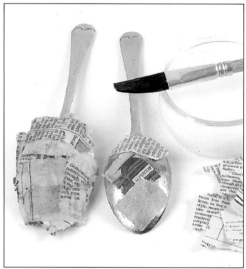

3

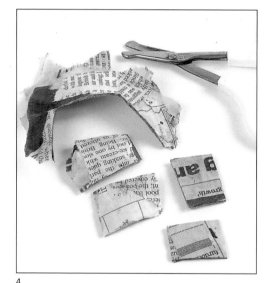

4

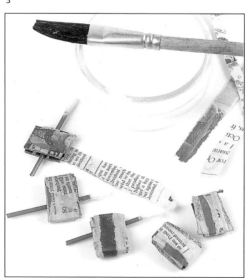

5

6

1 Make five round papier mâché pulp beads. Remove the ends from five cotton swabs and apply petroleum jelly as a releasing agent to the stems. Roll a ball of pulp in the palm of your hand and push it onto one stem; repeat for the other four stems. Leave to dry for about a week.

2 The second bead used is a layered tubular bead. Prepare another six cotton swabs in the same way as before. Apply PVA medium to the newspaper strips with a flat-ended brush. The technique used to produce these beads is easy: simply wrap the strips around the cotton swab stem, building up about six layers of newspaper. Leave to dry for four to five days.

3 The final bead is made from flat-layered papier mâché built up on the back of dessertspoons. Apply petroleum jelly as a releasing agent to the back of six spoons and then paste on the newspaper squares with PVA medium, following the method for layering papier mâché onto a mold (*see p. 110*). Build up eight layers, drying for several hours between layers.

4 When the papier mâché is hard, remove from the spoons. Then cut trapezoid shapes 1⅛in (3cm) x ¾in (2 cm) x 1⅛in (3cm) x ⅝in (1.5cm).

5 Brush more newspaper strips with PVA medium and tape the two halves of the bead together, using a cotton swab as a spacer.

6 Experiment with different designs for the beads by threading on a thong. Then remove them and apply a coat of gesso. Then decorate with the poster paints and finish each bead with five coats of polyurethane varnish, leaving to dry between coats as detailed in the manufacturer's instructions. Finally, thread the beads on a thong.

MATERIALS

Papier mâché pulp
(see pp. 107-8)

Petroleum jelly

Cotton swabs

Thinned PVA medium (see p. 107)

Flat-ended pastry brush

¾in (2cm) newspaper strips
and squares (see p. 107)

6 dessert spoons

Scissors

Leather thong
(from craft stores)

Acrylic gesso

Various paintbrushes

Red, dark brown, green, light
blue, and yellow poster paints

Polyurethane varnish

ADVANCED LEVEL

AFRICAN BEAD NECKLACE

This bright, colorful necklace would look particularly good worn with T-shirts in bright, primary colors. It is assembled from three contrasting types of beads, and reflects the same ethnic theme as the African Bangle (*see pp. 138-9*). Once again vibrant poster colors have been used in various spot and stripe designs on a strong base color: the round beads have been given a yellow base with dark-brown spots; the tubular beads a dark-brown base with green stripes, and the flat beads have a red base with yellow and blue stripes. When painting stripes onto the tubular beads, apply them in two sections, front then back, to avoid any smearing and blurring.

An easy way to varnish the beads is to thread each one onto the stem of a cotton bud, which is held upright in some modeling clay. You can then varnish them on both sides.

Once finished, the beads can be threaded onto a leather thong. To achieve other effects you might like to experiment with different types of boot laces, ribbon, and the various strings found in variety stores.

1 The snake in this project is made up from six sections, each decreasing a little in size. Draw the sections for the snake onto the cardboard with a marker pen. The head section is 2¼in (6cm) and the final tail piece is 1in (2.5cm). Your measurements need not be exact, but use these as a guide. Cut out the sections using a craft knife.

2 Mold some papier mâché pulp onto the top surface of each section to a depth of up to 1in (2.5cm). Create a forked tongue and features on the snake's face, and extend the final tail piece into a point. Leave all the pieces to dry for about a week.

3 When the papier mâché has dried, turn each section over. Then paste PVA medium onto the newspaper strips and apply five layers to each base, following the method for layering papier mâché onto a mold (see p. 110).

4 To make large eyes for the snake, model a pulp bead onto a cotton-swab stem with one end removed, first smearing with petroleum jelly as a releasing agent. After about a week, slice the hard bead in half and attach each piece to the snake's face with PVA medium.

5 Lay out the sections of the snake to see how it will fit together, then apply a coat of gesso to all sections. When dry, decorate with the bright poster colors. To finish apply five coats of polyurethane varnish, leaving to dry between coats as detailed in the manufacturer's instructions. Finally, assemble the snake by attaching screw eyes to the sections and linking them together with a couple of jump rings. Attach a magnet with glue to the base of each section and hold firmly to secure. Then place the snake on the refrigerator.

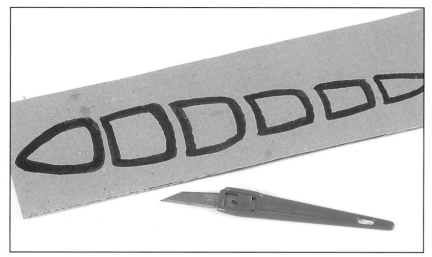

1

2

3

SNAKE FRIDGE MAGNET

This bright snake with its vivid jungle colors won't be missed by anyone as it slithers across the front of the refrigerator! Paint each poster color separately onto the gesso undercoat. The "V" snake pattern painted in red, bright blue, lime green, and purple has a bold, dynamic effect. Paint the eyes in yellow to stand out and add some black to the tongue to highlight the red "Y" shape of the fork. You may, of course, prefer to paint bright spots or scales on this vibrant snake rather than the design here.

4

MATERIALS

Cardboard

Marker pen

Craft knife

Papier mâché pulp
(see pp. 107-8)

Thinned PVA medium (see p. 107)

Flat-ended pastry brush

Short newspaper strips,
(see p. 107)

Cotton swabs and petroleum jelly

Acrylic gesso

Various paintbrushes

Red, purple, lime-green,
yellow, bright-blue, and black
poster paints

Polyurethane varnish

Screw eyes and jump rings

Small magnets

Strong metal glue

5

151

CROSS-STITCH

MATERIALS AND TECHNIQUES

MATERIALS AND TECHNIQUES

For those new to cross-stitch there may be references to threads, types of stitches, materials, equipment, and some techniques that you are not familiar with. The following pages go into detail, explaining some of the terms and techniques you will encounter.

FABRICS

Counted cross-stitch is worked on fabrics that have easily discernible vertical and horizontal threads. These fabrics are usually of two types: blockweaves, such as Aida and Binca; or evenweaves, such as linen.

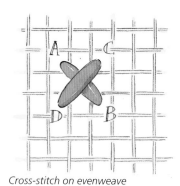

Cross-stitch on evenweave

BLOCKWEAVES

Blockweaves look as if they are woven from thin strips of material. Where the vertical and horizontal strips cross, they form a square with a hole at each corner. Cross-stitches are formed by using these holes to sew through, and each single stitch thus sits neatly over a single block (*see left*).

Since they are so easy to use, blockweaves are the most popular fabric for counted cross-stitch, and they are available with different numbers of holes per inch (hpi). The number of holes per inch determines how many stitches you can make per inch, and it is this that dictates the size and delicacy of your stitched piece. The complete range of sizes runs from 6 hpi Binca to 22 hpi Aida. There

Cross-stitch on blockweave

are also a range of linens, from very coarse to quite fine, so you have a lot of scope when it comes to choosing the fabric to work on.

For many cross-stitchers, 14 hpi Aida is a favorite. The squares are big enough to work easily, yet small enough to give good design detail. Binca, which is a good fabric for children, also lends itself to advanced projects, and should not be overlooked.

However, blockweaves can also be sized not by their hpi but by the number of squares per inch—known as the "count." To all intents and purposes, there is no difference between squares and holes per inch, and if you come across the term 14 count Aida, for example, it is exactly the same as 14 hpi Aida.

EVENWEAVES

Evenweaves have the same number of threads running vertically and horizontally. But since they are not woven in blocks they are not as easy to work on as blockweaves. Each stitch is usually worked over two vertical and two horizontal threads (*see left*), and since you have to decide on these yourself, you need to be very accurate with your counting.

Linen is a lovely fabric to work on, but it is expensive. However, you can buy evenweaves in cotton and rayon mixtures and both give very good results.

One fabric that looks like a blockweave but is, in fact, an evenweave, is Hardanger. This is woven in pairs of threads and looks as if it is made up of blocks.

CANVAS

There are three main types of canvas: single (mono) canvas, woven from single threads; interlocked canvas, woven from threads that are locked at the intersections (*see right*); and double (Penelope) canvas (*see right*), which has pairs of threads running horizontally and vertically.

Single and interlocked are graded according to the number of threads per inch, and double by the number of holes. There is a good choice of size, ranging from 22 gauge, for very fine work in cottons, to 7 gauge, for work in wool.

PLAINWEAVES

Since they are so densely woven, many plainweaves are not suitable for counted cross-stitch. However, by using waste canvas you can embroider "impossible" fabrics—such as cotton sheeting, denim, silk, or jersey—with ease. Waste canvas is a special double canvas recognizable by the blue threads running through it. It is loosely woven and held together with water-soluble glue. To use it, cut off a piece larger than your design and tack it firmly to the material. Then, stitch over the waste canvas as if you were cross-stitching ordinary double canvas, but go through the plainweave material as well. Stitches should be firmly placed, but not too tight.

When finished, trim off the excess canvas, dampen the whole area to dissolve the glue bonding the threads, and pull them out from behind the stitches.

KNITTED FABRICS

To work on fine knitted fabric, use the waste canvas method. Larger knits can be used directly as a background for counted cross-stitch—you simply need to get your eye in. If you look at stocking stitch, you will see that each stitch looks a little heart-shaped. With some imagination, transform that heart into a square, like the blocks you see on blockweaves. You then make one cross-stitch over each knitted stitch.

Sometimes, the stitches are longer than they are wide, so do a test by counting stitches up and across. If there is too much variation in the number of stitches along and number of rows up, the design may distort. If so, use the waste canvas method.

Knitted fabrics can stretch, so it may be best to tack interlining behind the design area before starting. Then cross-stitch your design through both knitting and interlining. When you have finished, cut off any excess interlining from around the design area. The interlining that is left acts as a permanent backing to your design and holds the knitting stable when you wear and wash the garment.

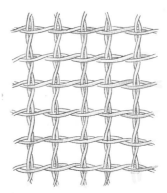

Interlocked canvas

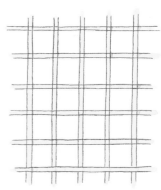

Double canvas

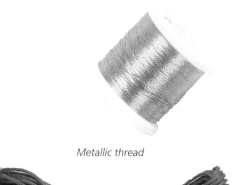

Metallic thread

Stranded cotton

Coton à broder, or
Self-embroidery cotton

Marlitt

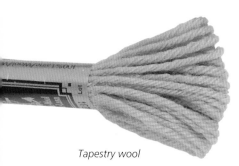

Cotton perle

Tapestry wool

THREADS

In early samplers and cross-stitch, silks and wools were popular threads. But as each generation has taken up this craft, so devotees have used the materials that were most easily accessible at that time.

STRANDED COTTON

The most popular thread today is stranded cotton. This is available in a wide range of more than 300 colors and, on the whole, is very economical to use.

Before starting to work, cut the lengths of cotton you need and separate them into their component 6 strands. Then work with the required number of strands—however many needed to give good coverage. If you are still learning, trying to keep a consistent tension and an even finish, it is best to practice with the standard combination of two strands of cotton on 14 hpi Aida.

When it is worked, stranded cotton has a dull shine. Knowing this, you can create a variety of effects by working with different numbers of threads on the one design. For example, to get the effect of distance or shadow, work the foreground in two strands and the background in one.

STRANDED SILK

Silk is more expensive and has fewer colors than stranded cotton, but it gives a richer and deeper finish. Work stranded silk in the same way as stranded cotton, or mix the two in the same design. Marlitt can be substituted for stranded silk.

FLOWER THREAD

Cotton flower thread is not divisible and is softer than stranded cotton. Although the range of colors is not as extensive as with cotton thread, its palette is more natural and earthy. There are bright colors as well, but the thread's matte finish means that it works very well with linens and evenweaves to give an antique or rustic flavor to your work.

PERLE COTTON

This is a thick and wonderfully silky thread. Again there is a large range of colors and you can buy it by the skein or on card reels. Perle cotton is ideal for bulky borders or abstract designs and always gives a richness to your designs.

SOFT EMBROIDERY COTTON

This is rather like a bulky version of a flower thread—the sort of thing that you might have experimented with when you first learned to stitch. It has an even, matte sheen, and some of the canvas projects in this book would work very well on a small-gauge canvas using this thread.

METALLIC THREAD

This is, for the most part, composed of fine strips of metal, such as aluminum. The weights and thicknesses of this thread vary greatly and there are always new ones appearing on the market. Gold, silver (which can be seen at the center of the picture on the facing page), bronze, and copper are the most popular colors. Metallic threads are well worth experimenting with.

WOOL

Wool is one of the most adaptable and enduring of threads. The two basic weights for cross-stitch are crewel and tapestry. Crewel is the finer of the two and works well on linens and natural fabrics. In this chapter the tapestry weight has been used for the canvas and plastic canvas work. If you want to use crewel wool instead, practice with combining two or three lengths where it is recommended that you use one length of tapestry wool.

Knitting wool in 4-ply or double knit can be used for cross-stitch. Try to avoid acrylic or acrylic/wool mixes, since these may "bobble."

BEADING

This popular Victorian technique has once again appeared to become one of the more exciting techniques used by today's stitchers. You will find that there are many projects available that call for dense bead work, and others in which the design is in cross-stitch and beads are used to provide detail and highlighting.

DIFFERENT TYPES OF STITCH

All of the projects in this chapter can be undertaken using just a small number of different stitches, most of which you will already be familiar with.

CROSS-STITCH

A cross-stitch is made in two movements, from two diagonal stitches crossing over each other. The result is a symmetrical, almost square, stitch. If working on a block-weave, the stitch lies over one block; on an evenweave, it lies over a block made from two horizontal and two vertical threads.

To work one cross-stitch, bring the needle up through the fabric at A and across and down at B (see left). This gives the underneath half of the stitch. Then, bring your needle up at C and down again at D for the top half of the stitch. The front of your work shows a whole stitch; the back two vertical stitches.

In most instances you will be able to work in rows, not in individual stitches. Not only is this easier and quicker to do, it also gives a more even finish to your work. First, work all the underneath half of the stitches (see below). Then return, working the top half of the stitches.

Cross-stitch

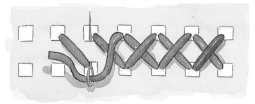

Row of cross-stitches

HALF CROSS-STITCH

Sometimes you may need half cross-stitches—perhaps for an area of shading. Stitches should go in the same direction, or the work will look uneven. Get into the habit of working them in the same direction.

QUARTER STITCH

These are very small stitches and are usually made to fill in gaps—in making three-quarter cross-stitches, for example. Quarter stitches are worked from the corner of a block to the center (see left).

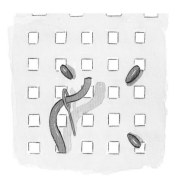

Half cross-stitch

Quarter stitch

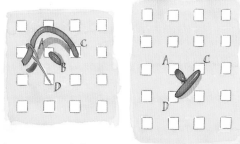

Three-quarter stitch

THREE-QUARTER STITCH

Three-quarter stitches are made from a combination of quarter and half stitches and are used for adding detail. Work the quarter stitch first (see above), from A in the corner to B in the middle. Then work the half stitch from C to D. The quarter block not worked can be left or filled in with the color of the surrounding area.

BACKSTITCH

These are usually worked in one strand, if you are using stranded thread. Backstitches are often used for outlining and should be done after the cross-stitching. They appear on the front of the work as a smooth line.

Backstitch

FRENCH KNOT

To make a French knot, bring the needle up through the fabric, keeping the thread taut (see right). Twist the needle around the thread, once, twice, or three times, depending on the size knot. Push the needle through the fabric close to where it emerged. When halfway through, pull the thread tight, making the knot, and push the needle and thread to the back.

LONG STITCH

A quick way of filling in background is with long stitches. The stitches can be vertical, horizontal, or diagonal and, unlike backstitch, they can cover more than one block of fabric (see right).

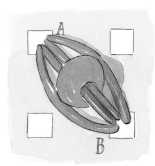

Fixing beads

FIXING BEADS

Traditionally, beads are fixed to the design by a half cross-stitch (*see opposite*). Bring your needle to the front where you want the bead, as if forming an ordinary half cross-stitch. Pick up the bead with the needle and thread it on to the yarn. Pull the yarn through and make sure the bead sits well on the fabric. Then complete the half cross-stitch.

However good your tension, using this method the beads will tend to wobble on the finished item. To prevent this happening, there is an alternative method. Use either sewing cotton or the yarn you are cross-stitching with, and double it so that you are working with two strands (*see left*). Fix the thread to the back of your work and pull it through to the front where you want the bead to be. Pick up the bead and finish the half cross-stitch, as above.

Then, bring the needle through at A again, take the thread over the top of the bead so that one strand lies on the left of it and one on the right, and complete the half cross-stitch. This second stitch on either side of the bead anchors it firmly in position and makes your work more even.

STARTING AND FINISHING

When starting or finishing a piece of work, the thread should not be secured on the back of the material with a knot because this may show through on the right side. To start, either run your new thread behind the stitches you have already worked, or hold the last 1in (2.5cm) of your thread behind your work and make sure it is secured by your new stitching. To finish, run your thread carefully through the backs of the stitches you have already worked (*see below*).

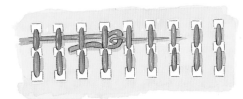

Starting and finishing

French knot

Long stitch

SIZES

One of the fascinating things about counted stitch is that, once you have a charted design, you can work it on any count fabric you like without having to do any complicated recalculations. Whatever count you choose, the design will look the same—just smaller or larger, depending on whether you have chosen fabric with fewer or more hpi.

With a little basic arithmetic, you can work out your design area quite easily. For example, if your design is 126 stitches wide, it will be 9in wide if you work on 14 hpi fabric. In other words, if there are 14 stitches to the inch, you need 9in to work 126 stitches, or $126 \div 14 = 9$.

Work the same design on 16 hpi fabric, however, and it will be approximately 8in wide ($126 \div 16\ 7.875$). So the rule is: divide the number of stitches by the hpi to obtain the size in inches.

NEEDLES

There are no hard and fast rules regarding the size of the needles you should use for each fabric but, generally speaking, a size 24 needle (blunt ended) is best for medium-gauge work; a tapestry needle is necessary for the canvas and plastic canvas projects; and a number 8 crewel is recommended on finer linens and 18 count Aida. Obviously if your needle distorts the fabric at all, or leaves a gaping hole, then choose a smaller size. On the other hand, don't use a needle that is too small on canvas projects, as this will damage the threads and give you poor coverage of the canvas.

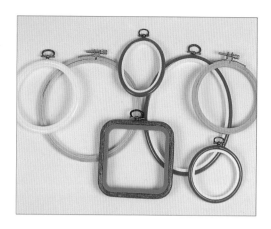

HOOPS AND FRAMES

Some cross-stitchers prefer to work with the fabric stretched taut in a frame or hoop (*see above*) in order to achieve an even tension; others prefer the freedom of working with the fabric loose. Embroidery hoops are the traditional equipment for light-weight fabrics but, especially on smaller projects, you can use a flexi-hoop (*see opposite*). A tapestry frame may be useful if you are working on a large piece of material but it is not very portable and, since setting it up takes quite a while, it might actually dampen your enthusiasm. The best advice is to experiment to find the method you are most comfortable with. Start off with a small hoop and, if it seems unsuccessful or awkward, try without it. Remember, it is very important that you enjoy your stitching. Finally, if you do work with a hoop, the fabric will definitely need washing afterward because the hoop will leave a "shadow image" behind.

PREPARING FABRIC

Work out the size of your design and add on at least 2in (5cm) all around before you cut your fabric. For example, for a design measuring 8 × 10in (20 × 25cm) you need to cut the fabric to 10 × 12in (25 × 30cm). To prevent it fraying, you can edge the fabric with blanket stitching, tack all the way around with ordinary sewing thread or hem the piece.

Next, fold the fabric in half both vertically and horizontally and tack along these folds in a thread color that will show clearly, marking the middle lines. Where they cross is the center of the fabric and this is where you will usually begin stitching your design. You will have to remove these stitched lines when you have finished your work, so remember not to sew through, or too tightly over, them while you are working your design.

If you are working with canvas, bind the edges with masking tape and then mark the middle with an indelible pen. For projects worked on plastic canvas, cut the canvas neatly with sharp scissors and carefully trim off any spikes so that you leave your work smooth-edged.

USING THREADS

The thread you use often suggests the best method of working. For example, if you are using wool, cut what you need from the ball or skein as required, restricting yourself to 15-16in (40cm) lengths to prevent tangles. If the wool starts to unwind as you are stitching, simply tie it off at the back and start stitching again with the other end of the wool that is still intact. With stranded cotton, and most other threads, 8in (20cm) lengths are about right—you will not have to rethread too often and they should not become tangled. If the thread does start to twist, simply hold the fabric and let the needle and thread hang down loosely to unwind.

THREAD ORGANIZER

If you are working with a large number of threads and are worried about mixing up similar colors, consider using a thread organizer. You can easily make one yourself by punching a strip of cardboard with holes. Cut a couple of lengths of a particular color thread, feed them through one of the holes, and write that color's number alongside it. Repeat this process with each color you are using in the design.

When you divide your threads, the individual strands can be safely stored on the thread organizer until needed. This method saves you the bother and annoyance of hunting around the room for all those oddments of thread, and also helps you to avoid the dreaded workbox tangles.

FINISHING

When you have completed a project, the chances are that it will have picked up odd bits of dirt and dust along the way. Washing it before mounting will remove this grime and show off your stitching to the best possible effect.

WASHING

Use lukewarm water and mild laundry detergent. Rinse thoroughly in cool water and, should any of the colors look like they are running, keep rinsing until you are sure it has stopped. If you don't, you may be left with ghostly shadows around the strong colors.

USING A FLEXI-HOOP

Flexi-hoops are a quick and easy way of finishing and presenting your work. There are two hoops; the inner hoop is made of a rigid material and the outer, more flexible ring, is stretched over it. Pull the hoops apart and, using the inner ring as a template, cut a piece of backing felt, or some other fabric, to fit the outside diameter. Place your washed stitching centrally over the inner ring and then refit the outer one, pulling it on from the front. Now adjust the position of your work by pulling the material by its edges. When satisfied, trim the excess fabric (*see below*) down to 1in (2.5cm).

Next, lay your backing felt or fabric over the back and, using a running stitch around the edge, cover the stitching on the rear of the design.

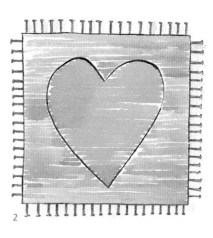

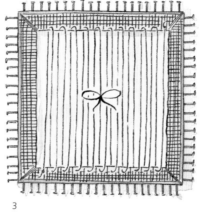

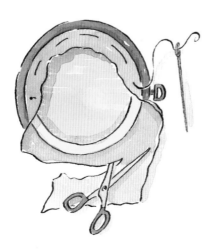

LACING AND FRAMING

Frames normally have a recess in the back for the glass and a piece of cardboard. Cut a piece of cardboard to fit this recess, allowing for the thickness of the fabric as it folds around the sides. Leave extra space around the design since all frames, except clip-frames, overlap your work a little.

Place your work, face up, with the design centered over the card and fold the fabric around the back of the card. Place pins through the fabric and into the edge of the card at the middle of each side (1). Using more pins, ease the fabric around the card (2). Next, turn your work over and, with a needle, secure sewing cotton to the top corner of one of the side flaps. Then work down, sewing from side to side and from bottom to top, at 1in (2.5cm) intervals (3). Keep the thread taut enough to pull the fabric tight without distorting its shape. You will end up with a grid effect of threads. Remove the pins and you are ready to frame your work (4).

FINISHING TIPS

● After washing in mild detergent, lay a thick towel on an ironing board or table and place another, thin towel or cloth over it.

● Gently squeeze—do not wring—your work, place it on top of the towel with the design face down, and press it with a warm iron. The towel cushions your work, preventing the stitching from being squashed flat.

● Iron out any creases in the fabric and, when it's dry, your work will be ready for lacing (*see left*).

MAKING CUSHIONS

Many of the projects in this chapter would make excellent cushions, which are a perfect showcase for displaying your stitching.

First, choose a backing fabric that will contrast, or coordinate, with your stitching. Then decide what opening method you are going to use to allow for washing at some later date. If you choose a zip, place this along a center seam and secure it, making sure that it will open on the outside of the cushion. An alternative to a zip is the button back, where three button-holes with covered buttons create the center seam. Finally, there is the folded overlap, which avoids any complicated sewing.

BASIC TECHNIQUE

Place the right sides of your stitching and backing together and pin them round the edge of the stitching, or a marked-out edge if there is an allowance of fabric around the design. It is always best to leave a "breathing space" around an open design (where not all the fabric is stitched), as cropping in too close might spoil the effect. With a fully stitched piece, the design will go right up to the edge of the finished cushion.

Working outward from the center seam, sew securely along the outside edges. Cut these outside edges to within about ½in (1cm) of the canvas or fabric, cutting the corners at 45° to give a neater edge when it is finished. When you do turn the work inside out, ease out these corners with a pencil for a perfectly expert finish.

To add the final detail, you can sew a piece of braid or cord around the edge of the cushion, but remember to buy a little more than you think you need—the corners always seem to use up more than you expect. Start the cord halfway along one side, not at a corner, since this will help you to disguise the join more effectively. Alternatively, you can add piping to finish off your cushion's edges, as was done on the tile cushion project seen on pages 170-1.

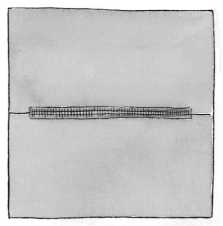

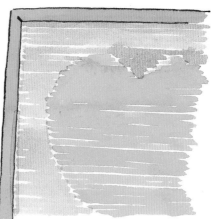

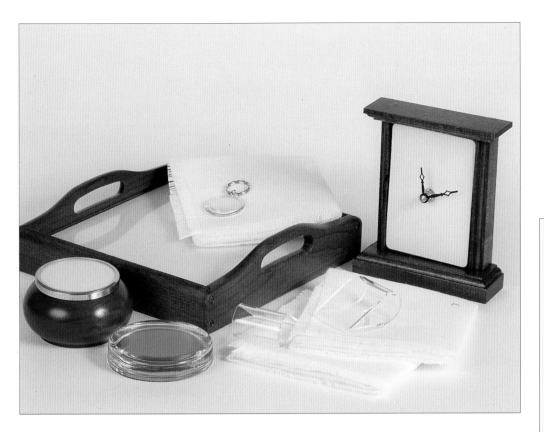

USING THE CHARTS

Each square on the charts accompanying the projects in this chapter represents one complete cross-, or X-shaped, stitch, and the accompanying color bars give the Anchor color reference numbers used in the example piece. To find out the DMC equivalents of these, see pages 206-7. A full square represents a whole cross-stitch and where two colors occupy the same square then one is a quarter stitch and the other is a three-quarter stitch. To control the color balance of your work, stitch the color you want to give more prominence to the three-quarter stitch.

Some cross-stitchers like to work all the stitches of one color before starting the others. However, this can lead to mistakes when you have a large area to cover. It is better, therefore, to work each small area of one color and then change the thread to work the adjacent stitches in the next color. For example, you might work one petal of a flower and then change color to stitch the center, and so on. Building up the design in this way will help to make sure that the finished piece is accurately worked. You may like to use a ruler to mark off each area of the chart as you complete it, and only concentrate on one section of it at a time.

DISPLAYING YOUR WORK

Many craft supply stores, wool and embroidery specialists and mail order outlets dealing with craft materials often carry a large range of "blanks" into which your finished cross-stitch pieces can be inserted (*see above*). Many of the projects featured in this chapter make use of these products and, once they are assembled, your stitching will look indistinguishable from that produced by a professional craft worker.

If you intend to use one of these for your stitching, first buy the one you want and then size your design so that it will fit comfortably within the display area of that particular piece. Each comes with complete assembly instructions.

Just a few examples of the hundreds available are shown here and you will need to obtain a catalog to see all your options.

POINTS TO REMEMBER

● Don't start or finish your work with a permanent knot.

● Don't take thread across an area behind your work that will not be stitched over, as the thread may show through on the right side of your work.

● Make sure that your tension is even and uniform throughout—neither too tight nor too loose. Working in a hoop or frame may help.

● To keep your stitching neat, sew all the bottom diagonals of the cross-stitches in one direction and all the tops in the alternative direction. Be consistent!

CROSS-STITCH

PROJECTS

INSTRUCTIONS

Number of stitches: 90 × 110.
Finished design size: 8⅕ × 10in
(20.8 × 25.4cm) on 11 hpi Aida.
Prepare your fabric (*see pp.
154-63*). Find the center of your
material and start stitching from
the center of the design.

EASY LEVEL

NUMBERS AND LETTERS SAMPLERS

There are hundreds of styles of numbers and letters to choose from, and a few are given on pages 204-5. You can take the examples illustrated here as your guide, copying both the style and colors, or borrow any of the elements and then freely adapt them.

Think about the colors of the numbers or letters, how they will work both within the design and the sampler's wider setting. Work the design out before beginning, using a page of printed graph paper to act as a guide. The two samplers here are the same design size and both have been stitched in 11 hpi Aida, which really is the largest fabric you can use for anything described as a serious project.

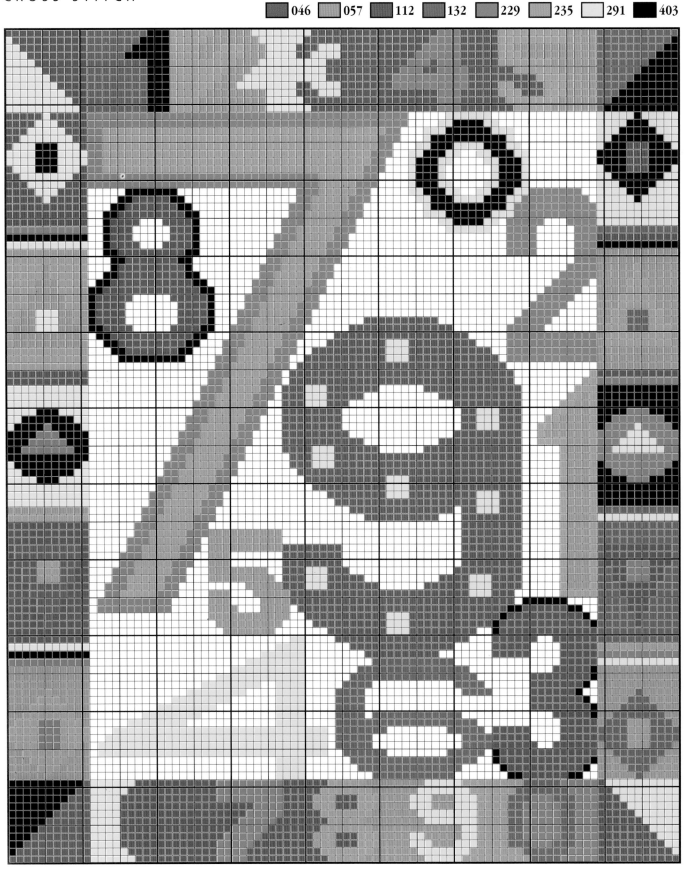

046 057 112 132 229 235 291 403

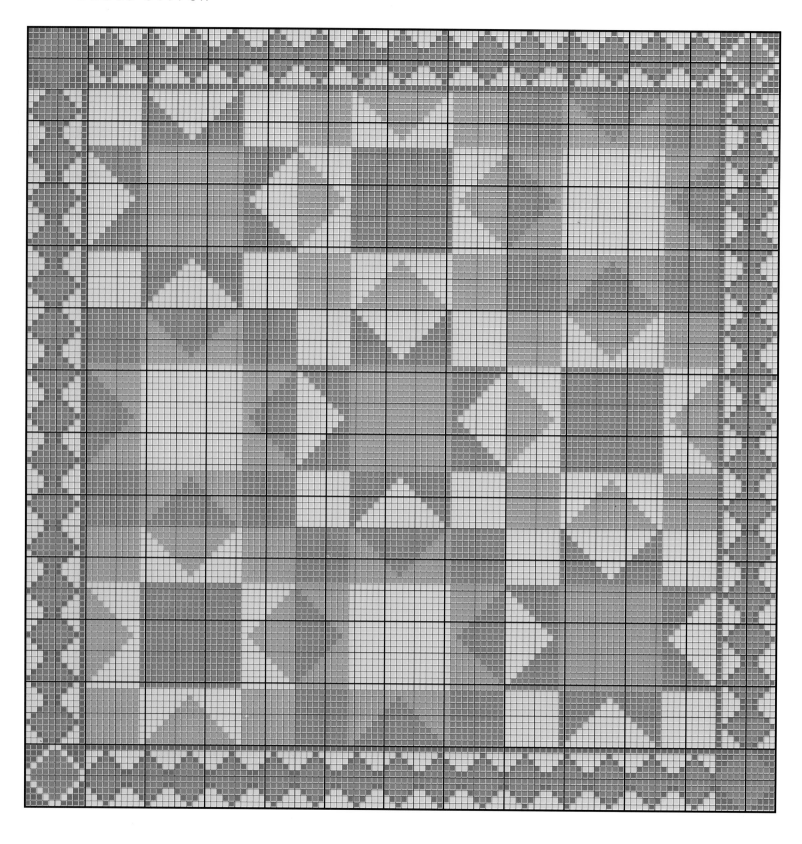

1014   175   123   306

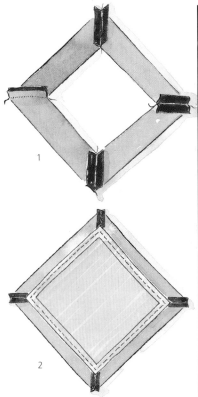

1

2

MATERIALS

Fabric: 10 × 10in
(25.4 × 25.4cm) 18 hpi Aida

Contrasting/toning fabric
for assembly

Needle

Thread: Stranded cotton—4
skeins of each color. Use 3
strands for the cross-stitch

INSTRUCTIONS

Number of stitches: 125 × 125.
Finished design size: 7 × 7in (17.8
× 17.8cm) on 18 hpi Aida. Prepare
your fabric (*see pp. 154-63*), find
the center of your fabric and start
stitching from the center of the
design.

Cut four pieces of velvet and stitch
them together as shown (1), to
make a 4in (10cm) border around
the finished piece. Place the
finished piece face down over the
center of the fabric border (2), and
stitch it to the inside edge of the
border, leaving one stitch all
around the cross-stitch panel.

TILE CUSHION

The type of geometric patterns seen in this piece can be found in the work of many British Victorian tile designers. You do need to concentrate when working on a symmetrically designed piece such as this but, on the positive side, the design is easy to stitch as long as you keep your stitching and tension even. The finished piece will look extremely effective when displayed in your home and, importantly, it will also make you a long-wearing cushion cover.

As with many of the projects in this chapter, you could easily adapt the design to make an entirely different piece, such as a table mat, or use just part of the pattern to make a smaller item, such as a brooch. This same design would make a stunning rug if it were worked in wool on 7 hpi canvas.

Either copy the color scheme pictured above or, as always, look for your inspiration elsewhere—your own home, for example. You could choose colors that coordinate with your furniture, for example.

EASY LEVEL

STARRY THROW

Travelers in previous centuries often brought back bolts of exotic cloth from different parts of the world and draped them luxuriantly over their furniture. Now you can enjoy the same effect—without going to the ends of the earth to achieve it.

Rather than using just an ordinary piece of fabric to cover a chair or sofa, you can produce an ethnic-inspired design that will turn an inexpensive length of material into an exclusive throw. The fabric chosen for this example is plain, but you could just as easily pick a tartan, stripe, or check.

Many furnishing fabrics come in 48in (1.2m) widths, so if you want to cover a large chair or sofa you may need to join two pieces together. Then you need to decide where you want to position the motifs. Because you cannot use ordinary stitching methods on these fabrics, the waste canvas method was used (*see p. 155*). Upholstery braid will give the edges a professionally finished look, and the result is ideal for covering a piece of furniture that is showing a little wear and tear.

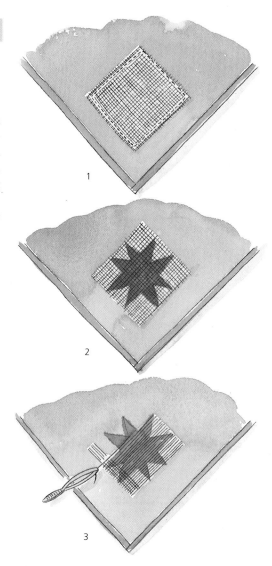

1

2

3

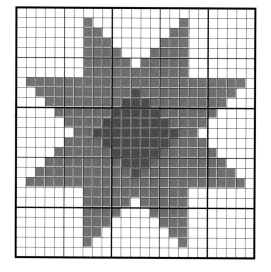

MATERIALS

Fabric: Fabric for the throw depends on size required, plus waste canvas

Needle

Thread: Stranded cotton—1 skein of each color for 2-3 motifs. Use 2 strands for the cross-stitch

INSTRUCTIONS

Number of stitches: 23 × 23.
Finished design size: $2^3/_4 \times 2^3/_4$in (7 × 7cm) on 8-9 gauge waste canvas (*see p. 155*). Don't forget, before you start, always wash your fabric to avoid it shrinking or running.

Edge your chosen fabric and then position the waste canvas where you want the first design. Pin and tack it securely (1). Now you can stitch your chosen design, making sure you stitch through both the canvas and the fabric (2). Once you have finished one element of the design, simply repeat the process by tacking fresh waste canvas wherever you want to position the next motif.

Next, dampen each piece of canvas with a wet sponge to dissolve the glue, and then begin the process of removing all the strands of canvas. A pair of tweezers is what you need here (3). Pull out each canvas thread, but don't pull too hard or you could distort the design. If the canvas still seems too stiff, just dampen it again and gently ease out the threads. Sometimes the glue leaves a stain; if so, wash the throw before using it.

922
978

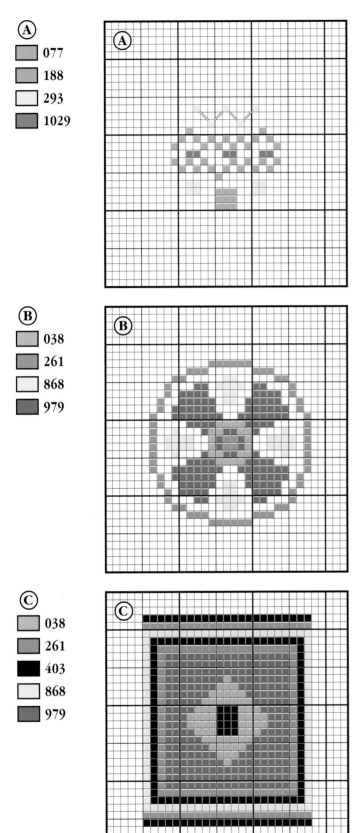

Ⓐ
- ▨ 077
- ▨ 188
- ▢ 293
- ▨ 1029

Ⓑ
- ▨ 038
- ▨ 261
- ▢ 868
- ▨ 979

Ⓒ
- ▨ 038
- ▨ 261
- ■ 403
- ▢ 868
- ▨ 979

KEY RING FOBS

One of the unwritten laws is that keys always multiply. The ones on your key ring will simply continue to increase in number until finally you need to split them up into different categories and bunches—home and auto keys together, for example, and, on another, all those annoying little keys that probably belonged to luggage and attaché cases you threw away years ago.

So as one bunch of keys becomes several, what do you do? You need more key rings, and that's where this project comes to the rescue. You could easily adapt almost any design from this chapter by experimenting with a higher count fabric to reduce the size of the motif, or just follow these charted patterns, which have been especially designed to fit into the type of standard-sized key ring holders commonly available from craft materials supply stores.

To find out how many stitches will fit into your key ring holder, lay the cardboard insert from the fob on the fabric, or some appropriately sized graph paper, draw around it, and then count off the number of stitches.

INSTRUCTIONS

Parts of other designs in the chapter have been used for each key ring. They have had to be adapted slightly to fit the space—for example, the rectangular design from the border of the numbers sampler had to be extended slightly. If you would rather make other choices, look through the different projects until something catches your eye, and then adapt it to fit the space you have available.

MATERIALS

Fabric: Fine Aida, Hardanger or evenweave—anything from 18 hpi

Needle

Thread: Oddments of stranded cotton or flower threads. Use 1 thread of stranded cotton for a delicate result

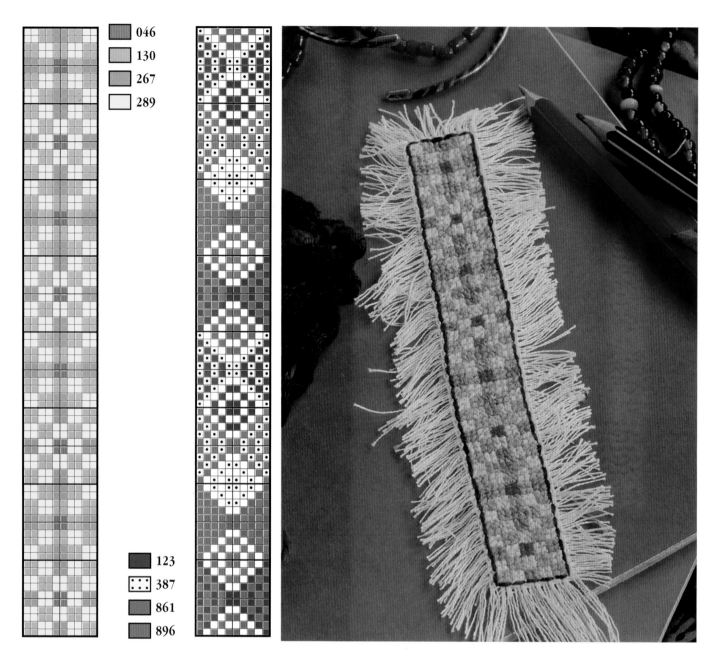

	046
	130
	267
	289

	123
	387
	861
	896

MATERIALS
Fabric (both wristbands):
9 × 3in (22.9 × 7.6cm)
14 hpi Aida
Ribbon or felt for backing
Needle
PVA glue
Thread: Stranded cotton or
flower threads—remnants only
required. Use 2 strands for the
cross-stitch

EASY LEVEL

CHILD'S WRISTBANDS

Small pieces of cross-stitch are ideal for using up remnants of material and threads. And the wristbands you see here demonstrate that it is possible to achieve excellent results from cross-stitch, even if you are a total novice. To prove this, two nine-year-olds, who had never done any cross-stitch before, were given graph paper and told to choose colors and designs, and stitch a pattern. Without any help, they came up with these two excellent pieces of work.

Not only are their designs lively, showing good color sense, they are also well stitched, have excellent tension, and are even neat on the backs. If you have yet to try your hand at this absorbing craft, hopefully this project will inspire you to make a start.

INSTRUCTIONS

Number of stitches (both
wristbands): 80 × 10. Finished
design size: 5¾ × ¾in (14.6 ×
1.9cm) on 14 hpi Aida. To stitch
the designs here, find the center
of your fabric and stitch from the
center of the chart.

To design your own, choose
between four and six colors,
decide on its dimensions, and mark
the outline on graph paper.
Backstitch around the finished
piece to give a firm edge. Cut
some ribbon or felt to fit and glue
it to the back of the wristband.
Choose stranded cotton in a color
that complements the design, and
sew it through both ends (1).
When you have enough, divide the
strands into three groups and plait.
Finish off with a knot and cut the
strands to leave a tassel (2). Or, cut
the Aida ⅓in (1cm) from the
edges, remove unworked threads
on all sides to produce a fringe,
and fold the fringe back and glue
it down. To hold the band on, sew
on small snaps at the ends (3).

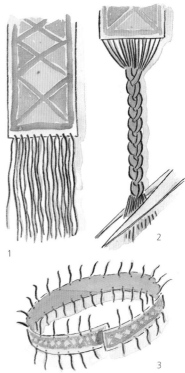

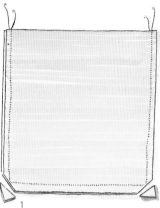

1

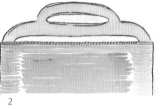

2

INSTRUCTION

Number of stitches: 68 × 75.
Finished design size: 11⅜ × 12½in
(29 × 31.7cm) 6 hpi Binca. Prepare
your fabric (see pp. 154-63), find
the center of your fabric and start
stitching from the center of the
design.

Cut a backing piece the same size
as the worked piece. Place it face
to face and stitch around two sides
and the bottom. Miter the bottom
corners (1), turn right side out and
press. Cut 2 lining pieces ⅛in
(3mm) smaller and stitch around
three sides. Place the lining (inside
out) inside the bag. Hand stitch the
top of the outer bag to the lining
bag through the slot in the
wooden handle (2).

MATERIALS

Fabric: 15 × 8in (38 × 20.3cm)
6 hpi Binca, plus lining and
backing fabric

Needle

Thread: 2 skeins of 147, 265,
243, and 1 skein of each of the
other colors. Use 6 strands for
the cross-stitch

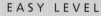

EASY LEVEL

CACTUS BAG

Cross-stitch techniques have been used to
bring out the bulkiness and spiky quality of
the cactus motif used on this bag. The large
stitches lend themselves to these characteris-
tics of the plant and also make for a quick-
to-complete project. All six strands of the
thread were used, so there is no dividing up
to be done for this project. A piece like
this is great for a child's first attempt at
cross-stitch, and the subject matter is interesting, too. There is no need to use all four
of the cactus motifs; if you want, you could
simplify the design and decide to use just
one of them.

If you decide to create a new species of
cactus, stitch the pot first and keep a uniform thickness for the plant.

| | 039 | | 147 | | 218 | | 243 | | 265 | | 303 | | 382 | | 897 |

BABY'S TOWEL

So that this chapter has something for everyone, here is a project for the smallest of kindergarten kids, even if they are too young to stitch it themselves.

Bright colors and faces are guaranteed to attract the attention of babies and toddlers. These farmyard faces have been designed to be worked on to a child's towel for added fun at bath time. Many towels can be bought with Aida panels already sewn in, ready for the cross-stitcher, and this type has been used here to show off a range of motifs for youngsters.

For an older child, a flower motif might be more appropriate; and if you can find other items—such as baseball caps—which also incorporate panels of Aida or linen, then you can try adapting any suitable design to suit the wearer. You don't have to worry about keeping the cross-stitch out of the way of dirt and grime. Both the fabric and the threads suggested here are washable and colorfast.

When you have worked on an Aida panel set into a towel, it is sensible to sew a panel of matching Aida on to the reverse in order to hide the back of your stitching.

MATERIALS

Fabric: Towel with Aida inset, plus matching Aida back panel or other suitable fabric

Needle

Thread: Stranded cotton—1 skein of each color. Use 2 strands for the cross-stitch and 1 for the backstitch

INSTRUCTIONS

Number of stitches: 113 × 23.

Finished design size: 8 × 1⅝in (20.3 × 4cm) on 14 hpi Aida (inset in towel).

Find the center of the Aida strip and start stitching from the middle of the central motif. Carefully arrange the outside motifs in the space that is left, making sure that they are lined up accurately with the central design. You can cover the back of your work by stitching on a piece of Aida, ribbon, or other fabric cut to size.

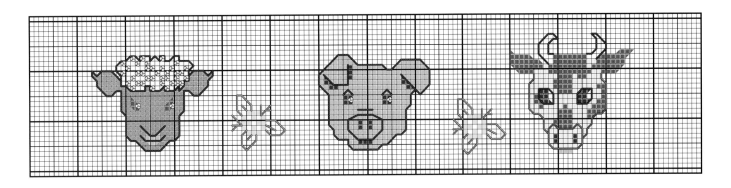

	23		258		289		370		398		401		926

712 Random French knots in one strand

INSTRUCTIONS

Number of stitches: 140 × 162.
Finished design size: 7³/₄ × 9in
(19.5 × 22.8cm) on 18 hpi Aida.
Start stitching 3in (7cm) from the
top of the fabric at the center of
the design.

Cut out a piece of cardboard the
same size as your stitched fabric
(1). Place the stitched work face
down with the cardboard mount
on top, making sure that the card
covers the design. Miter the
corners and cut a cross in the
middle, as shown (2). Using
double-sided tape, secure the
outer sides and fold the inner
fabric over the card and stitch (3).
Make a backing piece and support
as shown. Glue this to the frame,
leaving an opening at the bottom
to slide through a photograph (4).

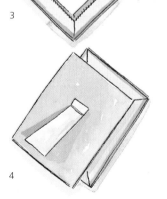

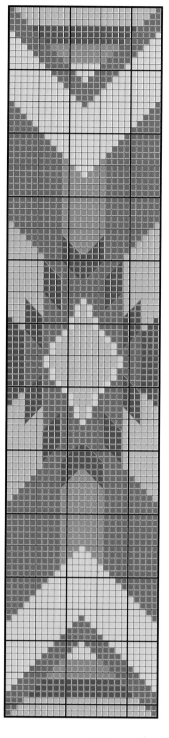

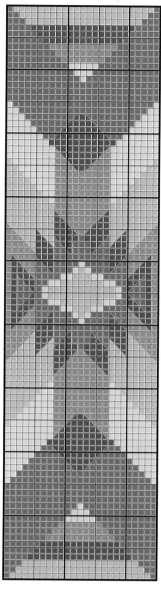

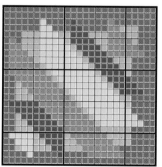

	262
	832
	853
	187
	341

MATERIALS
Fabric: 11 × 12in
(28 × 30.5cm) 18 hpi Aida
Needle
Thread: 3 skeins of each color.
Use 2 strands for the
cross-stitch

INTERMEDIATE LEVEL

ETHNIC FRAME

Brightly colored rugs and hangings are used by different cultures throughout the world. From India and Asia to Europe and the Americas, styles may vary but the desire to bring rich colors together with robust patterns seems to be universal.

Taking an ethnic theme as a starting point, this decorative frame brings a taste of foreign lands into your home. As well as using it to frame a suitable photograph, it would also make a particularly attractive mirror frame. Don't forget to have the glass sides ground smooth to remove those sharp edges that could cut into the stitching or backing material.

To reduce the overall size of the frame you could omit matching elements on each side. Tack out the edge of the design area in a contrasting thread color before starting. Don't stitch through this thread, as it will have to be removed before making up.

183

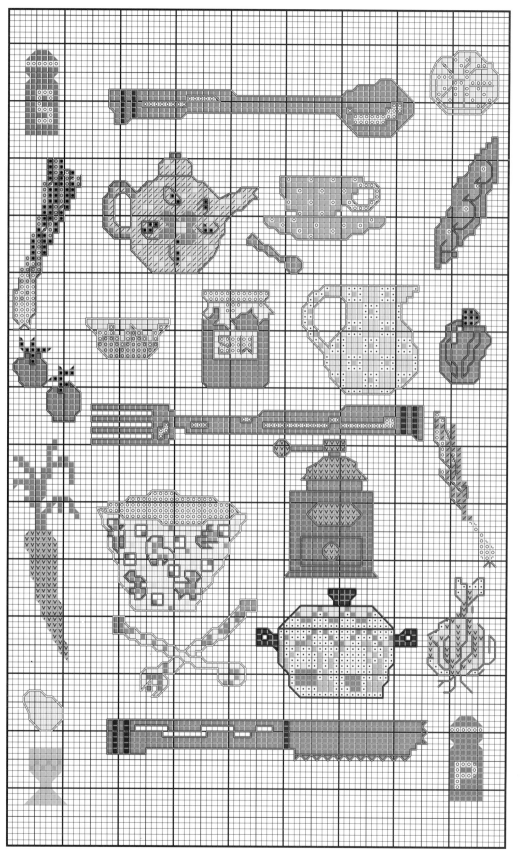

MATERIALS
Fabric: 14 × 10in
(35.5 × 25.5cm) 14 hpi Aida
Needle
Thread: 1 skein of each color.
Use 2 strands for the cross-stitch and 1 strand for the backstitch

INSTRUCTIONS

Number of stitches: 157 × 88.
Finished design size: 11⅕ × 6⅓in
(28.5 × 16cm) on 14 hpi Aida.
Prepare your fabric (*see pp. 154-63*), find the center of your fabric and start stitching from the center of the design.

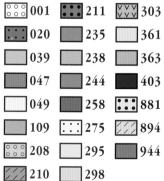

001	211	303
020	235	361
039	238	363
047	244	403
049	258	881
109	275	894
208	295	944
210	298	

KITCHEN SAMPLER

Anything connected with the kitchen can be included on this sampler. In the middle of the design shown here, space has been left on the preserving jar for you to include your initials, but you could as easily stitch your full name, the date, and the address of your home at the bottom of the design.

Feel free to substitute any of the suggested objects for ones you prefer. You could also take one or two of the motifs and use them on their own. They make excellent cut-outs—treat one with needlework finisher, attach a magnet, and you have a perfect refrigerator magnet to hold your grocery list or notes to the family.

MATERIALS

Fabric: 8 × 8in (20.3 × 20.3cm)
18 hpi white Aida

Needle

Thread: 2 skeins of each blue,
2 of white and 1 of each of the
other colors. Use 2 strands for
the cross-stitch

INSTRUCTIONS

Number of stitches: 99 × 99.
Finished design size: 5 x 5in
(12.7 × 12.7cm) on 18 hpi Aida.
Prepare your fabric (*see pp. 154-
63*). Stitch the check section first,
starting at the bottom center, and
leave at least a 3in (7.5cm) border
from the edge of the fabric.

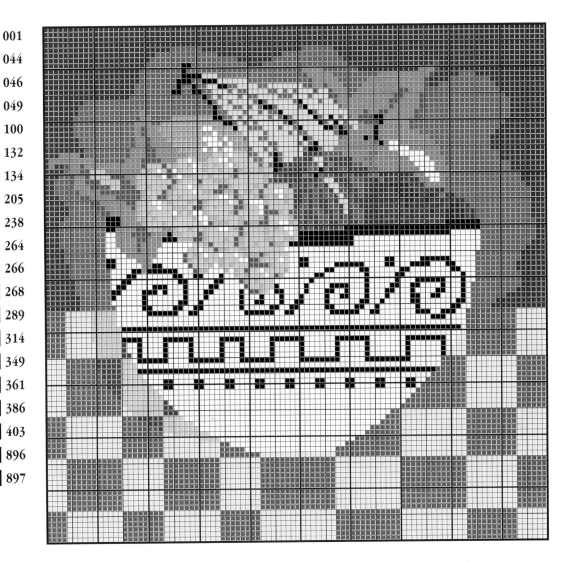

☐	001
■	044
■	046
▦	049
■	100
■	132
■	134
■	205
☐	238
☐	264
☐	266
■	268
☐	289
■	314
■	349
■	361
☐	386
■	403
■	896
■	897

INTERMEDIATE LEVEL

FRUIT BOWL PICTURE

Good enough to eat—that's what this cross-stitch bowl overflowing with luscious fruit looks like. The fruit in this picture really comes to life when stitched at the size illustrated here.

Traditional cross-stitch samplers often kept the objects depicted quite small, and this resulted in a lot of the background showing as plain material. Here, the approach is thoroughly modern—treating the fabric with an all-over technique, keeping to a single, dominant subject, and mixing a palette of vividly colored threads for the fruit as a contrast to the stark black and white of the fruit bowl.

One advantage of a design on this scale is that the three-dimensional effect really has impact, lifting the fruit and bowl away from the background of bright squares. The disadvantage of this, however, is that there is a lot of careful, concentrated stitching required—but the results will more than justify all the effort you put in.

To create a really dramatic finished result, you could mount the piece in an attractive wooden frame and then hand paint, or spray, in a bold color that contrasts or coordinates with the fruit in the picture.

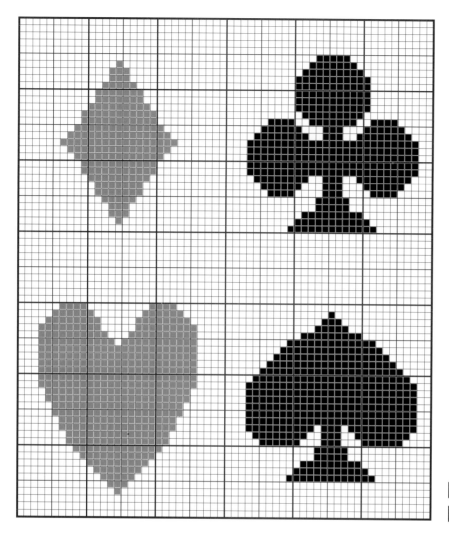

PLAYING CARD CUSHION

This project is an example of how, by borrowing designs and symbols from everyday objects, you can produce really eye-catching cross-stitch results. The impact of this cushion stems primarily from the contrast provided by the alternating black-and-white backgrounds and the black and red of the symbols themselves.

Although plain blacks and whites have been used for the cushion, there is no reason why you should not achieve equally good results from a fabric with a small pattern, or even one with an interesting texture. To carry the playing card theme even further, when you come to make up the cushion try to find a fabric for the reverse that mimics the geometric patterns often found on the backs of real playing cards.

� 046	
■ 403	

INSTRUCTIONS

The seam allowance throughout for this playing card cushion is about 1in (2cm).

You will need six black squares and six white squares, each measuring about 4 × 4in (10 × 10cm). Using the waste canvas method (*see p. 155*), work the hearts and diamonds in red on the black fabric, and the clubs and spades in black on the white fabric. You should end up with three of each symbol. Remove the waste canvas by damping it with a wet sponge and carefully pulling out the strands one at a time from behind your stitching with a pair of tweezers or your fingers. Place a piece of thin cardboard with an 8 × 8in (20 × 20cm) hole over the square of fabric and, using pins, mark the outer edges (1). Pin and stitch together the 12 squares making up the border in the order indicated (2). Cut the center piece square of fabric and then pin and tack it to your border. Stitch on the wrong side and then back the cross-stitching with a suitable fabric to make it into a cushion cover (*see pp. 154-63*).

MATERIALS
Fabric: 20in (50cm) white plainweave; 20in (50cm) black plainweave; 40in (1m) contrasting color for the center and back
Needle
Thread: Stranded cotton—2 skeins of each color. Use 2 strands for the cross-stitch

1

2

188

TEA COZY

To keep the tea warm while it infuses in their teapots, the British traditionally use a warmer called a "tea cozy." This simple and very effective tea warmer has been inspired by a traditional patchwork pattern known as "tumbling blocks." Just like cross-stitch, patchwork goes back a long time. You will find literally hundreds of traditional and contemporary designs to choose from if you are interested, and many of these have successfully crossed over into other craft forms. And because patchwork is made up of geometric shapes, it is relatively easy to adapt and chart to use it for a cross-stitch project.

The most striking thing about a well-executed tumbling blocks pattern is that, no matter which way up you look at it, it always has a pronounced three-dimensional quality. This is an important factor to consider when choosing colors for your cross-stitch version. To make sure you maintain the geometric ambiguity, it is vital that you select threads by tone, not just by color. That is to say, you should choose a dark color, a light color, and medium color. Whether they are pinks, blues, yellows, or a mixture of all three, is not so important. So if you have a good eye for threads, and you have a good selection from which to choose, you could easily work this project out of remnants.

Any repeat pattern would look good on this tea warmer. Look at traditional patchwork designs for inspiration, and then get to work on graph paper and design your own.

| ■ 214 |
| ■ 216 |
| ■ 218 |

MATERIALS
Fabric: 20in (50cm)
11 hpi Aida.
Suitable backing fabric
Padding and lining
Bias binding 1in (2.5cm) wide
Needle
Thread: Stranded cotton—4 skeins of each color. Use 4 strands for the cross-stitch

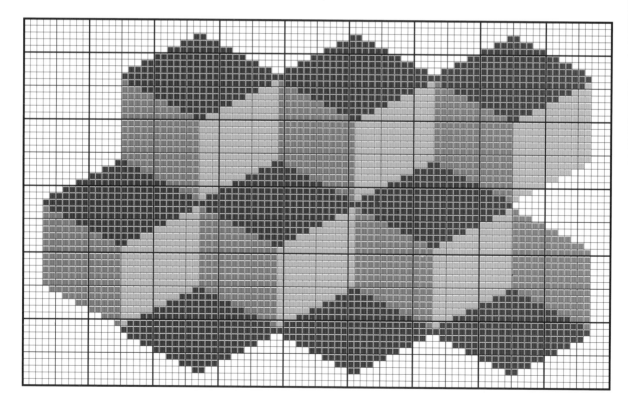

INSTRUCTIONS

Number of stitches: 144 × 112. Finished design size: 13 × 10in (33 × 25.4cm) on 11 hpi Aida. Start by working the bottom dark line of diamonds 1½in (4cm) from the bottom of the fabric. Level up the bottom edge by in-filling with the light and medium colors. Work upward until you have finished the fifth line of dark diamonds. Using your stitching as a template, trace the curve for the corner and draw it on to the fabric, starting at the point of the end diamond. Turn the tracing over and draw on to the other side to mark the other corner. Continue the tumbling blocks pattern up to the edges you have marked, using quarter and three-quarter stitches (*see pp. 154-63 for details*) where necessary. Wash and dry the finished embroidery.

To make up the tea cozy, cut out the backing fabric and 2 pieces of padding to the same size as the cross-stitched piece. Tack the padding to the wrong side of the worked piece and to the backing fabric. Place the worked piece on the backing piece, tack the right sides together, and then stitch through all of the layers around the sides and top. Cut nicks in the curved seam, turn the piece the right side out, and press. Make up the lining in the same way, but without the padding.

Place the lining inside the outer layers, turn under the edges, and slip stitch them together. To finish it off, trim with bias binding around all the seams.

OVEN GLOVE

An oven glove is used practically every day, and because it has to cope with hot pans and spilled foods it needs to be robustly made.

The pineapple was chosen as a motif for this glove because the coolness of the fruit seems a perfect foil for boiling pots and dishes. Use this suggestion or select a motif of your own that fits in with your kitchen's decorative scheme. Whatever it is that you choose, the waste canvas technique (*see p. 155*) allows you to stitch on almost any fabric you like.

If you normally use a two-handed glove, then just make two gloves (one left-handed and one right-handed) and join them together with a length of the same fabric. If the glove ever gets beyond the easy-cleaning stage, carefully remove the material on the palm and sew on some new.

MATERIALS
Fabric: 9 × 14in
(22.9 × 35.6cm) calico,
plus waste canvas
Lining and padding
Needle
Thread: Stranded cotton—1
skein of each color. Use 2
strands for the cross-stitch and
1 strand for the backstitch

INSTRUCTIONS

Number of stitches: 63 × 40.
Finished design size: 5 × 3⅜in
(12.7 × 8.6cm) using 12 hpi
waste canvas.

Tack the waste canvas to the
calico, leaving plenty of room all
around for the stitching. Work the
design in the center of the canvas
(see p. 155 for using waste
canvas). When you have finished
the cross-stitch, remove the waste
canvas. To make a glove-shaped
template, draw around your hand
on a piece of paper and add 2in
(5cm) all around. Transfer this on
to a piece of cardboard, and cut
out the shape.

Cut out the backing piece of calico
to the same size as the worked
piece. Also cut 2 pieces of
padding. Place the worked piece
face down on the backing piece
and then place the 2 pieces of
padding between them. Machine
stitch around the sides and top (1).
Cut nicks around the curved areas
and turn right side out. Cut 2
pieces of lining fabric and stitch
the right sides and top together.
Place the lining pieces (inside out)
inside the glove, turn edges in
around the wrist and stitch them
together. For a decorative finish,
hand stitch around the outside of
the glove (2).

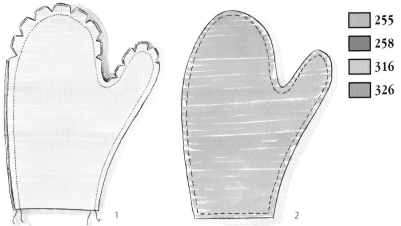

▨	**255**
▨	**258**
▨	**316**
▨	**326**

WEDDING AND BIRTH CARDS

The wedding card part of this project is designed to be worked in shades of pink and green, and the birth card in pinks and yellows. To give the wedding card extra sparkle, stitched rings using metallic gold threads have been added. You can always add other details such as names and dates in your own choice of lettering styles, some examples of which are given on pp. 204-5.

To mount your finished work you can buy ready-made card mounts or, if you have stitched the design on a fine fabric, you could cut your own mounts from this card.

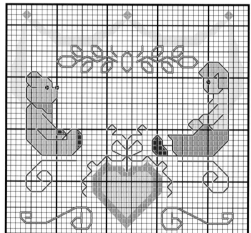

MATERIALS
Fabric:

7 × 7½in (17.8 × 19cm)

18 hpi Aida

Needle

Thread: Stranded cotton—1 skein of each color. Use 1 strand for the cross-stitch and 1 strand for the backstitch

INSTRUCTIONS

Number of stitches (both cards): 42 × 46.

Finished design size (both cards): 2⅜ × 2½in (6 × 6.4cm) on 18 hpi Aida.

Prepare your fabric (*see pp. 154-63*), find the center of your fabric and start stitching from the center of the design. Add names, dates and so forth in the spaces. Work out any lettering and numbers on graph paper first and then work from the center on the design.

024
262
260
261
293
403
914
Gold
French
knot

019
026
112
145
205
236
275
293
343

MATERIALS

Fabric: 11 × 13in
(28 × 33cm) 16 hpi Aida

Needle

Thread: 1 skein of each color.
Use 1 strand for the
cross-stitch and 1 strand for
the backstitch

INSTRUCTIONS

Number of stitches: 116 × 151.
Finished design size: 7¼ × 9½in
(18.5 × 14cm) on 16 hpi Aida.
Prepare your fabric (*see pp.
154-63*), find the center of your
fabric and start stitching from the
center of the design.

FESTIVAL
SAMPLER

In the sampler pictured here you can probably see the design influences of the early
1950s, and all around is evidence of the new
style introduced in that boom period following the war.

Here, you can see updated lettering and
traditional sampler motifs used to create a
vigorous mix of moving swirls, of numerals
and alphabets, all anchored to the central
star and colored bar. To provide variety,
there is also lots of backstitch to enhance the
three-dimensional quality of the piece.

If you are inspired, you can extend the
border down to give yourself more room,
and then include such information as
names, anniversary dates, or addresses, using
the alphabets and numerals on pages 204-5.
You could also substitute any of the other
motifs from this chapter or favorite ones of
your own.

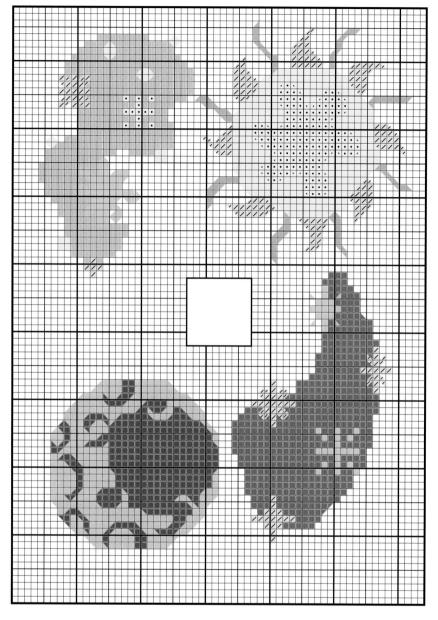

SUN AND MOON CLOCK

Next time you get the opportunity, take a close look at the face of an old grandfather clock. Often they have intricately engraved patterns, or they may be hand painted with colorful scenes or motifs worked in enamels.

As its inspiration, this project uses one such face worked in cross-stitch. As you can see from the photograph of the finished piece, this clock face features attractive sun and moon motifs, which are traditionally used symbols to illustrate the passing of day and night. But, although this project is intended to become a real working clock, it does not feature any numerals, so timekeeping will have to be approximate.

The working parts of the clock can be bought from craft materials supply stores (*see p. 163*), and they should also be able to supply a clear Plexiglass cover to protect your work from dust. Alternatively, you can buy any similarly sized clock movement with a plain face and mount your work around its face. If you want a more accurate timekeeper, take the appropriate numerals from one of the sets supplied on pages 204-5, and experiment with graph paper until you have them positioned properly.

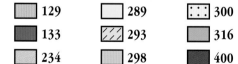

▨	129	▢	289	⬚	300
■	133	▨	293	▧	316
▨	234	▢	298	■	400

INSTRUCTIONS

Number of stitches: 78 × 58.
Finished design size: 5⅝ × 3¼in
(14.25 × 8.25cm) on 18 hpi Aida.
Prepare your fabric (*see pp. 154-63*). Start by stitching the top left-hand figure, leaving a generous amount of Aida as a border.
Place the other designs carefully and then, when the stitched piece is finished, carefully follow the instructions accompanying the clock for assembly.

MATERIALS
Fabric: 9 × 7in (22.8 × 17.8cm)
18 hpi cream Aida

Needle

Thread: Stranded cotton—1 skein of each color. Use 2 threads for the cross-stitch

FAIR ISLE BILLFOLD

This good-looking and practical billfold is a freestyle design loosely based on a Fair Isle pattern, but here it has been brought up to date by stitching on to a piece of black 14 hpi Aida. The black fabric background gives this piece a solid look and lets the jewel-like colors really sing out. For all its good looks,

this billfold is tough enough to stand up to normal wear and tear, and a press-and-touch fastener has been added. This is simple to sew on and fastens the billfold closed in an instant.

Although this design is intended for a billfold, you could easily alter its proportions and construction to make it into a case for spectacles or a cover for a personal organizer. If you place a circular or rectangular panel of different-colored thread into the design, you could then add your initials or phone number.

063
094
132
188
279

MATERIALS

Fabric: 2 pieces 10½ × 5½in
(26.5 × 14cm) and 1 piece
10½ × 3½in (26.5 × 9cm)
14 hpi Aida

Needle

Thread: Stranded cotton—1
skein of each color. Use 2
strands for the cross-stitch and
2 strands for the backstitch

INSTRUCTIONS

Number of stitches: 56 × 130.
Finished design size: 4 × 9¼in (10
× 23.5cm) on 14 hpi black Aida.
Following the charted design and,
leaving about a ½in (1.5cm)
border, cross-stitch on one of the
larger pieces. When this is
complete, fold it over and hem all
around, leaving 2 squares of Aida
as a border. Press it flat.
Fold over and press under a hem
on the second large piece of Aida,
so that it matches the embroidered
piece for size.
Fold over and stitch a hem on one
long side of the narrower piece of
Aida, and then fold over and press
a hem on the other three sides,
matching the ends and bottom to
the larger pieces. With hems facing
each other, pin all the pieces
together and stab stitch through
the holes, 1 hole in from the edge
all around. Finally, stitch press-and-
touch fastening on the ends as a
fastener for the billfold.

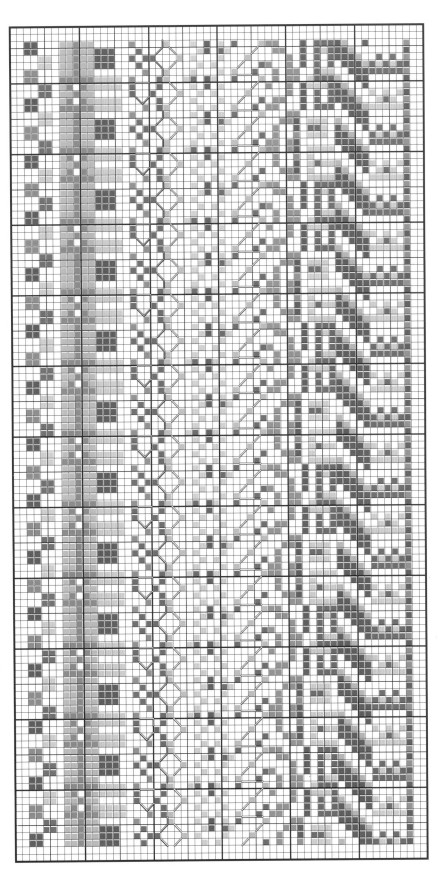

DINOSAUR T-SHIRT

Although dinosaurs have enjoyed an immense revival in popularity in recent years—even more so after the film Jurassic Park—they have long been a favorite with children. The dinosaur featured on this T-shirt is pretty loosely based on a stegosaurus, which, with its row of spinal plates, would have been about the size of a two-floor house.

An advantage of cross-stitching is that there is a wide range of good-quality, fashionable children's clothes to which you can add your own designs. Using the waste canvas technique (*see p. 155*), this dinosaur has been stitched on to a cotton T-shirt. That means that when it becomes dirty you can throw it into the week's laundry along with all the other clothes.

If you like the result achieved here, why not work similar designs on to other articles of clothing as well?

INSTRUCTIONS

Number of stitches: 32 × 55.
Finished design size: 2¼ × 4in
(5.7 × 10cm) on 11 hpi canvas.
Decide where you want to stitch
the dinosaur design and tack on
a piece of waste canvas in that
position. Stitch the design and
then remove the waste canvas.

MATERIALS

Fabric: T-shirt and
11 hpi waste canvas

Needle

Thread: Stranded cotton—1
skein of each color. Use 2
strands for the cross-stitch and
1 strand for the backstitch

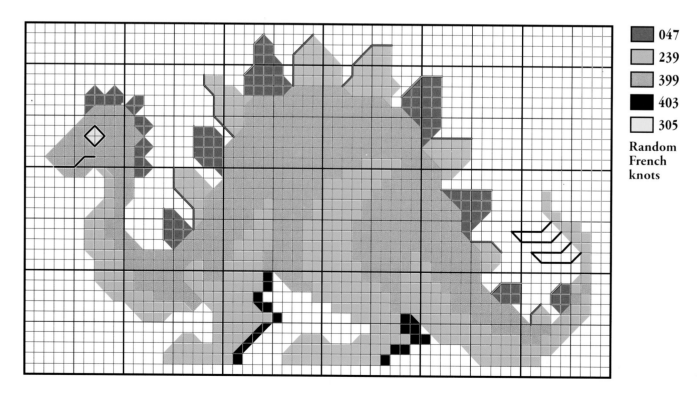

■	047
▨	239
▨	399
■	403
□	305

Random French knots

ALPHABETS

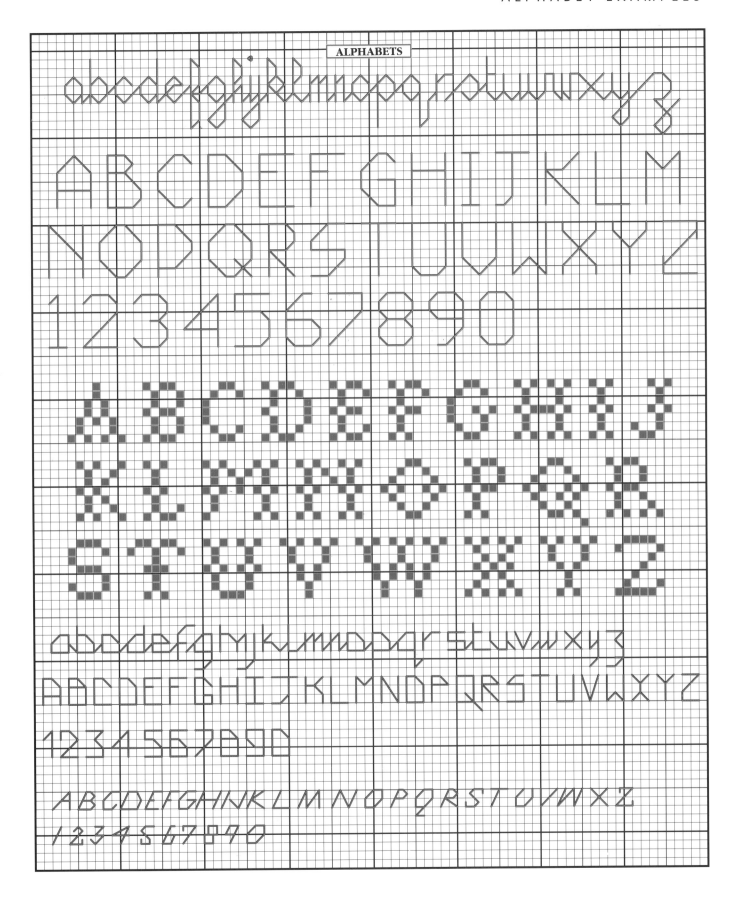

ALPHABETS

CONVERSION CHART

All of the threads referred to in the charts of this book are produced by Anchor. The other major thread producer is DMC. Use the following chart to buy DMC equivalents, but bear in mind that color matches may only be approximate.

ANCHOR	DMC	ANCHOR	DMC	ANCHOR	DMC	ANCHOR	DMC
1	Blanc	75	3354	145	799	228	700
2	Neige	76	3731	146	798	229	700
6	754	77	3350	147	797	230	909
8	353	78	3350	148	311	238	703
9	352	85	3609	149	336	239	702
10	351	86	3608	150	823	240	955
11	350	87	3607	152	939	241	954
13	349	88	718	158	828	242	913
19	347	89	917	159	827	243	912
20	816	95	554	160	813	244	911
22	815	96	554	161	826	245	700
23	819	97	553	162	825	246	699
24	818	98	553	164	824	253	772
25	776	99	552	167	3766	254	907
26	894	100	552	168	807	255	907
27	893	101	550	169	806	256	906
28	892	102	550	170	517	257	906
29	891	104	210	185	964	258	904
35	3705	105	209	186	959	259	772
40	893	107	552	187	958	260	3348
41	892	108	211	188	943	261	989
42	309	109	210	189	943	262	3363
43	816	110	209	203	954	263	3362
44	814	111	208	204	913	264	3348
46	666	112	208	205	912	265	989
47	304	117	794	206	564	266	3347
48	963	118	793	208	563	267	3346
49	3689	119	333	209	562	268	3345
50	605	120	794	210	562	269	895
52	957	121	793	211	561	278	472
54	956	123	791	212	561	279	472
59	326	127	939	213	504	280	581
65	600	128	800	214	368	281	580
66	3688	129	809	215	320	288	445
68	5687	130	799	216	367	289	307
69	3685	131	798	217	319	290	973
70	3685	132	797	218	890	291	444
72	902	133	796	225	954	292	3078
73	3689	134	820	226	702	293	727
74	605	144	3325	227	701	295	726
297	444	369	435	860	3363	930	825

ANCHOR	DMC	ANCHOR	DMC	ANCHOR	DMC	ANCHOR	DMC
298	972	370	434	861	3363	933	3774
300	3078	371	433	862	3362	936	632
301	745	372	738	868	3779	939	793
302	743	373	3045	869	3042	940	792
303	742	374	420	870	3042	941	791
304	741	375	420	871	3041	942	738
305	725	376	842	872	3041	943	436
306	783	378	841	873	327	944	869
307	783	379	840	874	834	945	3046
308	782	380	898	875	504	956	3047
309	781	381	938	876	503	968	224
310	780	382	3371	877	502	969	3727
311	676	386	746	878	501	970	315
313	742	387	Ecru	879	500	972	3687
314	741	388	3782	880	951	975	775
316	740	390	3033	881	945	976	3325
323	772	391	3782	882	3064	977	334
324	721	392	642	883	407	978	322
326	720	393	640	884	400	979	312
328	3341	397	762	885	3047	1201	48
329	947	398	415	886	3046	1202	106
330	947	399	318	887	422	1203	57
332	946	400	317	888	420	1204	107
333	608	401	413	890	729	1206	115
334	606	403	310	891	676	1207	116
335	606	410	995	892	225	1208	52
336	402	433	996	893	225	1210	113
337	922	778	951	894	224	1211	91
338	921	779	926	895	223	1213	125
339	920	830	3033	896	3721	1215	122
340	919	831	612	897	221	1216	94
341	918	832	3032	898	611	1217	104
347	402	842	3013	900	648	1218	105
349	301	843	3012	901	680	1220	51
351	400	844	3012	903	3032	4146	754
352	300	845	3011	905	3031	5968	355
355	975	846	936	906	869	5975	356
357	300	847	3072	907	832	8581	646
358	433	848	927	914	407	9575	758
359	801	849	927	920	932		
360	898	850	926	921	931		
361	738	851	924	922	930		
362	437	852	3047	923	699		
363	436	853	613	924	580		
365	435	854	3012	925	970		
366	739	856	3011	926	822		
367	739	858	524	928	747		
368	437	859	523	929	813		

PATCHWORK

MATERIALS AND TECHNIQUES

MATERIALS AND TECHNIQUES

In the eighteenth and nineteenth centuries in Britain and America, patchwork was a craft of economy and utility, especially among poor folk who lived in the country. Housewives carefully hoarded every tiny scrap of precious material left over from dressmaking, and, when enough was saved, the pieces were sewn by hand to make quilts and coverlets. Nothing was ever wasted. Even the quilt backs were pieced, and the padding was often tufts of sheep's wool gleaned from boundary fences.

In those days, design in patchwork was dictated by the limitations of what little material was available. Keeping people warm in bed at night was its most important function. Nowadays, there is no reason not to recycle old clothes and scrap bag bits, but in addition to recycled material, fabric is available that is designed, dyed, and printed especially for patchwork. Patchwork has been elevated from simple utility to an interesting craft. With an unlimited palette to choose from, the patchworker can let the design dictate the material, rather than the other way around.

BUYING PATCHWORK FABRIC

The best place to buy fabric for patchwork projects is in specialty patchwork stores. There you can find the best selection of prints and colors of the good-quality cotton dress-weight material that is ideal for the craft, as well as rotary cutting equipment, padding, wider inexpensive fabric for quilt backs, marking pens and pencils, books, and other items to help you in your work. Also, you will find that the store owners are usually patchworkers themselves, who gladly pass on tips to customers.

CHOOSING PATCHWORK FABRIC
In this chapter, details are given of how much fabric you need for each project. Unless otherwise stated, the measurements are given for 100% cotton fabric which is 45in (115cm) wide. For best results the fabric should have a good, tight, and even weave.

Most of the projects need pieces that are less than 18in (0.5m) in length. In ordinary fabric stores you can usually only buy materials in longer lengths. If you need 9in (0.25m), you

have to buy a long piece of material measuring 45in x 9in (115cm x 25cm). For patchwork, a much more convenient size is called a "fat quarter." A fat quarter is 18in (0.5m) of fabric cut in half the "fat" way to measure 18in x 22in (46cm x 56cm). Most patchwork stores have a big selection of precut fat quarters to choose from, and will also cut fat quarters from the bolt for you, if necessary.

Some of the projects in the book call for a "fat eighth" which is about half the size of a fat quarter, i.e., 11in x 18in (28cm x 46cm). These measurements are for your guidance only—normally the smallest size piece you can buy in a patchwork store is a fat quarter.

If you want your quilt or patchwork item to be washable, it is very important to prewash and iron all cotton fabric before cutting piecing. This will guard against shrinkage and ensure colorfastness.

DIFFERENT FABRICS
Some projects are made from material not normally associated with patchwork, such as wool or silky fabric. If you are prepared to take extra care when dealing with bulky seams or shiny, slippery material, you can create a really individual item. There are no hard and fast rules about material you can use for patchwork, so let your imagination be your guide.

If you make a project that you want to quilt, you will need some kind of padding. Padding adds texture and warmth to a quilt, and a square of padding under the patchwork top of a cushion cover makes it fit better on the pad.

Padding comes in various weights and in different materials. For most projects the padding used is made from soft polyester in the 2oz (50g) weight, referring to its weight per square meter. This lightweight padding is normally bought in 36in lengths, 54in (140cm) wide, but is also available in patchwork stores in various larger-sized pieces suitable for bed quilts.

For small items such as cushion covers that have been quilted by machine, squares of the medium weight 4oz (100g) padding are used. Although this heavier padding is warmer and gives a nice high "loft" to your quilting project, it is difficult to quilt by hand.

USING YOUR SEWING MACHINE

Before this century, women sewed by hand, not from choice but because there was no alternative. With the invention of the sewing machine, seamstresses preferred to make garments and soft furnishings by machine, not only because it was quicker this way, but because the stronger seams created a much longer-lasting object.

In Britain, in particular, a patchwork tradition of sewing together hexagonal shapes had already been established before people acquired sewing machines. Hexagons, which need oversewing, are quite difficult to join by machine, so it was accepted that "hexagons" were synonymous with patchwork, and that machine patchwork was "wrong." A craftsperson might create a beautifully designed and technically well-sewn piece of patchwork, but be criticized because it was not hand-sewn or based on hexagons.

Nowadays, attitudes have changed and most people realize that good patchwork design is more important than how many stitches to the inch or centimeter you can hand sew, and there is a real interest in finding new patchwork designs and methods. This is not criticizing sewing by hand. Always choose the sewing method and the design you prefer. For many patchworkers, a happy compromise for those who enjoy hand sewing is to piece by machine and quilt by hand.

USING GOOD EQUIPMENT

Most of the projects in this chapter are pieced and quilted by machine, so adapt your sewing preference to the instructions given. There are, however, a few tips about machine patchwork that you should note. You do not need a modern, expensive sewing machine, but keep your machine regularly oiled and remove any fluff that accumulates in the bobbin case. You can do intricate piecing with a straight-stitch machine as long as you can create an even, tight stitch that does not pucker and that looks as good on the back as the front.

For patchwork made with ordinary dress-weight material, a sharp sewing machine needle is recommended. Unless the project instructions state otherwise, set your stitch length to about 10 stitches to the inch.

PATCHWORK SEAMS

Unless otherwise noted for a particular project, all seams for the patchwork, whether sewn by hand or machine, are ¼in (6mm). The only real rule in patchwork is accuracy. If your seams are not all ¼in (6mm), the patches will not fit together and, even after pressing, the blocks will not lie flat. So take care to sew an accurate ¼in (6mm) seam at all times.

The best way to gauge a ¼in (6mm) seam is by using a ¼in (6mm) foot, i.e., a presser foot whose sides are exactly ¼in (6mm) away from the needle. Many sewing machine manufacturers make a ¼in (6mm) foot especially for patchworkers.

Without this special attachment, there is another method of gauging the seam allowance with your presser foot. With many machines it just involves finding a point of light on the "toe" of the presser foot that is ¼in (6mm) away from the needle. Line up this point of light with the patch's raw edge, or with the diagonal line on a R.I.T. (Right-angled Isosceles Triangle) Square grid. If that doesn't seem to work, you can try "swinging" the needle a bit to the left or to the right.

Whichever method you use for these seams, please practice on a scrap of fabric until you can get it right. Remember that a tiny discrepancy on each patch makes a significant difference on a large project.

EVEN STITCHING

If you wish to quilt by machine, it is vital that the tension between the needle thread and the bobbin thread is correct. The stitches formed on the quilt back must be as good as those on the top, and a badly running machine may skip stitches or form loops. As quilting is a decorative technique as well as a method of holding quilt layers together, it is better to quilt by hand than to use a machine that can't form good stitches. Always test machine-quilting stitches on a sample "padding sandwich" before quilting a patchwork project.

For straight-line machine quilting, better results are achieved with a "walking foot" or an "even-feed" foot. For freehand, decorative machine quilting, you need a darning foot and the facility to lower the feed-dog of the machine (*see p. 219*).

> ### TIPS
>
> • Always adjust your sewing work table to the correct height for you, sit comfortably and work under a good light.
>
> • Arrange your ironing table in reach of the sewing machine, or have a little pressing board and small travel iron right next to your machine, so that you can press your patchwork as you sew.

USING A ROTARY CUTTER

The introduction of rotary cutting equipment in the 1980s really revolutionized traditional patchwork methods. Before then, patchworkers had to trace around templates onto the fabric, carefully measuring seam allowances for each little piece and then individually cutting out the shapes with scissors. This method was not very accurate, it was very time-consuming, and it was wasteful of fabric.

Luckily for patchworkers, there are now rotary cutters, quilter's rulers and self-healing mats to make the chore of cutting out pieces for patchwork much easier, quicker, and more accurate, without the use of templates. A rotary cutting set is expensive but is worth the investment if you get interested in patchwork.

A rotary cutter is a tool with a very sharp circular blade, a little like a pizza cutter, which can cut through several layers of fabric at the same time. Rotary cutters come in different sizes and grip styles, and blades are replaceable.

A rotary cutter must be used with a self-healing mat, which is made of a special kind of rubber that both protects the blade and provides a good surface for cutting. The mat is printed with grid lines to help you keep your pieces square. For your first mat, the most convenient size is 17in x 23in (43cm x 58.5cm); this is long enough to cut strips from a folded piece of 45in (115cm) wide fabric, yet small enough for the mat to be easily portable. Please take care to store your self-healing mat flat and out of the way of direct sunlight.

Transparent quilter's rulers come in all shapes and sizes, for slicing, chopping, trimming, and measuring, but to start with choose a ruler at least 24in (61cm) long and 5in (13cm) or 6in (15cm) wide. You can use it as a straightedge and for measuring, and, together with the rotary cutter, it enables you to cut geometric pieces accurately without marking and without templates.

Most quilter's rulers are calibrated only in inches. Therefore it is strongly recommend that you use the imperial measurements given for projects in this book which use the quilter's ruler. (Left-handed patchworkers may find it useful to recalibrate their quilter's rulers with a permanent marking pen, so that the measurements read from the left-hand side when they are cutting out.)

If you haven't used a rotary cutter before, it is a good idea to practice on a large scrap before cutting good fabric. Iron the scrap and lay it squarely on the mat. Place the ruler on top of the fabric so the right-hand edge of the ruler is just covering the left-hand edge of the fabric. The lines of the ruler should line up with the grid lines on the cutting mat.

First trim away the raw or selvage edge as follows. Pull away the guard protecting the blade of the rotary cutter. Hold the cutter at about a 45° angle and flat against the edge of the ruler as shown in Fig. 1. Press down hard on the ruler with your left hand to stop it slipping and push the rotary cutter forward, starting your cut before you reach the fabric and continuing past the fabric at the other end. (Left-handers should reverse this procedure: cut on the left-hand side of the ruler on the right-hand edge of the fabric.) After a few cuts you will feel how much pressure is necessary to cut cleanly in one go.

When you are making a long cut, you sometimes need to move your hand on the ruler to keep it steady along the cut. Leave the blade in the cut, reposition the ruler back onto the line if necessary, move your hand upward on the ruler, and continue cutting.

USING A RULER AS A STRAIGHTEDGE

When you are cutting out R.I.T. Squares (*see p. 214*) or other fabric pieces with drawn lines, place the right edge of the ruler exactly on the

Use a rotary cutter on a protective self-healing mat to cut material easily and quickly. Transparent quilter's rulers can be bought in different shapes and sizes.

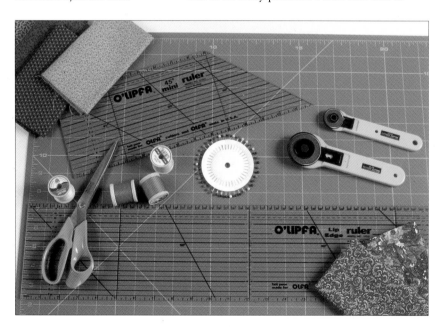

1

2

3

4

line you want to cut. First trim away the margins around the grid, and then cut out the patches. With R.I.T. Squares, make sure you cut on all the drawn lines (*see Fig. 1*).

MEASURING STRIPS AND SQUARES
If your piece of fabric is wider than your cutting mat, fold it in half so that the fold line is on the straight of the grain. Place the fold line on one of the horizontal grid lines of the mat with the edge you want to cut on the left. First trim off any raw edge as described above. Remove the ruler and pull the cut piece away without disturbing the larger piece.

To cut strips, move the ruler over the fabric with the trimmed edge aligned with the measurement on the ruler that you want to cut. For example, if you want to cut a strip 3½in wide, place the 3½in line of the ruler on the

left-hand edge of the fabric and cut. As before, be sure to avoid disturbing the large piece (*see Fig. 2*). Pick up the ruler and remove the cut strip before measuring and cutting the next strip.

To cut square shapes, stack up all your cut strips so they are even with a horizontal line on the mat and with the left-hand edges lined up. Trim off any raw edges on the left, if necessary. Then move the ruler over the strips so that the measurement you want is lined up with the left-hand edge of the strips (*see Fig. 3*).

CUTTING ANGLED PIECES
To cut fabric pieces at an angle, lay the strip or strips across the board and trim the left-hand edge as above. Place the line of the desired angle, printed on the ruler, either on a vertical or horizontal line on the mat and cut (*see Fig. 4*).

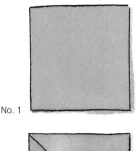

No. 1

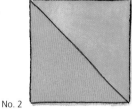

No. 2

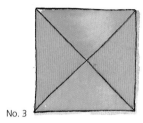

No. 3

MACHINE PATCHWORK WITH R.I.T. SQUARES

R.I.T. (Right-angled Isosceles Triangle) Squares is a patchwork method designed especially for the sewing machine. It involves sewing triangular-shaped fabric pieces together before cutting them out, and is a very quick and accurate way to make the three types of patches shown on the left. You can then use these patches to create many different American block or border designs, or to build up patchwork designs of your own invention.

Many of the patchwork projects in this book use the R.I.T. Square method. It's much quicker and more accurate than old-fashioned patchwork methods where you have to trace and cut out all the pieces of material separately, and sew them by hand over little cards.

The R.I.T. Square method involves drawing a simple grid on your fabric. As in hand-sewn patchwork, you use templates to make R.I.T.

Squares, but the templates are really just measuring tools to help you draw the grids.

A 2-inch set and a 3-inch set of R.I.T. Square templates are reproduced for you to make 2in and 3in patches (about 5cm and 7.5cm) (*see pp. 224-5*). Even though the three templates that make up each set are different sizes, the patches all end up the same size, so that they are easy to sew together using a ¼in (6mm) seam allowance. You can produce the same block patterns with either size of template set; the 2-inch set is useful if you want a smaller scale of block or border.

To make the templates, photocopy the set you want to use or copy them onto tracing paper (*see pp. 224-5*), stick the diagrams onto stiff cardboard, and then cut out the templates carefully with a craft knife. Alternatively, you can obtain the 3-inch set of R.I.T. Square templates in heavy-duty plastic, together with instructions and many pattern suggestions from good craft stores.

HOW TO MAKE R.I.T. SQUARES

MATERIALS

No. 1, 2, and 3 templates from 3-inch set of R.I.T. Squares

Five contrasting cotton fabric scraps: 1 4in (10cm) square piece for No. 1 patch, 4 4¾in x 9in (12cm x 23cm) pieces for No. 2 and No. 3 patches

Ballpoint pen, scissors

Quilter's ruler, rotary cutter, cutting mat (optional)

Matching sewing thread

Steam iron, pins

1 To practice the R.I.T. Square method, make this traditional "Ohio Star" block with one No. 1, four No. 2, and four No. 3 patches. Make the No. 1 patch by tracing around the No. 1 template with the pen and cut out on the lines. Alternatively, use your rotary cutter to cut a 3½in (9cm) patch (*see p. 212*).

2 To make No. 2 and No. 3 patches, always remember to draw, sew, and cut. Place two fabric pieces for No. 2 patches right sides together. To make four No. 2 patches, place two fabric pieces right sides together. Draw a line on the back of the lighter-colored fabric about ¼in (6mm) from top (*Fig. A*). This guide line keeps the grid square and is trimmed after sewing.

3 Place No. 2 template up to the guide line and draw around it twice to make a grid of two squares (*Fig. B*). Leave trimming margins at the fabric's edge. Draw diagonal lines from the corners of the two squares. Pin pieces together, and then sew a line ¼in (6mm) away from each side of diagonal line (*see p. 211 for gauging a ¼in [6mm] seam with a machine*). At the end of the V-shaped line, don't cut the threads, but turn the work around 180° and then continue sewing on the other side of the line (*Fig. C*).

4 To finish the four No. 2 patches, remove pins and cut on drawn lines with rotary cutter or scissors (*Fig. D*). Discard trimming margins, and keep big scraps for other projects. Each square traced makes two patches because fabric is doubled. Open patches (*Fig. E*) and press seams toward darker fabric.

5 To make four No. 3 patches follow Steps 2 and 3 but use No. 3 template, and draw two diagonal lines across each square (*Fig. F*). Sew as Step 3, stitching on each side of one diagonal line in each square. Cut out eight small pieces on lines (*Fig. G*).

6 Open up half pieces (*Fig. H*) and press seams toward darker-colored fabric. Sort pieces into two mirror-image rows (*Fig. I*). Taking a pair of pieces from one row at a time, sew together, using a ¼in (6mm) seam so that darker

triangles are opposite. Don't cut threads between patches, just sew up a long "kite tail" (*Fig. J*). Cut four patches apart, pressing seams to one side.

7 Assemble Ohio Star block. Put nine patches down to form design (*Fig. K*). With a ¼in (6mm) seam, sew patches together to make three rows. Press seams in opposite direction, then sew rows together, matching seams. To make other R.I.T. Square blocks, note the number of different patches in each block and multiply it by the blocks in the project. (With No. 2 and No. 3 patches you draw only half the patches needed.) Normally, the grid depends on the patch total and fabric shape. For example, you can make about 40 3in (7.5cm) R.I.T. Squares from two fat quarters (*see p. 210*). In each relevant project, there is a diagram showing the grids.

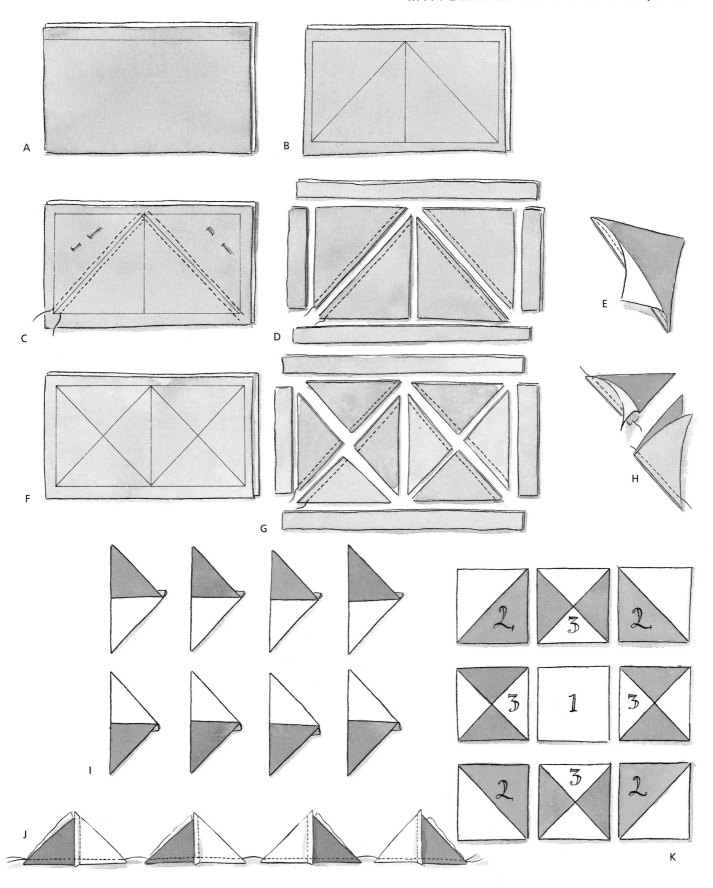

FOUNDATION PIECING

Foundation piecing is a method that takes you a step beyond R.I.T. Squares, because it allows you to join up odd-shaped pieces, and to piece very sharp points and very small blocks accurately. It also gives you a chance to use up all those spare little bits in your scrap bag and to cope with sewing difficult fabrics like silks and taffetas.

With foundation piecing you sew the patchwork pieces onto a background of

paper or cloth which has the design drawn or printed on it. The foundation adds stability to the block, so you can piece lightweight or slippery fabrics with ease. You simply sew on the lines of the design and, with paper piecing, when the block is finished you just dampen and tear the paper away.

In this book we have included two Foundation projects for you to try: the Waterlily Cushions (*see pp. 256-7*) and the Cottage Tea Cozy (*see pp. 262-3*).

For paper piecing use lightweight translucent paper such as waxed paper. For cloth foundations, choose a lightweight but tightly woven fabric such as curtain lining. First photocopy or trace the foundation design onto a sheet of ordinary paper—this will reverse the image and your master design. Then cut the required number of foundation squares, making them about ½in (1.3cm) larger all around than the design. Tape the master design to the back of the cloth or paper foundation, place on a light box or up to a window, and with a ruler and fine-tipped pen, draw each copy. It is easier to draw on a cloth foundation if you first apply spray starch. Be sure to number the areas of the master, and of all the foundation squares.

Before you start sewing, place your iron near your work table, as well as a lamp without a shade and a bin for scraps.

CRAZY PATCHWORK

Crazy patchwork is easy with a machine and makes use of a mixture of silk, brocade, velvet, and other fabric scraps not normally suitable for patchwork.

1 Cut out a selection of crazy pieces in various geometric shapes that measure at least 2in to 3in (5cm to 8cm) wide. Then cut out a foundation base for the patchwork, which includes seam allowances, from a piece of mediumweight iron-on interfacing.

2 Pin a crazy piece in middle of the foundation's shiny side. Choose next contrasting colored piece. Pin, right sides together, on top of first, so raw edges meet. Sew with ¼in (6mm) seam and finger-press outward. Each new piece must cover at least one raw edge of piece or pieces below it. Seam as above, or turn in raw edge of next piece on one or two sides and oversew. When fully covered, press (with cloth) to bond patches to interfacing. Decorate seams with hand or machine embroidery, if desired. Trim base edges.

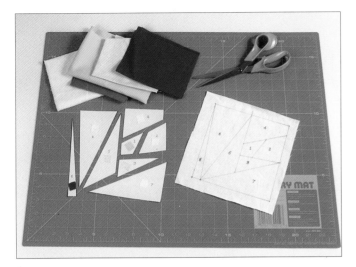

1

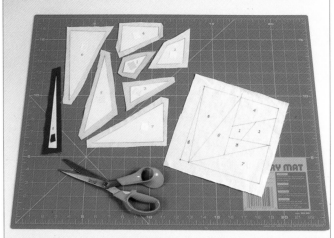

2

3

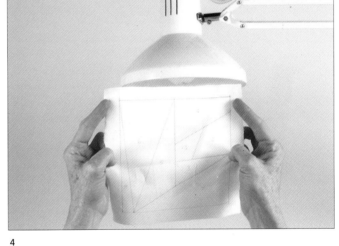

4

FOUNDATION PIECING METHOD

MATERIALS
Colored fabric pieces
Paper foundations with design
Scissors, clear adhesive tape or
spray adhesive, lamp, pins
Sewing machine
Matching sewing thread
Steam or travel iron

1 Decide which fabric colors will cover each area of the design. As a reminder, tape a tiny swatch of each color to numbered areas of your master design (*Fig. 1*). Cut out pieces of the master design along lines in order to use each numbered piece as a template (*Fig. 2*).

2 Stick each template face up with rolled-up clear adhesive tape on the back of correct fabric and roughly cut a piece at least ⅜in (8mm) larger all around than the template (*Fig. 3*). If you are making more than one block, make sure you cut enough pieces for each one. (You can also temporarily stick the templates by spraying the back of the templates with some adhesive.)

3 Starting with Piece 1, remove the paper template, hold the foundation up to the light, and place the piece on the blank side of the foundation right side up so that it covers Area 1. Pin in place. Take Piece 2. Holding foundation up to the light, first hold Piece 2 so that it covers Area 2, right side up. Then turn it over Piece 1 so the edge of the paper template is on the line between Area 1 and Area 2 (*Fig. 4*). Remove template and pin in place.

4 Turn the foundation over and sew on the line between 1 and 2. (Start and finish stitching just a little beyond the line.) From the right side of the foundation again, remove the pin and fold Piece 2 back along the seam line, checking with the light that you have completely covered Area 2. Then fold the piece back and trim the seam to about ¼in (6mm). Press Piece 2 right side out again.

5 Take the next piece and repeat Steps 3 and 4 until all the pieces have been sewn on. Sew all around the block about ⅛in (3mm) outside the marked line. Join blocks together, or attach borders, by sewing on the lines around the blocks. Stick pins through at the corners to make sure that the corners and lines align. If you are using a paper foundation, tear it away from the block. (This is easier if you dampen it first.)

217

QUILTING

Quilting is the technique of holding together layers of cloth, usually with a filling of padding, either by working utilitarian straight-lines running stitches or by decorative stitching, by hand or by machine. Quilting your patchwork project is not necessary, but it adds an extra dimension to your work.

Another way of holding layers of patchwork together is by "tying." Patchwork and quilting are really two separate crafts that are often combined to make "patchwork quilts."

Many modern patchworkers make a happy compromise between machine sewing and hand work by piecing by machine and quilting by hand. Hand quilting is very relaxing, and it is satisfying to see your beautiful quilting patterns building up. Machine quilting, which is much quicker and enables you to quilt easily over bulky seams, requires some practice.

Before quilting you need to prepare the quilt or other project by tacking the top layer together with the padding and the backing fabric (*see p. 221*). Decide which areas of your patchwork project you want to quilt. You may decide to quilt in straight lines around the patches of a patchwork block or border to add texture to the design. With hand quilting this is usually done by stitching about ¼in (6mm) away from the seam, so you avoid the bulk of sewing though the extra layers. With machine quilting, you can sew right in the seam line.

Alternatively, you might like to try a fancy quilting design. Choose one that fits the area you want to quilt and that enhances the patchwork. You can either buy a ready-cut quilting stencil from a patchwork store, or you can make your own from a design you have drawn or copied from a patchwork book. Designs for hand quilting should be smooth and flowing and not too intricate.

Designs for machine quilting can be much more intricate, but should have continuous lines with as few starts and stops as possible (*see Jacob's Ladder Cot Quilt pp. 240-1*).

When hand quilting, it is easier to stitch fancy quilting designs on plain blocks or borders rather than over pieced areas of the design. Also, quilting shows up much better on plain fabric than on prints.

MAKING A QUILTING STENCIL

A purchased quilting stencil has channels cut out around the design, through which you mark the fabric. To make your own stencil, you need a sheet of tough, but thin, transparent plastic just larger than your chosen design. Enlarge or reduce your design, if necessary, by photocopying and tape to the back of the stencil plastic. With needle pricks about ⅛in (3mm) apart, make holes by hand or machine through the lines of the design. If you are using a machine, remove thread from needle and bobbin and prick through with a medium needle.

MAKING A "POUNCE" BAG

To make marks on the fabric through the pricked holes in your stencil, you will need a pounce bag. Cut a piece of loosely woven material about 4in (10cm) square. To mark on dark-colored fabrics, place about a teaspoonful of cornstarch in the middle of the square and tie up the square to make a bag. To mark light-colored fabrics, use ground cinnamon.

For drawing quilting designs you need a marker that draws on fabric without dragging and has a clear line that is easy to remove after quilting. You can find all sorts of markers in specialty patchwork stores such as white, yellow, or silver pencils to mark on dark-colored fabric, and water-erasable pens for lighter fabrics.

TRANSFERRING THE DESIGN

To transfer your design onto a quilt, you need your quilting stencil, a pounce bag (only if you are using your own, pricked stencil), and a marking pen or pencil.

Place the quilting stencil over the area to be quilted and hold in place with adhesive tape. If you are using a pricked stencil, pounce through the design by bouncing the pounce bag against the stencil so that the dust penetrates the holes or channels and forms tiny dots on the fabric's surface. Remove stencil, and draw over pounced design with your marker. With a bought stencil, just use the marker to draw the design. Straight lines can be marked with a marker or with ¼in (6mm) masking tape (available from patchwork stores).

HAND QUILTING

You need short, fine size 10 or 12 quilting needles, quilting thread (which is slightly heavier than ordinary sewing thread), two thimbles (one for your sewing hand and one to stop the needle pricking your other hand), and a quilting hoop.

Place the area to be quilted in a quilting hoop to hold the fabric taut. Thread the needle with a short length of quilting thread and make a small knot. The thread is usually the same color as the background, but you can choose a contrasting color for extra impact. At the beginning of the quilting design, pull the thread through from the back and "pop" the knot through just the back layer of fabric. Taking short stitches through all the layers of fabric, load the needle with several stitches at a time before pulling the thread through. At the end of the design, tie off the thread and hide the end in the padding.

MACHINE QUILTING

There are two ways of quilting by machine—either straight-line quilting, which is a more utilitarian technique, or fancy quilting, which is done with free-motion stitching.

STRAIGHT-LINE MACHINE QUILTING

Most of the patchwork projects in this chapter are machine quilted with straight-line quilting. There is a sewing-machine attachment called a "walking foot" or an "even-feed" foot, available from your sewing machine dealer, which works by feeding the top layer of fabric under the foot at the same time as the bottom layer. You should use a walking foot for straight-line machine quilting if possible to avoid any puckering and pulling of the fabric.

After putting together your quilt (*see p. 221*), study the patchwork and decide where the design can be enhanced by a line of quilting. Thread the needle with a sewing thread to blend with the patchwork's colors, and fill the bobbin with a color to match the back. If you are quilting over many different colors, you can use transparent nylon quilting thread in the needle.

Set the stitch length to about 10 stitches to an inch or 2.5mm and check your stitches on a little sample "padding sandwich" to make sure

that the tension is correct. Begin by making several stitches in place in order to lock the stitches and then sew along your planned route, keeping close to the seam lines, but on the flatter side opposite to which the seams have been pressed. This technique is called "stitch-in-the-ditch." When you come to a corner, put the needle in the down position, turn and continue sewing. Try to plan a route with as few starts and stops as possible. When you get to the end, stitch in place as before and clip the thread ends close to the work.

When you are quilting the middle of a large item, such as a bed quilt, roll up the sides tightly and hold it in place with bicycle clips.

FANCY MACHINE QUILTING

Once you have gotten used to freehand quilting, you will find that you can easily quilt quite intricate designs and you can easily move the fabric in any direction.

Thread the machine as for straight-line quilting. Before you begin, read the instructions in your sewing machine manual about darning. It is not possible to do free-hand machine quilting with an ordinary presser foot, so replace this with a darning foot that allows free movement of fabric beneath it. Also lower or cover the feed-dog.

Practice free-motion quilting on a sample "padding sandwich" and do the following exercises until you feel confident about trying machine quilting on your patchwork. First, grip the sandwich firmly with both hands and sew some free-hand "squiggles" and loops by moving the sandwich round and round under the needle. You will soon discover how to form even stitches and smooth curves by varying the speed with which you move the fabric under the needle, and how fast you run the machine. Next draw a quilting pattern on the padding sandwich. Practice as above, trying to keep the stitches on the pattern lines. However, it is more important to keep your quilting line smooth. Fix the stitches at the top and bottom of the designs by sewing a few stitches in place. Occasionally check the tension at the back.

Remember, you can move the fabric in any direction under the needle so, when you get to the end of a curve, leave the needle down and turn the work for you to see your next line. If you wear lightweight rubber gloves for freehand quilting, you can grip the quilt more easily.

A continuous line design for freehand machine quilting, seen opposite, is used in the Flying Geese Throw (see pp. 230–31). The line design above features in the Jacob's Ladder Crib Quilt (see pp. 240-1).

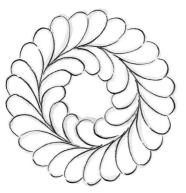

A typical hand-quilting design that could decorate any plain-material quilt.

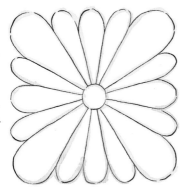

A hand-quilting design in Jacob's Ladder Crib Quilt (see pp. 240-1).

PRESSING AND "BLOCKING" PATCHWORK

Your iron is as important a tool as your sewing machine for neat and accurate patchwork. Always set up your ironing table near the sewing machine so that it will be easy for you to press your patchwork pieces as you sew.

Before you cut or mark fabric, it is important to press it. If your fabric is rather flimsy, a treatment with spray starch makes cutting and piecing easier.

PRESSING SEAMS
Generally speaking, in patchwork you do not have to press seams open, but toward the darker side of the seam. Also, when sewing rows of patches together, avoid bulky seams wherever possible by pressing the seams of alternate rows of patches in opposite directions (*Fig. A*). In doing this, you will sometimes have to break the rule about always pressing seams toward the darker side.

With some patchwork blocks, whichever way you press, it is impossible to avoid lots of seams converging in the same place. To reduce the bulk in this situation, you can sometimes clip the seams so that they change direction (*Fig. B*).

BLOCKING
It is a good idea to draw a grid on your ironing table cover as an aid to pressing and blocking. It almost always happens, however carefully and accurately you sew, that long rows or borders of patches end up being rather crooked. It is important to block the patchwork row before you continue sewing.

Lay the row or border on the ironing table so that it is lined up with one of your grid lines (*Fig. 1*). Pin the row in place along the top and bottom into the pad of the table surface. Press down firmly with a steam iron to straighten the row firmly against the grid line (*Fig. 2*).

PUTTING TOGETHER THE LAYERS OF A QUILT

Before quilting or tying your quilt, and before putting on the binding, you must secure together the patchwork top, the padding and the backing fabric by making a "quilt sandwich." The usual way to do this is by tacking. Press the top and back well to eliminate any wrinkles or creases. Cut the

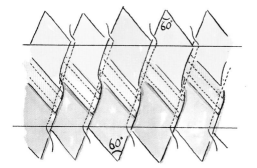

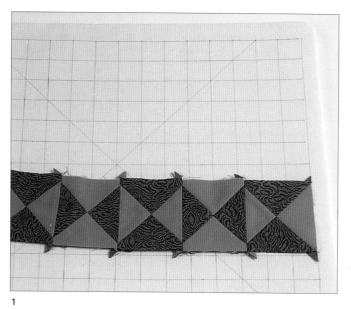

1

2

back a little larger all around than the patchwork and lay it face down on the floor. Cut a piece of padding the same size and lay it on top of the back. Center the top over the padding, smoothing out the layers to avoid any unsightly wrinkling.

Tack the three layers together as follows. Thread a long needle and stitch from the middle of the quilt diagonally out to the corners. Then make a grid of horizontal and vertical lines. The tacking lines should be at least 6in (15cm) apart.

Tack all around the edge too (*Fig. A*). If your machine has a zig-zag stitch, it is a good idea to zig-zag all around the raw edges of the top. You are now ready to start quilting, either by hand or machine.

USING "STICKY PADDING"

Another way of securing quilt layers together is called "sticky padding," and is ideal for machine quilting. With this method you can actually glue the layers together with spray adhesive (available from graphic art stores).

Prepare the patchwork, back and padding as above. First protect the floor with a large plastic sheet, and open windows to provide good ventilation. Lay the padding on the sheet. Lay a length of dark thread across the middle of the padding in both directions. Hold the thread in place by winding around a pin at each end.

Spray the padding all over with the adhesive. Place right sides together, fold the patchwork top in half first one way and then the other way. Lay the folded edges up to the thread lines on one quarter of the padding and then drop the patchwork onto the sticky surface (*Fig. B*). You will need a friend to help you if your quilt is very large. Unfold the patchwork onto the rest of the padding, smoothing down any unattractive wrinkles with your hand. (You can lift the patchwork up and lay it down again if any puckers do start to appear.)

Repeat this procedure with the backing fabric. You may find it necessary to pin all around the edges before zig-zagging around the raw edges of the top.

Trim away any excess padding and backing fabric up to the zig-zag line. Quilt in your pattern as desired (*see pp. 218-9*).

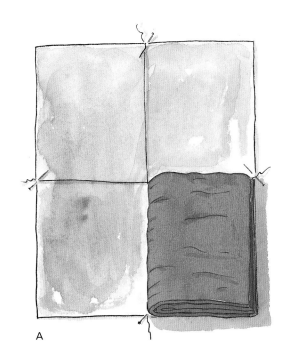

A

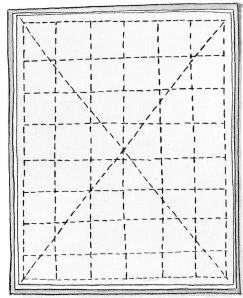

B

BINDING A QUILT

Here is a simple method of binding a quilt with one fabric strip. The corners are folded in using a method that produces a neat miter. The binding is sewn first to the back of the quilt by machine. It is then folded over to the front, and this edge is either sewn down with tiny zig-zag machine stitches, or by hand using blind-stitching. You do not have to cut binding for a quilt on the bias unless the quilt edge itself is curved.

A   B   C   D

E   F   G   H

SEWING ON A BINDING

MATERIALS
Fabric strips for binding
Sewing machine
Matching sewing thread
Steam iron, pins

1 Cut enough strips of fabric to stretch all around your quilt plus about 15in (40cm) for joining the strips and for turning corners. Cut strips four times the finished width of the binding. The bindings for most of the quilts in this chapter are ¾in (2cm) wide, so the strips are cut 3in (8cm) wide. Cut off ends of the strips at a 45° angle and join them diagonally,

right sides together (*Fig. A*). On the wrong side of the strip, draw a line down the middle, turn in raw edges up to the line, and press with a steam iron (*Fig. B*).

2 Thread the needle to match the binding, and the bobbin to match the quilt top. From the back of the quilt, start sewing on the binding halfway along one side leaving about 3in (8cm) free. Sew on pressed line with the binding raw edge in line with the edge of the quilt.

3 At the corners, fold the binding diagonally outward at 45°. Press fold with your finger

and mark fold line with a pin (*Fig. C*). Sew right up to pin, then backstitch a few stitches, raise the needle and pull the threads out a bit without cutting.

4 Remove pin and fold binding outward again on same fold line (*Fig. D*). Turn the quilt and fold binding back inward so that the new fold is even with the quilt edge. Start sewing again on pressed line, right from quilt edge (*Fig. E*) Repeat for all four corners.

5 When you reach the starting point, turn in the end of the first raw edge. Cut off excess binding, leaving 2in (5cm) overlap

and lay new raw edge on top (*Fig. F*). Continue sewing until binding has been attached all around.

6 To sew the binding to the front, rewind the bobbin with thread to match binding. Turn quilt right side up and fold binding over so that the folded edge meets the stitching line. Sew with tiny zig-zag stitches overlapping folded edge (*Fig. G*).

7 When you get to the corners turn quilt and fold binding to form a miter (*Fig. H*). Pin folded corner in place as you sew. If you prefer, you can hand sew binding into place with blindstitch.

FINISHING CUSHIONS

Making a cushion back is easy and adding a zipper makes the cushion easy to remove (see below). You can also add a professional finish by edging cushions with piping. To cover the piping cord, use a similar weight fabric to that of the cushion cover. Strips to make the piping can be cut from the cushion back fabric, or you can use one of the patchwork front fabrics. As a general guide, ½yd (0.5m) of 45in (115cm) wide fabric is enough for two cushion backs and piping for two 15in (38cm) square cushions.

You can buy piping cord by the length in fabric stores in several widths, but the No. 4 size (which is ³⁄₁₆in [4mm] in diameter) is ideal for cushion making.

It is easiest to use your quilter's ruler and rotary cutter (*see pp. 212-3*) to cut the strips for encasing the piping cord; 1¼in (3.5cm) is the correct width for No.4 cord. You do not have to cut the strips on the bias unless your item has lots of curves. You need to use the zipper foot attachment on your sewing machine to encase the piping and to sew it to the cushion.

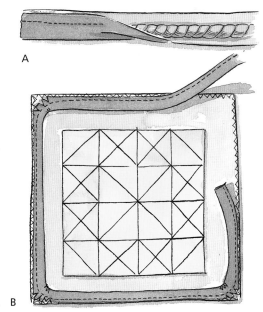

A

B

C

MATERIALS
No. 4 piping cord to go round cushion
Matching fabric strips
Quilter's ruler, rotary cutter (*see pp. 212-3*), cutting mat
Sewing machine with zip foot attachment
Matching sewing thread
Finished cushion

that the top is 1in (2.5cm) larger than the finished cushion size. Zig-zag around raw edges. Place one end of encased piping about halfway along side of the cushion top, lining up raw edges (*Fig. B*). Leaving about first 2in (5cm) unsewn, stitch close to the piping.

3 Stop sewing 1in (2.5cm) from the first corner and backstitch about 1in (2.5cm). Clip piping in several places where it will bend around the corner, right up to the stitching line of the casing. Continue to sew, rounding off corners. When you are nearing the beginning again, stop sewing and cut casing to overlap the other end by about 1in (2.5cm) and the piping so that it meets other end (*Fig. C*). Finish sewing.

SEWING ON PIPING

1 Cut the No. 4 piping cord to go around your cushion, plus an extra 2in (5cm). Cut strips of fabric 1¼in (3.5cm) wide and long enough to go around your

cushion, plus about 5in (12cm) for seams. Cut off ends of strips at a 45° angle and join right sides together (*Fig. A on opposite page*). Press seams open. Enclose the piping cord inside the piping strip, and sew with a fairly long stitch

(*Fig. A*), using a zipper foot so that you can sew close to the cord inside the casing.

2 Prepare the completed cushion top (and padding if quilted) by trimming raw edges so

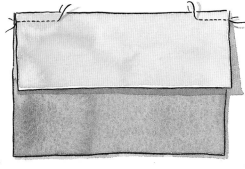

A

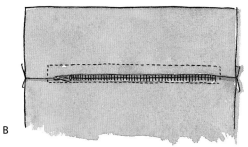

B

INSERTING A ZIPPER AND SEWING ON BACK

MATERIALS
Steam iron
1 zipper, two-thirds of cushion width, pins, sewing machine
Fabric rectangle for cushion back (to size of finished cushion plus 1in [2.5cm] width and 2in [5cm] length)
Matching sewing thread, cushion pad

1 To insert a zipper, fold over one-third of fabric, right sides together (*Fig. A*). Press. Sew a ½in (1.3cm) seam with gap for zipper. Slit fold; press open. Place zipper

under opening with lower fold level with teeth and pin. With zipper foot, stitch close to fold along zipper length and across zipper end. Turn and sew other side ⅜in (9mm) from fold, then across puller end (*Fig. B*).

2 To sew on a cushion back, open zipper, and pin the back to the front, right sides together. If unpiped, sew with ½in seam, rounding off corners. Clip the seam allowance at the corners up to the stitching line, trim padding, and then turn out. Press the cushion back and insert cushion pad. If piped, make as above, sewing with zipper foot on piping stitching line.

Project templates

2-INCH SET OF R.I.T. SQUARE
TEMPLATES (see pp. 214-5)

3-INCH SET OF R.I.T. SQUARE
TEMPLATES (see pp. 214-5)

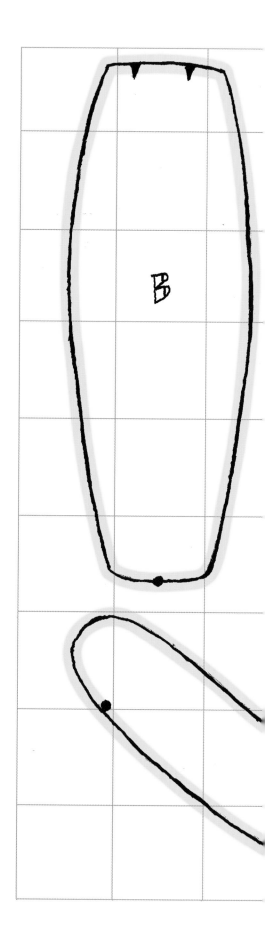

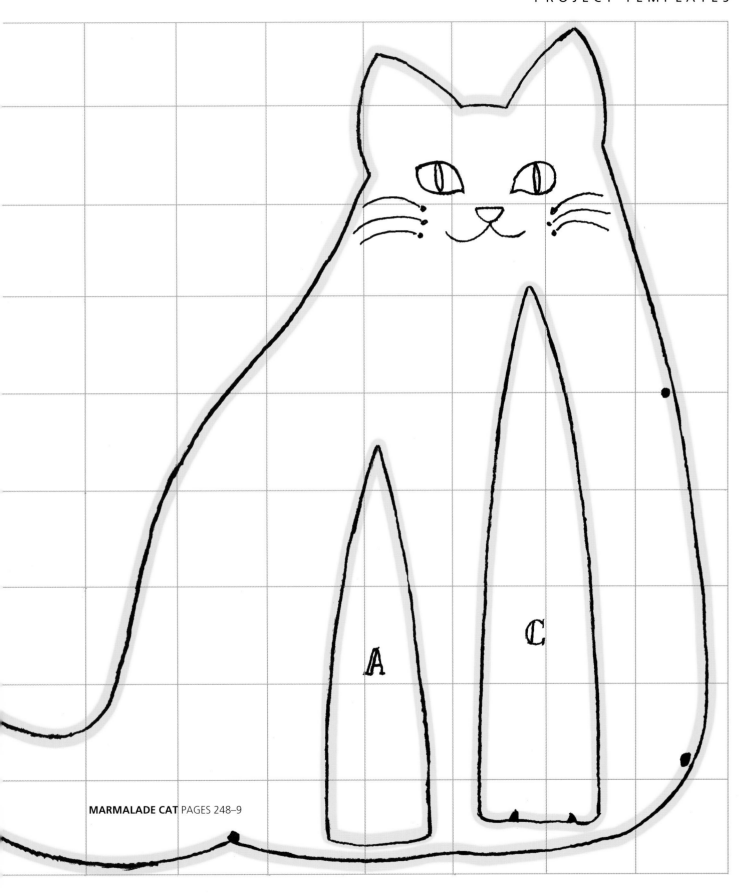

MARMALADE CAT PAGES 248–9

PATCHWORK

PROJECTS

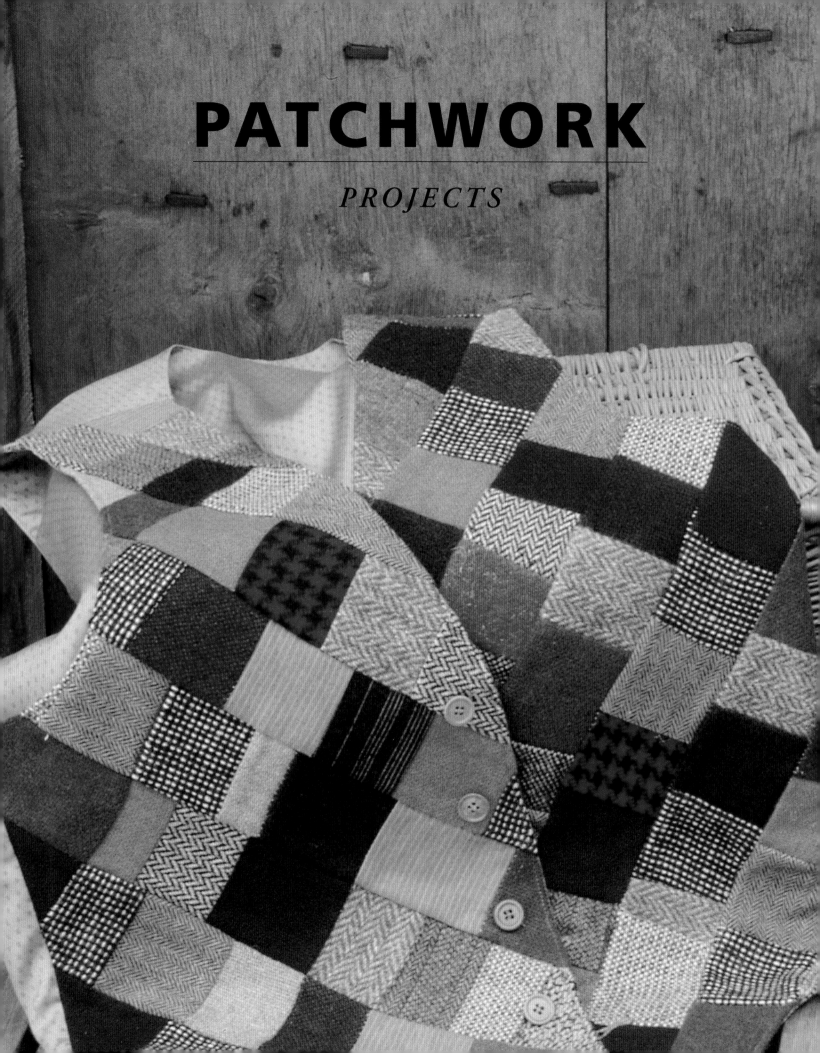

PATCHWORK

A

B

C

D

E

F

MATERIALS

finished size: 29in x 34in (73.5cm x 86cm)

18in (0.45m) of mid-blue print cotton fabric

1 fat quarter (*see p. 210*) each of white and dark-blue cotton fabrics

12in (0.3m) of white cotton fabric for sashing and borders

12in (0.3m) of dark-blue cotton fabric for binding and straps

36in (0.9m) of toweling

36in (0.9m) of 4oz (100g) polyester padding

No. 2 template from 3inch-set of R.I.T. Squares (*see pp. 224-5*)

Ballpoint or fine felt-tip pen

Rotary cutter (*see pp. 212-3*)

Quilter's ruler, cutting mat

Matching sewing thread

Steam iron

1 For six boats, you need 24 No. 2 R.I.T. Square sails. From the mid-blue print fabric and the fat quarter of white fabric cut pieces 13in x 18in (33cm x 46cm) as in Figs. A and C. Press pieces right sides together and use No. 2 R.I.T. Square template to draw a grid of 12 squares (*Fig. D*). Sew and cut (*see pp.214-5*). All seams are ¼in (6mm) unless otherwise stated. Press seams toward darker side with a steam iron.

2 From mid-blue print fabric and the fat quarter of dark-blue fabric cut pieces 9in x 18in (23cm x 46cm) as in Figs. B and C. Draw, sew and cut six No.2 R.I.T. Squares as in Step 1 to make six bows and six sterns (*Fig. E*).

3 From remaining piece of dark-blue fabric cut three strips 3½in (9cm) wide. From each strip cut two pieces 6½in (16.5cm) long for the boats (*Fig. B*). From remaining mid-blue print fabric,

228

cut four strips 3½in (9cm) wide and 22in (56cm) long. From each strip cut three 6½in (16.5cm) lengths for the sky (*Fig. C*).

4 Join the sails to make a pair for each mast. Sew together the sky patches and the sails, and sew the bow and stern to each boat. Press seams toward the darker side. Join the sail portion to the boat portion of each block, matching seams. Press the blocks.

5 From the white fabric for sashing, cut five long strips 2¼in (5.75cm) wide. From the ends of four strips cut four pieces 12½in (32cm) long and sew them between blocks (*Fig. F*). Press seams toward sashing. Cut three strips to same length as the columns of boats and sew to each side of the columns (*see Fig. F*). Press seams toward the sashing.

6 Cut two strips to length of patchwork width and sew to top and bottom. Press seams toward the borders. Cut a strip 3in x 44in (7.5cm x 112cm) long from dark-blue fabric for straps. Fold in half lengthways, then fold edges into foldline. Stitch close to edge along each side. Cut two straps 18in (46cm) long.

7 Cut toweling pieces and padding to patchwork size. Pin the padding to wrong side of toweling. Fold under the ends of the straps and sew to right side of the toweling (*Fig. G*). Make a quilt sandwich (*see pp. 220-1*). Machine quilt using the "stitch-in-the-ditch" method (*see p. 219*) around each block (avoiding straps at back). From the dark-blue fabric, cut four 2in (5cm) wide strips for a narrow ½in (1.3cm) binding. Sew on binding (*see p. 222*), but don't sew over straps. Fig. G shows you how to fold the mat.

EASY LEVEL

BABY CHANGING MAT

This versatile sailing boat changing mat, which has an absorbent toweling back and handy carrying straps, can be folded up to hold everything a baby needs on a day out. The six boat blocks are easy to make in the cotton fabrics, using the R.I.T. Square method (*see pp. 214-5*). The fabrics specified are all 45in (115cm) wide unless otherwise stated. Be sure to wash them all before you start sewing the mat.

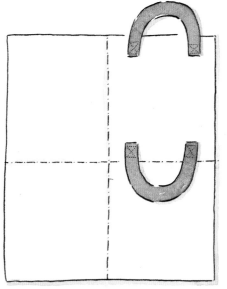

G

229

MATERIALS

finished size: about 49in x 58in (124cm x 148cm)
36in (1m) of white cotton background fabric
8 fat eighths (*see p. 210*) of assorted dark- to mid-green print cotton fabrics
18in (0.5m) of mid-green cotton fabric for narrow framing
41in (1.05m) of pale-green cotton fabric for sashing and wide border
56in (1.5m) of 60in (150cm) wide toning backing fabric
56in (1.5m) of 54in (140cm) wide 2oz (50g) polyester padding
23in (0.6m) of dark-green print cotton fabric for binding
No.2 template from the 3-inch set of R.I.T. Squares (*see pp. 224-5*)
Ballpoint or fine felt-tip pen
Rotary cutter (*see pp. 212-3*)
Quilter's ruler, cutting mat
Matching sewing thread
Steam iron
Quilting materials (optional) and design (*see pp. 218-9*)

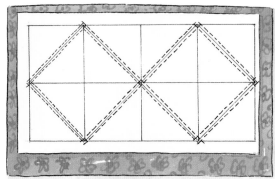

A

B

1 First make the geese as follows. From the white cotton fabric, cut eight pieces about 8½in x 16½in (22cm x 42cm). Place one of the pieces right sides together with one of the green print fabrics. Use the No. 2 R.I.T. Square template as a guide to draw a grid of eight squares (*Fig. A*). Sew and cut (*see pp. 214-5*) to make 16 No. 2 patches. All seams are ¼in (6mm). Press the seams toward the light color with a steam iron.

2 Sew the patches together to make 8 geese (*Fig. B*). Press the seams open. Repeat with the remaining seven green print fabrics to make 64 geese.

3 Arrange the 64 geese on the floor randomly into four rows of 16 geese as shown in the photograph. Place two "twin" geese in each row. This step takes quite a long time because you have to check that no twins are adjacent and that there is a nice balance of the prints overall. Sew up the four rows of geese, matching the vertical seams. Clip off the points at the top and press seams downward. Use the steam iron to block the rows by stretching or easing the geese in each row to fit along a straight line drawn on your ironing board.

4 Now make the narrow framing. From the mid-green fabric cut 11 strips 1½in (4cm) wide and about 44in (115cm) long. Sew nine strips together end to end, press the seams open, and divide them into eight pieces of equal length. Cut all pieces to the exact length of a row of geese and sew them to each side of each row keeping the rows straight. Press seams outward.

5 From the pale-green fabric, cut four strips 3½in (9cm) wide and about 44in (115cm)

long. Sew them end to end and press the seams open. Cut three strips exactly the length of a row of geese and sew one between each row. Press the seams toward the narrow framing. Cut the remaining two mid-green framing strips to the exact width of the patchwork and sew to top and bottom. Press the seams outward.

6 Make the wide border next. From the pale-green fabric cut 5 strips 4½in (11.5cm) wide and about 44in (115cm) long. Cut two strips exactly the width of the patchwork and sew to top and bottom. Press seams toward the narrow framing. Sew the remaining three strips together, end to end. Cut two strips exactly the length of the patchwork and sew one to each side. Press seams inward and press the whole quilt.

7 Make your "quilt sandwich" with the padding and backing fabric (*see pp. 220-1*). Quilt by hand or machine around the geese and on each side of each strip, using the "stitch-in-the-ditch" method (*see p. 219*). If you wish to add decorative quilting on the border and

sashing, transfer the quilting design with the "prick-and-pounce" method (*see p. 218*), and go over the lines with a quilt marker. Quilt along the marked lines. Cut six strips 3in (7.5cm) wide across the width of the dark-green print fabric for the binding and then sew on as described in the Binding a Quilt section on page 222.

FLYING GEESE THROW

The "Flying Geese" pattern used for this throw, which is ideal to put on a bed or sofa, is a traditional American patchwork design. Whereas many American designs, such as "Jacob's Ladder" (*see pp. 240-1*), are made up by repeating the same block, the Flying Geese pattern comes into the category of a strip quilt. Instead of using a block arrangement, the geese are placed together in long columns which are then separated by sashing. The border and sashing in this project are finished with decorative quilting which you can either stitch by hand or by machine. All the fabrics specified are 45in (115cm) wide unless otherwise stated.

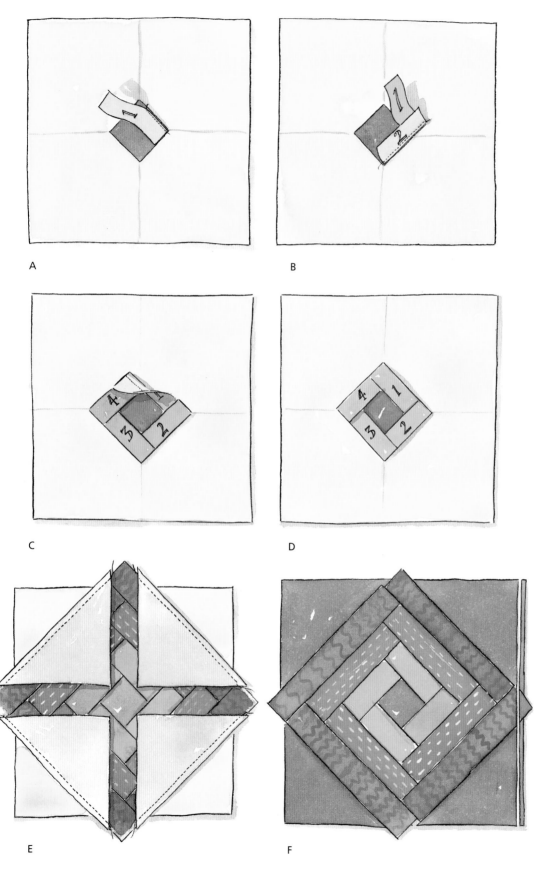

A

B

C

D

E

F

1 Mark the middle lines on the square of padding both ways with a felt-tip pen. Cut a 4½in (12cm) square of the bright floral fabric and pin it diagonally to the padding as shown in Fig. A.

2 From the gold fabric cut four strips 2½in (6.5cm) wide and 6½in (17cm) long. Sew the first strip to the middle square (Fig. A), taking a ¼in (6mm) seam allowance and leaving about the first 1½in (4cm) unsewn. Press the strip outward. Sew on the next strip of gold fabric as shown in Fig. B. Sew on the remaining strips of gold fabric in clockwise order, pressing each strip outward as you are sewing. Pin the unsewn end of the first strip over the fourth strip as shown in Fig. C and sew up to the first line of stitches. Press strip outward with steam iron (Fig. D).

3 Cut strips from the red fabric to the same width as the gold fabric, but make them about 10½in (27cm) long. Sew them on as Step 2, working out from the gold.

4 Cut strips from the green fabric to the same width, but about 12½in (32cm) long. Sew them on next to the red as Step 2.

5 Cut a 10in (26cm) square from the brown fabric. Fold the square diagonally both ways and cut on the fold lines to make four triangles. Pin the triangles to the block (Fig. E), sew, and press back outward.

6 Trim the block to 16in (41cm) square (Fig. F) and zig-zag stitch around the raw edges.

7 Make up the cushion cover with toning fabric, adding a back zipper opening as described on p. 21. Finally, insert the cushion pad.

MATERIALS

finished size: 15in (38cm) square

16in (41cm) square of 4oz (100g) polyester padding

1 fat eighth (*see p. 210*) each of floral print and four gold, red, green, and brown cotton print fabrics

16in x 18in (41cm x 46cm) square of toning cotton fabric for back

Felt-tip pen, rotary cutter (*see pp. 212-3*), quilter's ruler, cutting mat, matching sewing thread, steam iron

12in (30cm) matching zipper

15in (38cm) square cushion pad

EASY LEVEL

QUILT-AS-YOU-GO CUSHION

This cushion is very easy to make, but is no less attractive for its simplicity. It can really stand out when placed on a plain-colored sofa or you can make a feature of it on a bed with a white or cream bedspread. You can also try placing it on an old wooden chair in the kitchen to give it renewed life and some added color and texture.

The four strips of each color are sewn around the middle patch as if it is "woven." The middle square can be a scrap of fabric left over from your curtain making, while the four surrounding strips could be self-color prints in colors picked out from the floral piece.

The fabric strips are pieced directly onto a square of padding, so you are in fact quilting the cushion top as you sew the patchwork. With piecing by sewing machine, it only takes about 20 minutes to complete the top.

You can use the same method of patchwork to create a large quilt. Just make as many blocks as you need for the quilt and simply stitch them together. Then add some backing fabric and quilt by hand along the seams where all the blocks join.

233

AMISH CUSHIONS

When you use the R.I.T. Square method of sewing patchwork together (*see pp. 214-5*), it is often just as easy to make two or more blocks as it is to make one. This is certainly the case with these two Amish cushions—a traditional Star block, shown in the photograph, and a Diamond block, shown on page 235. They both have the same middle pattern, but the outer patches have different colors and pattern arrangements.

To follow the Amish tradition, choose plain, bright colors for these cushions, such as fuchsia, magenta, black, royal blue, aqua, scarlet, and purple. The Amish people always avoided yellow and white. For a stunning larger project, you could repeat the blocks to create your own quilt design.

MATERIALS

(to make two cushions)

finished size: 15in (38cm) square

8 fat eighths *(see p. 210)* of royal blue, turquoise, bright pink, black, maroon, scarlet, purple, and lilac cotton fabric

18in (0.45m) of 45in (115cm) wide toning blue cotton fabric for back and piping

Two pieces of 4oz (100g) polyester padding 16in (41cm) square

No. 2 and No. 3 templates from the 3-inch set of R.I.T. Squares *(see pp. 224-5)*

Ballpoint or fine felt-tip pen

Rotary cutter *(see pp. 212-3)*

Quilter's ruler, cutting mat

Matching sewing thread

Steam iron

Quilting materials *(see pp. 218-9)*

3½yd (3.2m) of No. 4 piping cord

2 matching 12in (30cm) zippers

2 15in (38cm) square cushion pads

1 Make enough No. 3 R.I.T. Square patches for both cushions as follows. Place the pieces of royal blue and turquoise fabric right sides together. Using the No. 3 R.I.T. Square template as a guide, draw a grid of four squares on the turquoise fabric *(Fig. A)*. Sew and cut as described on pages 214-5. All seams are ¼in (6mm). Join to make eight No. 3 patches.

2 Make the patches for the Star block. From the black and bright pink fabrics, cut pieces 9in x 11in (about 23cm x 28cm) and place right sides together. Using the No. 2 R.I.T. Square template, draw a grid of four squares on bright pink fabric *(Fig. B)*. Sew and cut as described on pages 214-5 to make eight No. 2 patches. Cut four 3½in (9cm) squares from the black fabric to make No. 1 patches. Lay the patches for the Star block on the table as in Fig. C, making sure that you have the patches the right way round. Sew them together in rows. Press seams of alternate rows in opposite direction with a steam iron. Sew the rows together, matching seams. Press block.

3 From the maroon fabric, cut four strips 2¼in (6cm) wide. Cut two strips to the width of the block and sew to top and bottom. Cut two more strips exactly the length of the block and sew to each side. Press seams outward. Make the No. 1 and No. 2 patches for the Diamond block exactly as described in Step 2 above, but use the scarlet and purple fabrics. Assemble them as shown in Fig. D. Use the lilac fabric to make the border. Press the block.

4 Now quilt your cushion blocks. Place each piece of patchwork on a square of padding and pin to secure. Quilt by hand in straight lines about ¼in (6mm) away from the seams in the areas shown in the photographs. The color of the quilting thread can either match or contrast the patchwork. Mark a centered 16in (41cm) square on the quilted blocks, trim away any excess material, and zig-zag stitch around the edges of the blocks.

5 From the blue backing fabric, cut two pieces 16in x 18in (41cm x 46cm). From the remainder of the blue fabric, cut eight strips 1¼in (3.5cm) wide for the piping. Join and prepare the piping *(see p. 223)*, and sew to the patchwork with raw edges lined up. Make up the cushion covers with back zipper openings as described on page 223. Insert the cushion pads.

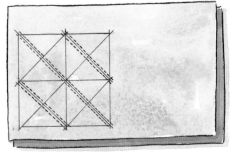

A

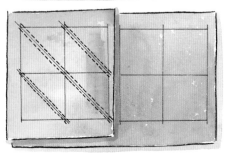

B

C

D

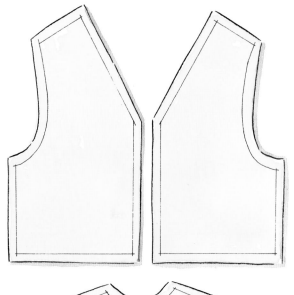

A

MATERIALS

Assortment of silk pieces to make 32 strips 2in x 22in (5cm x 60cm)
23in (0.6m) of 60in (150cm) wide lining fabric (in a toning color)
23in (0.6m) of 45in (115cm) wide soft cotton fabric for interlining
Vest pattern
Scissors
Rotary cutter (see pp. 212-3)
Quilter's ruler
Cutting mat
Matching sewing thread
Steam iron
Silver metallic thread for machine quilting
Vest buckle and buttons (as required)

1 Using the vest pattern, cut a back and a left and right front from the cotton interlining, including the normal ⅝in (1.5cm) seam allowances (Fig. A).

2 From your assortment of silk pieces, cut strips 2in (5cm) wide. If a silk strip is too short, you can join two different lengths together to add interest to the waistcoat, seaming them as Fig. B.

3 Taking ¼in (6mm) seams, sew the strips together to form "strippy" sheets large enough to cover the three interlining pieces plus about 1in (2.5cm) over all the way around (Fig. C). You need about eight strips to cover each front piece, and about 15 strips for the back. Choose the strips more or less at random, but with some contrast of pattern and color. Occasionally introduce a diagonally pieced strip. Press the seams open with a steam iron.

4 Thread your sewing machine with silver metallic thread. Pin the strippy sheets to the interlining pieces and quilt through the interlining with straight lines of stitching just to the left of the seam lines. Trim away the excess patchwork level with the edges of the interlining (Fig. D).

5 Make up waistcoat according to pattern. You can use leftover pieces to make a matching Strippy Silk Clutch Bag (see pp. 238-9).

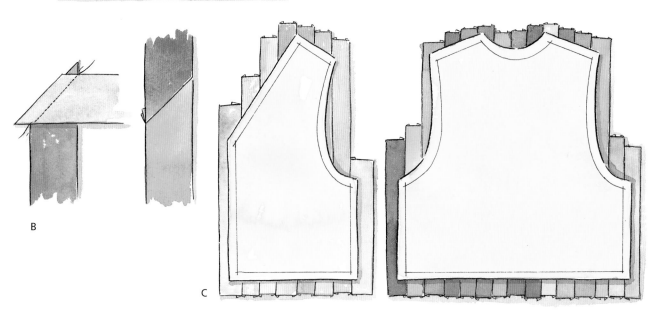

B

C

STRIPPY SILK VEST

This vest is made from beautiful silk pieces from Japan. You could use any pretty silk scraps, silk sample pieces, or even cast-off neck-ties. The vest would also be striking in some of the new ethnic or metallic prints available in patchwork stores.

Use a paper pattern to make up your vest. The vest pictured above contains a variety of silks about 6in x 22in (16cm x 60cm). However, if your pattern is larger, you will need to use more fabric.

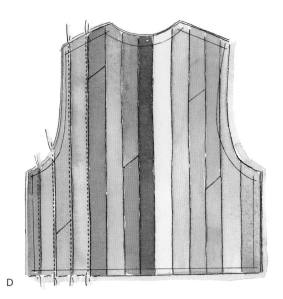

237

STRIPPY SILK CLUTCH BAG

Sew a matching clutch bag from silk pieces left over from the Strippy Vest on pages 236-7. Decorated with metallic thread and a novel "croissant" toggle button, it makes a really elegant accessory for an evening out.

The silk bag is so easy to piece together that you could run up several at the same time and give them to friends as presents. If the bag was made in more practical, washable fabrics, it would also be perfect to use as a cosmetic bag.

1 Cut eight silk strips 2in (5cm) wide and about 16in (40cm) long. Lay the first strip on the interlining, overlapping the left-hand edge by about ½in (1.3cm). Choose the next strip at random, but with some contrast of color and pattern. Lay it right sides together over the first strip and sew through interlining ¼in (6mm) away from the right-hand edge of the strips. Press the second strip over to the right with a steam iron.

2 Continue sewing on the rest of the strips in this way (*Fig. A*) until the entire piece of interlining is covered. Press well. Now decorate the patchwork piece

A

B

C

D

E

F

with some metallic thread sewn in a zig-zag stitch over the seam lines of all the silk strips.

3 Fold the patchwork right sides together to make a pocket 5½in (14 cm) deep and stitch very close to the interlining (*Fig. B*). Turn the raw patchwork edge over the interlining. "Sew off" a little triangle from the wrong side at each corner (*Fig. C*), trim off the corner, and turn right side out.

4 Cut the lining to the same size as the patchwork. Turn under the top edge of the lining pocket by ½in (1.3cm) and press. Sew each side of the lining pocket as in Step 3, but increase seam slightly so that the lining will be a little smaller than the bag. "Sew off" corners as previously.

5 To make a fastening loop, cut a scrap of silk that measures 2½in x ¾in (6.5cm x 2cm). Fold it in half lengthwise and then carefully fold the raw edges into the middle. Sew the folded edges together by hand with neat stitches. Hold the loop in place on the bag with a piece of clear tape.

6 With right sides together, sew the flap of the patchwork to the flap of the lining, around three sides, very close to the interlining, catching the fastening loop in the seam (*Fig. D*). Trim the corners, turn right side out and push the lining into patchwork pocket (*Fig. E*). Sew the folded edge of the lining to the inside of the pocket.

7 Apply the fusible web to half the length of the silk strip for the toggle as shown in Fig. F. Remove the paper backing and then fold the other half of the silk strip over and iron to create a double thickness. Cut a long triangle as shown. Roll up from the wide end as if you were making a croissant. Fix the point in position with a tiny scrap of fusible web. Finally, sew toggle onto bag.

MATERIALS
finished size: 10in x 5in (24cm x 12.5cm)
2in x 32in (5cm x 80cm) silk strips in each of four patterns
10in x 15in (25cm x 38cm) craft-weight non woven interlining or window cornice interlining
10½in x 15½in (27cm x 40cm) brightly colored silk for lining
Scrap of silk for fastening loop
1½in x 8in (4cm x 20cm) silk strip for toggle
1½in x 4in (4cm x 10cm) fusible web
Rotary cutter (see pp. 212-3)
Quilter's ruler
Cutting mat
Matching sewing thread
Steam iron
Metallic thread for quilting
Clear adhesive tapes

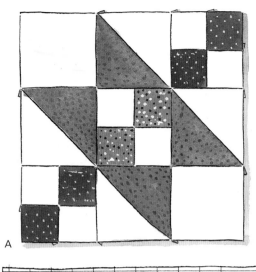

A

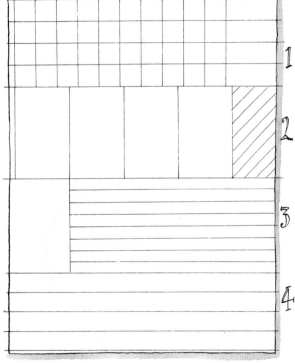

B

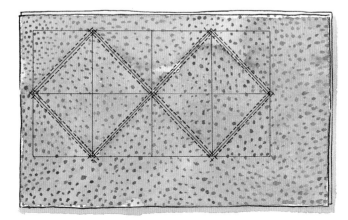

C

MATERIALS

finished size: about 41in x 50in (104cm x 127cm)

60in (1.5m) of white cotton fabric for background

3 fat eighths (see p. 210) of assorted navy print cotton fabrics

5 fat eighths of assorted mid-tone print cotton fabrics

12in (0.3m) each of navy print and light print cotton fabric for second and third border

54in (1.4m) of backing fabric (in a toning color)

48in (1.2m) of 54in (140cm) wide 2oz (50g) polyester padding

14in (0.35m) of maroon cotton fabric for binding

No. 1 and No. 2 templates from the 3-inch set of R.I.T. Squares (see pp. 224-5)

Ballpoint or fine felt-tip pen

Rotary cutter (see pp. 212-3)

Quilter's ruler

Cutting mat

Matching sewing thread

Steam iron

Quilting materials and design (see pp. 218-9)

1 The quilt is made up of 20 nine-patch blocks (Fig. A) using the R.I.T. Square method. Each block has two No. 1 patches (plain squares); make these 40 patches first. Using a rotary cutter, cut four

D

strips 3½in (9cm) wide from white cotton background fabric, then cut ten 3½in (9cm) squares from each strip (Fig. B1). If you don't have a rotary cutter, use the No. 1 R.I.T. Square template to trace patches and cut out with scissors.

2 From the white background material cut five pieces about 9in x 16in (23cm x 41cm) (Fig B2). Press one of white pieces right sides together with one of the mid-toned fabrics. Use the No. 2 R.I.T. Square template to draw a grid (Fig. C). Sew and cut (see pp. 214-5) to make 16 No. 2 patches. All seams are ¼in (6mm).

3 Repeat Step 2 with four other mid-toned print fabrics to make 80 No. 2 patches. Now make checkerboard patches for the "ladders." From the white fabric cut eight strips 2in (5cm) wide and 36in (90cm) long (Fig B3). Cut in half to make 16 strips about 18in (45cm) long. From each navy-print fabric cut five strips 2in (5cm) wide and about 18in (45cm) long. One white strip is left.

4 With right sides together, sew each white strip to a navy print strip along their lengths and press seams toward the darker side. Cut each strip-set into eight pieces 2in (5cm) wide. Choosing the three navy prints randomly, turn alternate pieces upside down and sew together in pairs, matching seams, to make 60 3½in (9cm) square patches (Fig. D). Clip seam at back and press each half toward darker side.

5 Now assemble blocks. Sew patches together (Fig. A). The four No. 2 patches should be the same, but the checkerboard patches should be placed so that there is a scattering of the navy

prints in each block. Press seams away from the No. 2 patches. Sew three rows for each block together; line up seams carefully. Press with steam iron. Place blocks on floor so that all checkerboard "ladders" are ascending in the same direction. Arrange blocks so that no identical ones are adjacent. Sew blocks together to make five rows, then sew rows together. Press well.

6 For first border, cut four strips from white fabric measuring 2½in (5cm) wide and about 45in (115cm) long (*Fig. B4*). Join together end to end. From this length, cut two strips to patchwork width and sew to top and bottom. Cut two more strips to patchwork length and sew to either side. Press seams outward. For second border, cut five

strips 1½in (4cm) wide and same length as first, from navy print, join and sew as Step 6. For final border, cut five strips 2in (5cm) wide and same length as first, from light print. Join and sew as Step 6.

7 Make a "quilt sandwich" with the padding and backing fabric (*see pp. 220-1*). Transfer quilting design on pages 218-9 onto the No.1 patches so that the hearts' bases meet at the checkerboard patches' corners. Quilt by hand or machine. The remainder of the quilt can be quilted by machine using the "stitch-in-the-ditch" method (*see p. 219*) around all the squares, triangles and borders. Then, cut out five 3in (8cm) strips across the width of the maroon fabric for the binding and sew as described on page 222.

INTERMEDIATE LEVEL

JACOB'S LADDER CRIB QUILT

The natural-colored cotton fabrics used in this crib quilt make a welcome change from the pastel or primary shades which are the usual favorites in a child's nursery. The "Jacob's Ladder" pattern is a traditional American nine-patch block design. Non-symmetrical blocks like these look best repeated in a quilt rather than used alone in a cushion or sampler, because the little squares and triangles join up to create interesting diagonals in two directions. The design is straightforward to make using the R.I.T. Square method (*see pp. 214-5*). The fabrics specified are all 45in (115cm) wide unless otherwise stated.

TRIP-AROUND-THE-WORLD THROW

The fascinating pattern displayed on this quilt is "Trip around the World"—a traditional Amish design. While the Amish always used plain fabrics in rich, jewel-like colors, the quilt in the photograph is made with a most unusual print fabric that is reminiscent of natural textures in bright sapphire shades. You could, however, use any interesting cotton fabrics as long as they range in tone from light to dark. You will need seven different tones for this quilt. Unless otherwise specified, the fabrics are 45in (115cm) wide.

Typically, the Trip-around-the-World design is always square. Imagine how time-consuming it would be to cut out and sew together individually all the 529 little squares that are included in this quilt! Fortunately for you, making this large throw is as easy as cutting strips with your rotary cutter, sewing them together and then "dicing" across them to produce the necessary rows of different-colored squares.

MATERIALS

finished size: about 54in x 54in (137cm x 137cm)

1 fat quarter (*see p. 210*) each of a very light-blue and a very dark-blue print cotton fabric

18in (0.5m) each of five other blue print cotton fabrics, ranging from dark to light blue

36in (1m) of blue striped cotton fabric for border

9in (0.25m) of dark-blue cotton fabric for corners

54in (1.4m) of 60in (150cm) wide, or 3yd (2.7m) of 45in (115cm) wide, backing fabric (in a toning color)

54in (1.4m) of 54in (140cm) wide 2oz (50g) polyester padding

18in (0.5m) of navy cotton fabric for binding

Rotary cutter (*see pp. 212-3*)

Quilter's ruler

Cutting mat

Seven small plastic bags labeled 1 to 7

Matching sewing thread

Seam ripper

Steam iron

Invisible nylon thread for machine quilting

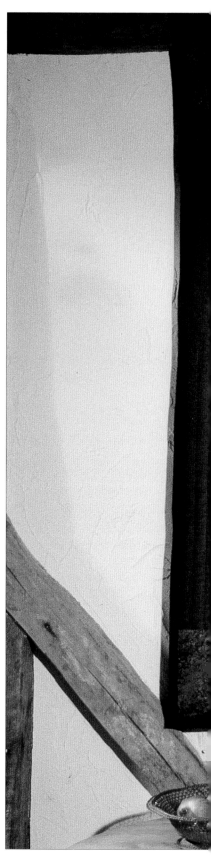

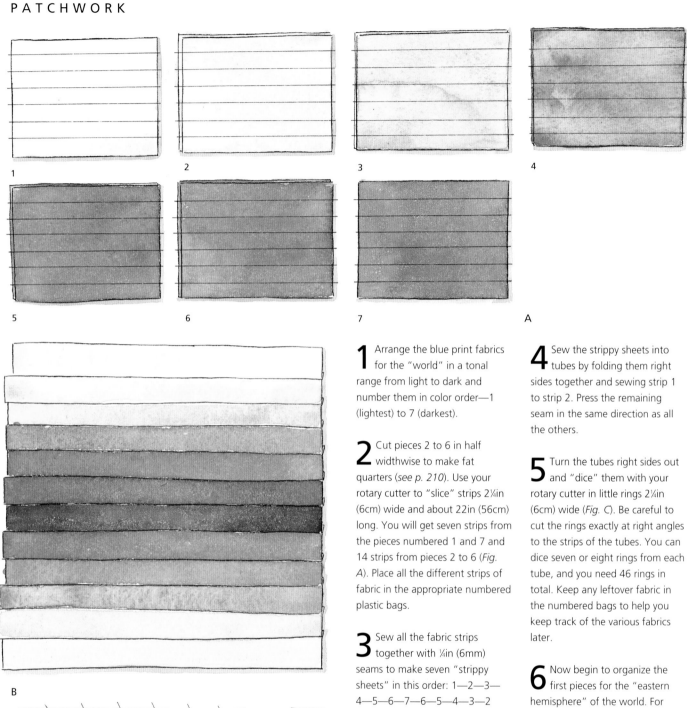

1

2

3

4

5

6

7

A

B

C

1 Arrange the blue print fabrics for the "world" in a tonal range from light to dark and number them in color order—1 (lightest) to 7 (darkest).

2 Cut pieces 2 to 6 in half widthwise to make fat quarters (see p. 210). Use your rotary cutter to "slice" strips 2¼in (6cm) wide and about 22in (56cm) long. You will get seven strips from the pieces numbered 1 and 7 and 14 strips from pieces 2 to 6 (Fig. A). Place all the different strips of fabric in the appropriate numbered plastic bags.

3 Sew all the fabric strips together with ¼in (6mm) seams to make seven "strippy sheets" in this order: 1—2—3—4—5—6—7—6—5—4—3—2 (Fig. B) and then press all the seams with a steam iron, making sure you iron them all in the same direction. When you are sewing, be careful not to stretch any of the strips, otherwise the sheets will not lie straight. Always start sewing from the same end and keep the ends even on one side (not all the strips will be exactly the same length).

4 Sew the strippy sheets into tubes by folding them right sides together and sewing strip 1 to strip 2. Press the remaining seam in the same direction as all the others.

5 Turn the tubes right sides out and "dice" them with your rotary cutter in little rings 2¼in (6cm) wide (Fig. C). Be careful to cut the rings exactly at right angles to the strips of the tubes. You can dice seven or eight rings from each tube, and you need 46 rings in total. Keep any leftover fabric in the numbered bags to help you keep track of the various fabrics later.

6 Now begin to organize the first pieces for the "eastern hemisphere" of the world. For Row 1, take a ring and hold it right side toward you with the seams toward the right; use seam ripper between Pieces 2 and 3. Turn the ring for Row 2 the other way round so that its seams go toward the left; use seam ripper between Pieces 3 and 4. Lay the pieces as in the chart on page 39. For each row, refer to the diagram, and use seam ripper between the patch

											border
3	4	5	6	7	6	5	4	3	2	1	2
4	5	6	7	6	5	4	3	2	1	2	3
5	6	7	6	5	4	3	2	1	2	3	4
6	7	6	5	4	3	2	1	2	3	4	5
7	6	5	4	3	2	1	2	3	4	5	6
6	5	4	3	2	1	2	3	4	5	6	7
5	4	3	2	1	2	3	4	5	6	7	6
4	3	2	1	2	3	4	5	6	7	6	5
3	2	1	2	3	4	5	6	7	6	5	4
2	1	2	3	4	5	6	7	6	5	4	3
1	2	3	4	5	6	7	6	5	4	3	2
2	3	4	5	6	7	6	5	4	3	2	1
1	2	3	4	5	6	7	6	5	4	3	2
2	1	2	3	4	5	6	7	6	5	4	3
3	2	1	2	3	4	5	6	7	6	5	4
4	3	2	1	2	3	4	5	6	7	6	5
5	4	3	2	1	2	3	4	5	6	7	6
6	5	4	3	2	1	2	3	4	5	6	7
7	6	5	4	3	2	1	2	3	4	5	6
6	7	6	5	4	3	2	1	2	3	4	5
5	6	7	6	5	4	3	2	1	2	3	4
4	5	6	7	6	5	4	3	2	1	2	3
3	4	5	6	7	6	5	4	3	2	1	2

ROW 1
ROW 2
ROW 3
ROW 4
ROW 5
ROW 6
ROW 7
ROW 8
ROW 9
ROW 10
ROW 11
ROW 12
ROW 13
ROW 14
ROW 15
ROW 16
ROW 17
ROW 18
ROW 19
ROW 20
ROW 21
ROW 22
ROW 23

2	1	2	3	4	5	6	7	6	5	4	3
3	2	1	2	3	4	5	6	7	6	5	4
4	3	2	1	2	3	4	5	6	7	6	5
5	4	3	2	1	2	3	4	5	6	7	6
6	5	4	3	2	1	2	3	4	5	6	7
7	6	5	4	3	2	1	2	3	4	5	6
6	7	6	5	4	3	2	1	2	3	4	5
5	6	7	6	5	4	3	2	1	2	3	4
4	5	6	7	6	5	4	3	2	1	2	3
3	4	5	6	7	6	5	4	3	2	1	2
2	3	4	5	6	7	6	5	4	3	2	1
1*	2	3	4	5	6	7	6	5	4	3	2
2	3	4	5	6	7	6	5	4	3	2	1
3	4	5	6	7	6	5	4	3	2	1	2
4	5	6	7	6	5	4	3	2	1	2	3
5	6	7	6	5	4	3	2	1	2	3	4
6	7	6	5	4	3	2	1	2	3	4	5
7	6	5	4	3	2	1	2	3	4	5	6
6	5	4	3	2	1	2	3	4	5	6	7
5	4	3	2	1	2	3	4	5	6	7	6
4	3	2	1	2	3	4	5	6	7	6	5
3	2	1	2	3	4	5	6	7	6	5	4
2	1	2	3	4	5	6	7	6	5	4	3

number in the left-hand column and the patch number in the right-hand column. Check the numbered bags to make sure you are using the seam ripper on the right color! The seams of the odd-numbered rows go toward the right and those of the even-numbered rows go toward the left. As the pattern of the eastern hemisphere starts to form, sew the rows together, matching the seams carefully.

7 When you get to Row 12, use the ripper between Pieces 1 and 2, but rip and discard Piece 1 (starred on the chart) and replace it with a little square cut from one of

the dark-colored fabrics. Continue sewing carefully following the numbered diagram exactly, until you have sewn together the 23 rows of the eastern hemisphere.

8 For the "western hemisphere," follow the instructions as for Step 6. However, reverse the colors of the rings and, for each row, rip and discard the patch in the highlighted column in the chart. Sew together the 23 rows with seams of alternate rows going in opposite directions.

9 Press all the horizontal seams of the eastern hemisphere upward and those of the western

hemisphere downward. Sew the two hemispheres together, being careful to match the seams. Press the world carefully.

10 Cut four strips 8in (20cm) wide from the blue-striped fabric for the border. (The width of the border can vary depending on the width of the stripes.) Cut the four strips to exactly the same length as the sides of the world. Then cut four dark-blue squares to match the width of the border strips. Sew two of the border strips to the opposite sides of the world. Sew the dark-blue squares to each end of the other two border strips and sew these to the remaining

two sides of the world, taking care to match up the seams neatly. Press the seams toward the border strips.

11 To finish, make your "quilt sandwich" with the padding and backing fabric (see pp. 220-1), joining the backing fabric if necessary. Machine quilt diagonally across the small squares using invisible nylon thread and around the borders using the "stitch-in-the-ditch" method (see p. 219). Cut six strips 3in (8cm) wide across the width of the navy fabric for the binding and then sew onto the throw as fully described on p. 20.

MAN'S WOOL VEST

Vests are a popular fashion accessory. Children want them in bright novelty prints, teenagers want them for school or college, women want them for evening wear and, finally, men want them. The favorite man in your life would gladly exchange his pin-striped version for this rustic weekend vest, made from wool fabrics gleaned from second-hand or garage sales. Only the fronts are made from patchwork; the back is made from some lining fabric.

Wool can be difficult to use for patchwork, because its heavy weight makes very bulky seams. It does require a lot of pressing with a steam iron, but the bulk of the seams adds an interesting texture to the patchwork, which does not then need to be quilted. Make sure that you press all the seams well in the same direction.

Use a paper pattern in the required size to make up the vest, remembering to allow enough wool scraps to fit the width of the vest fronts.

1 With pattern, cut a left and right front from interfacing without seam allowances. Draw diagonal lines with pen on the adhesive side of pieces (*Fig. A*), to help place patchwork strips.

2 Cut some wool strips 2½in (6cm) wide in a variety of colors. Cut pieces from the wool strips in different lengths from 1½in to 3½in (3cm to 9cm). Pick up small wool pieces at random for a good mix of color, texture and size and sew together in rows with ¼in

MATERIALS

27in (0.7m) of 35in (90cm) wide medium weight iron-on interfacing	
Wool scraps sufficient to cover two vest fronts	
64in (1.4m) of 60in (150cm) lining fabric (in a toning color)	
Vest pattern	
Scissors	
Felt-tip marking pen	
Rotary cutter (see pp. 212-3)	
Quilter's ruler	
Cutting mat	
Matching sewing thread	
Steam iron	
Vest buckle and buttons (as required)	

(6mm) seams to cover the vest fronts diagonally.

3 When you have four rows of patchwork pieces, check the lengths against the vest front (*Fig. B*). Sew them together so that brighter colors are scattered around, rearranging rows where necessary for a good balance. Press all the seams with a steam iron to one side.

4 Continue making rows of patches, sewing them together until you have enough patchwork for one vest front (*Fig. C*). Leave a good margin all around the shape for the seam allowance. Press patchwork well with the steam iron. Repeat for second vest front, slanting strips the other way.

5 Apply the interfacing pieces to the wrong sides of the patchwork. Trim any excess material, making sure you leave a ⅝in (1.5cm) seam allowance (*Fig. D*).

6 Make up vest back with lining fabric, and finish following the pattern instructions.

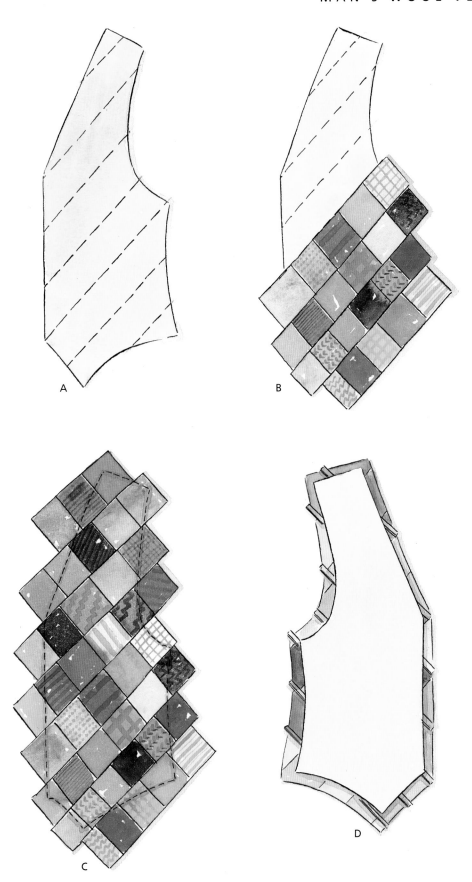

A

B

C

D

MARMALADE CAT

Cat lovers young and old will adore this cheeky ginger patchwork cat. The ideal pet, he won't leave hairs all over your furniture, nor sit on your newspaper when you are trying to read it!

The cat is made up in "strippy" patchwork in a variety of marmalade-colored prints, and its features are embroidered on. You could also use the same simple technique to make a child a cuddly teddy, an Easter bunny, or a dog, perhaps. Look in the pattern books at your local dress fabric store to get other ideas for making different types of stuffed animals.

A

MATERIALS
finished size: 14in (36cm) tall
1 fat quarter (*see p. 210*) in each of four marmalade-colored print cotton fabrics
Steam iron, rotary cutter (*see pp. 212-3*), quilter's ruler, cutting mat
Matching sewing thread, 23in (0.6m) of mediumweight iron-on interfacing
Photocopied pattern, water-erasable pen, blunt instrument
Black embroidery thread
8oz (200g) polyester toy filling
Ribbon and bell to decorate

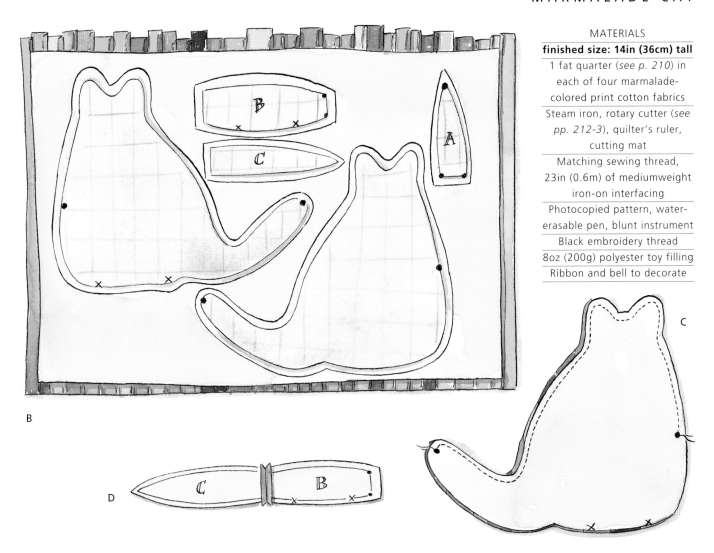

1 Press the four fat quarters together with a steam iron and cut through all layers at once with rotary cutter to make eight strips from each fabric 1½in (4cm) wide and about 22in (56cm) long.

2 Arranging the 32 strips in random order so that no two identical fabrics are adjacent, sew them together to make a "strippy" sheet (*Fig. A*) about 22in x 32in (56cm x 81cm). Use ¼in (6mm) seams throughout. Press seams to one side.

3 Cut out a piece of iron-on interfacing that is slightly smaller in size all round than the strippy sheet and then iron it to the wrong side of the patchwork so that you reinforce it.

4 Enlarge the pattern pieces for the cat by 165% (*see pp. 224-5*) using a photocopier. Trace them onto the wrong (interfacing) side of the patchwork, leaving at least ½in (12mm) between the pieces for seam allowances. The traced line will be your sewing line. Mark the large and small dots and stars (*Fig. B*). Cut out the pieces adding a ¼in (6mm) seam allowance all round.

5 To transfer the cat's face to the patchwork, pin or tape the design under the cat's head and then place the patchwork against a window. Copy the features with a water-erasable pen, then embroider by hand or satin-stitch by machine with some black embroidery thread.

6 Place the cat front and cat back right sides together. Stitch round the body on the sewing lines from the large dot on the front of the cat, over the ears to the dot that is at the tip of its tail (*Fig. C*). Clip the seams at the large dots. Then with right sides together, sew the front gusset (*A in Fig. A*) to the body from the small dots at the base to the large dot placed below the chin. Sew the tail gusset (*C*) to the base of the body (*B*) (*Fig. D*).

7 Cut extra pieces of interlining and iron in place on the front and back of the ears and on the base to reinforce them. Sew the base and tail to the cat's body, matching the dots. Leave a gap between "star" symbols.

8 Clip the seams to the sewing lines and trim closely around the ears and the end of the tail. Turn the cat so that it is right side out and, using a blunt pointed instrument, carefully push out the ears and the end of the tail. Stuff as firmly as possible with the polyester toy filling and then sew up the gap. To finish, decorate your marmalade cat with a pretty ribbon tied in a bow and a bell.

MATERIALS

finished size: about 37in x 44in (94cm x 112cm)

27in (0.7m) of dark-green print cotton fabric for stars

1 fat quarter (*see p. 210*) of brown print cotton fabric

5 9in (24cm) square scraps of very light print cotton fabric

1 fat quarter of large floral print cotton fabric

6 fat quarters in brown and brick-red cotton fabrics, or fabric scraps about 22in (55cm) long for 56 strips 1¾in (4.5cm) wide

9in (0.25m) of dark-green print cotton fabric for first border

18in (0.3m) of very light print cotton fabric for second border plus small brown print cotton scrap for corners

41in (1m) of backing fabric (in a toning color)

41in (1m) of 54in (140cm) wide 2oz (50g) polyester padding

14in (0.35m) of plain dark-green cotton fabric for binding

No. 2 template from the 3-inch set of R.I.T. Squares (*see pp. 224-5*)

White marking pencil and ballpoint pen

Rotary cutter (*see pp. 212-3*)

Quilter's ruler

Cutting mat

Steam iron

Matching sewing thread

WALLED GARDEN HANGING

This beautiful wall hanging in softly colored floral prints makes an eye-catching feature in any living room. It is based on a block pattern called "Ohio Star" and is a scrap quilt in the true sense of the word. You can use as many suitable cotton fabrics as you like—bits left over from dressmaking and second-hand sale bargains are ideal. Try to find fabrics that are of a similar weight, and remember to wash all scrap fabrics first to make sure they don't shrink or run. The "Walled Garden" design only really works successfully if you organize the fabrics so that the darkest tone forms the points of the star in the nine-patch block and the lightest tone creates the little diamonds. Consider the overall color carefully, too.

In the hanging in the photograph, dark-green stars are complemented by rich brick reds and browns. Choose a pretty floral print for the patches in the middle of the blocks. The fabrics specified for the hanging are all 45in (115cm) wide unless otherwise stated.

The Walled Garden hanging is made by the R.I.T. Square method (*see pp. 214-5*), using the 3-inch set. By using a No. 2 template (which is slightly smaller than a No. 3 template) to make a No. 3 patch, the size of the hanging is scaled down to create a more intricate-looking design.

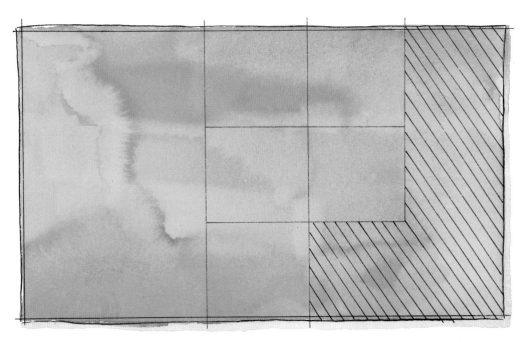

A

1 First make the points of the stars. From the dark-green fabric cut a piece 18in x 27in (46cm x 70cm) (*Fig. A*). Place it right sides together with the brown print fabric. With a marking pencil draw a grid of 20 squares (*Fig. B*). (Note that for this design you are using the No. 2 R.I.T. Square template for No. 3 patches rather than the No. 3 template.)

Sew and cut 80 half-patches with ¼in (6mm) seams (*see p.12*). Press seams with a steam iron toward the darker side.

2 From the dark-green print fabric cut five 9in (23cm) squares (*Fig. A*). Place one piece right sides together with one of the very light print fabric squares. Draw a grid of four squares using the No. 2 R.I.T. Square template as a guide (*Fig. C*). Sew and cut 16 half-patches. Press seams toward darker side. Repeat with other four light print fabric squares to make 80 half-patches.

3 To complete the stars' points, sew together half-patches from Step 1 and Step 2 so that the brown print and light print are

B

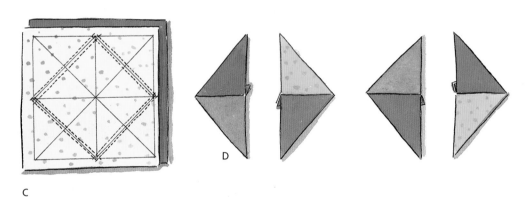

C

D

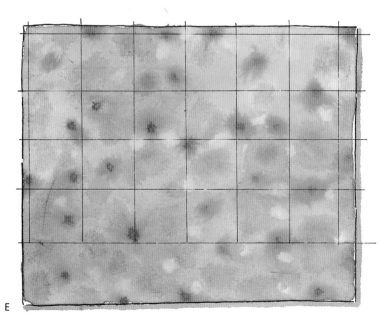

E

always opposite (*Fig. D*). Press seams to one side.

4 Now make middle square of each block. From floral print cut four strips 3⅛in (8cm) wide and 22in (56cm) long (*Fig. E*). From each strip cut five 3⅛in (8cm) squares.

5 Next make "strippy" sheets from brown and red fat quarters or scraps to cut corner squares. Cut 56 strips about 22in (60cm) long, 1¾in (4.5cm) wide. Sew 14 strips together randomly for a strippy sheet about 22in x 19in (60cm x 50cm). Make three more strippy sheets and press seams to one side. "Block" sheets (*see p. 220*) so that strips are straight.

6 From each strippy sheet, cut diagonal strips 3⅛in (8cm) wide (*Fig. F*). From each strip cut 3⅛in (8cm) squares, making sure that a seam runs from corner to corner on each square—you need 80.

7 Next, assemble blocks. Choose a patch with a different light print piece for each No. 3 patch in each block, and a good mix of scraps for each corner. Sew blocks together (*Fig. G*). First sew three patches to form rows and then sew rows together, matching seams. Make 20 blocks, and press.

8 Lay blocks on floor in five rows of four blocks each. Keep rearranging to make a good color balance in the scrap corners. Check that no two identical light prints are adjacent when No. 3 patches are together. Sew blocks together, in rows first, then pin rows, matching up seams. Press and block.

9 From the dark-green print for the first border cut four strips 1½in (4cm) wide. Cut two strips to patchwork's width and sew to top and bottom. Cut two more strips

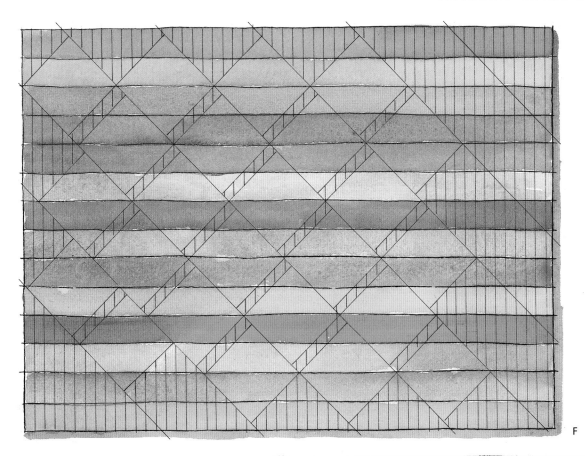

F

to its length and sew one to each side. Press seams outward.

10 From light print fabric for the second border cut four strips 2¾in (7cm) wide. Cut two strips to patchwork's width and two to patchwork's length. Cut four 2¾in (7cm) squares from brown print fabric. Sew two to each end of shorter strips. Sew the two longer strips to each patchwork side and press. Sew two shorter strips to top and bottom, matching corner seams.

11 Make your "quilt sandwich" with padding and backing fabric (*see pp. 220-1*). Quilt by machine around the points of the stars and borders, using the "stitch-in-the-ditch" method (*see p. 219*). Cut four 3in (8cm) strips across dark-green fabric's width for binding and sew on (*see p. 222*).

G

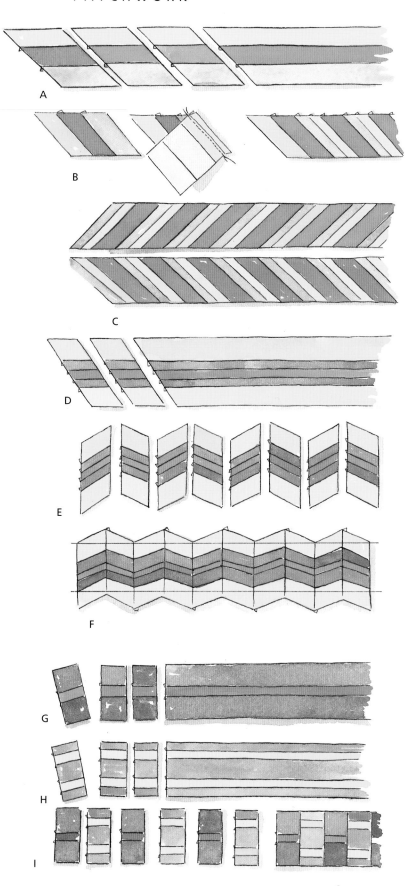

A

B

C

D

E

F

G

H

I

1 Make chevron band as follows. (Ideally use nonmetric measurements throughout this project.) Cut four strips each from the yellow and turquoise fabrics ¾in (2cm) wide and four from the crimson fabric 1in (2.5cm) wide. Sew the strips together to make four strip sets of the three colors as shown in Fig. A. All the seams are ¼in (6mm) unless otherwise noted. Press all seams with a steam iron in one direction and then block strip the sets so that they are perfectly straight.

2 Use your quilter's ruler and rotary cutter to cut the strip sets at a 45° angle and 1¾in (4.5cm) wide (*Fig. A*). Line up the 45° angle line of the ruler to one of the grid lines of your cutting mat for accuracy. Cut two of the strip sets angled toward the right and two angled toward the left. You can cut six pieces from each strip set. Sew the pieces together (*Fig. B*) to make two long bands. Press and block all seams of one band to the right, and those of the other to the left (*Fig. C*).

3 Trim each band to measure 1½in (4cm). Cut off angled section from the right-hand end and sew to the left-hand end to make ends straight. Sew the two bands together, using pins if necessary to make sure the stripes match up. Press middle seam open and block the band. Cut band to 12½in (32cm). From the royal blue fabric, cut two strips 12½in (32cm) long and ¾in (2cm) wide. Sew them both to each side of the chevron band.

4 Make zig-zag band as follows. Cut four strips of yellow fabric 1¼in (3.2cm) wide; four strips of royal blue fabric 1in (2.5cm) wide; and two strips of fuchsia fabric ¾in (2cm) wide. Sew the three colors

together to make two strip sets as shown in Fig. D. Place strips of one set to the right and the other to the left. Press seams of one strip upward and the seams of the other strip downward. Block the strip sets so that they are straight.

5 Cut pieces from strip sets at a 60° angle and 1½in (4cm) wide. Line up 60° angle line of the ruler with one of the grid lines of your cutting mat for accuracy. Cut one of the strip sets angled toward the right and the other angled toward the left. (You can cut the pieces from both strip sets at the same time by placing one upside down on top of the other.) You get about nine pieces from each strip set.

6 Sew pieces together alternately to make the zig-zag band (*Fig. E*). To line up seams, put a pin through ¼in (6mm) away from the raw edges of the pieces exactly where the seams should meet. Trim band exactly ½in (1.3cm) away from the tips of the blue points (*Fig. F*). Press and block band, and then cut to 12½in (32cm). From turquoise fabric, cut two strips 12½in (32cm) long and ¾in (2cm) wide. Sew to each side of the zig-zag band.

7 Make the woven band from two different strip sets as follows. For the first-strip set, cut two strips of turquoise fabric ¾in (2cm) wide, one strip of turquoise fabric 1¼in (3.2cm) wide and two strips of yellow fabric 1in (2.5cm) wide. For the second strip set, cut two strips of royal blue fabric 1½in (4cm) wide and one strip of fuchsia fabric ¾in (2cm) wide. Sew together to make two strip sets as shown in figs. G and H. Press all seams outward from the narrower strips and block strip sets so they are straight.

MATERIALS

**finished size: 12in (30cm)
square**

1 fat quarter (*see p. 8*) each of
yellow, turquoise, crimson,
royal blue, fuchsia, and black
cotton fabrics

Rotary cutter (*see pp. 10–11*)

Quilter's ruler

Cutting mat

Matching sewing thread

Steam iron, pins

54in (1.25m) No.4 piping cord

10in (25cm) black zipper

12in (30cm) square cushion
pad

8 Cut each strip set into pieces
1in (2.5cm) wide as shown in
figs. G and H. Sew pieces together
alternately, taking care that the
fuchsia stripe is in line across the
band (*Fig. I*). Press and block the
band well, then cut to 12½in
(32cm) long.

9 From crimson fabric cut two
strips 12½in (32cm) long and
¾in (2cm) wide. Sew to each side
of woven band. From black fabric
cut two strips 12½in (32cm) long
and 1¼in (3.2cm) wide. Sew
between the three bands as shown
in the photograph. Cut two black
strips 12½in (32cm) long and 2in
(5cm) wide and sew to top and
bottom of the block. Press well.
Trim finished cushion block to
12½in (32cm) square.

10 Cut cushion back and piping
strips from the remaining
black fabric, then prepare the piping
(*see p. 223*) and sew to the
patchwork top with raw edges lined
up. Make up the back with a
zipper opening (*see p. 223*), trim
back to 12½in (34cm) square and
sew back to cushion top. Insert
cushion pad.

ADVANCED LEVEL

SEMINOLE CUSHION

Three different Seminole bands are sewn together to make this bright cushion. Seminole patchwork involves joining long strips of fabric and cutting them into smaller pieces which are then sewn together in various ways to create hundreds of different "band" designs. This technique was developed by the Seminole Indians, a group of native Americans who were forcibly re-settled to swampy areas of Florida in the late nineteenth century. On acquiring hand- or treadle-operated sewing machines around this time, the Seminole women began to create designs or patchwork with brightly dyed cotton fabrics, based on geometric beadwork designs. These were then sewn into garments such as skirts and tops for women and shirts for men. Many items were sold as tourist curios. Contemporary quick-piecing techniques have their roots in Seminole patchwork, but unfortunately Seminole craftswomen had no rotary-cutting equipment to make their job easier!

Save your leftover bits from this project and use them to make pincushions, Christmas cards, Christmas tree ornaments and a Christmas stocking. You can also decorate guest towels, curtains and clothing with Seminole bands. Note that the strips for the pieced bands in the cushion are cut across the width of fat quarters of fabric, so they are all 18in (45cm) long.

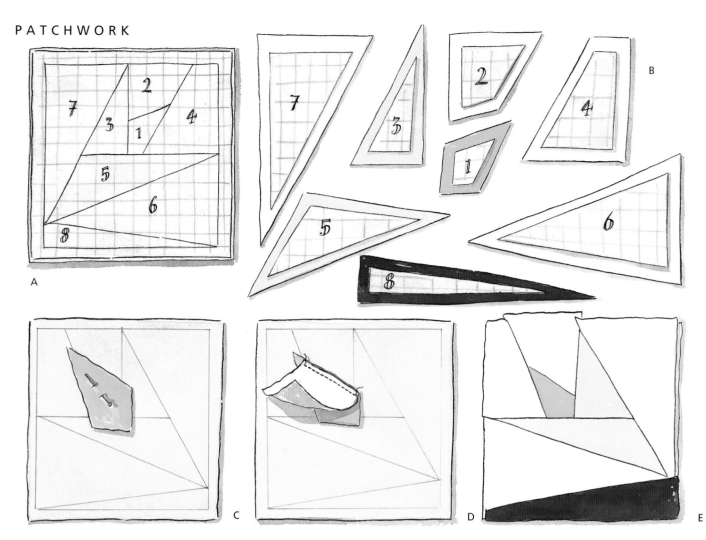

A

B

C

D

E

MATERIALS

(to make two cushions)

finished size: 15in (38cm) square

1 fat quarter (*see p. 210*) each of light- and deep-yellow and white cotton fabric

Big scrap of dark-blue cotton

18in (0.5m) of royal blue cotton fabric for borders and backs

14in (0.6m) white firmly woven cotton fabric for foundations (*see pp. 216-7*)

2 16in (40cm) squares of 2oz (50g) polyester padding

Photocopied design, spray starch

Light box, fine-tipped pen, ruler

Scissors, clear adhesive tape, matching sewing thread

Table lamp, pins, steam iron, 2 12in (30.5cm) matching zippers

3½yd (3.2m) No.4 piping cord

2 15in (38cm) cushion pads

1 Cut eight 7in (18cm) squares of foundation cloth. Enlarge Fig. F to twice its size (200%) on a photocopier to make master design. Transfer onto backs of the cloth foundations with a light box (*Fig. A*), or put on a window. (Tracing is easier if foundations are spray starched.) Number areas as shown.

2 Cut numbered areas of paper master design along lines to make templates. Stick these to reverse side of appropriate colored fabrics using rolled-up tape. For each block cut out eight fabric pieces around paper templates, leaving a seams margin of at least ⅜in (8mm) (*Fig. B*).

3 Remove paper template from Piece 1. Use your table lamp to check that you have correctly

placed the piece right side up on the blank side of the foundation squares so that it covers Area 1. Pin in place (*Fig. C*).

4 Take Piece 2 and, using your lamp to check its position, place it right side down over Piece 1 so that the edge of the paper template is on the line between Areas 1 and 2. Remove the template and then pin Piece 2 in position. From the back of the foundation square (i.e. on the side with the printed lines), sew on that line (*Fig. D*). Remove pin and fold Piece 2 over to cover Area 2. Check with the light that it is correctly positioned. Then fold Piece 2 back over Piece 1 again and trim the seam almost to the sewing line. Fold Piece 2 back over Area 2 and press well.

5 Repeat Step 4 with all eight pieces until first block is complete (*Fig. E*). Sew around block just outside square. Make four blocks in this way for each cushion. Join blocks, matching up seams. Cut strips 2in (5cm) wide and 18in (45cm) long from royal blue fabric. Cut two strips to block's width and sew to top and bottom. Cut two more strips to block's length and sew to sides.

6 Pin patchwork to a square of padding. Quilt around edges of white blocks using the "stitch-in-the-ditch" technique (*see p. 219*). Using deep-yellow fabric, prepare piping and sew to cushion fronts (*see p. 223*). Make up the cushion covers with back material, inserting a back zipper opening (*see p. 223*). Insert cushion pads.

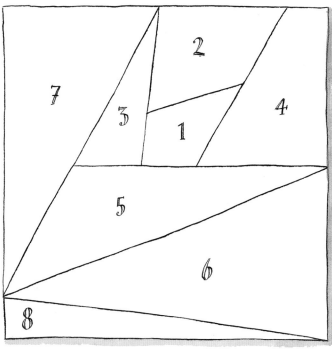

F

WATER LILY FOUNDATION CUSHIONS

These delightful cushions will give a summery atmosphere to any living room or bedroom. Four water lily blocks make up the cushions, pieced using the foundation method (*see pp. 216-7*). A cloth foundation is used here rather than paper, because it adds the extra stability needed for this larger design.

For a smaller project, you could scale the design down by half to make a delightful quilt for a doll's bed. For convenience, set up your work table with a lamp and have a steam iron nearby before you begin the project. All the fabric specified is 45in (115cm) wide unless otherwise stated.

1 Using your vest pattern, cut a left and right front from iron-on interfacing. From the lining fabric cut a left and right front and two backs. Be sure to include seam allowances (*Fig. A*).

2 From your assorted silky scraps, cut a selection of crazy patchwork pieces. The pieces need to be a minimum of 2in (5cm) wide in each direction.

3 Sew the crazy patches to the adhesive side of the two interfacing pieces with ¼in (6mm) seams (*see p. 216*). Place the patches in such a way that there is an interesting balance of colors and prints on both sides (*Fig. B*). Once both interfacing fronts are completely covered with crazy patches, including the seam allowances, press the fronts with a steam iron so that the patches bond with the the interfacing. You can then decorate the crazy patches with top-stitching, or with some hand or machine embroidery (*Fig. C*).

4 Make up the vest's back with lining fabric. Line and finish the vest following the instructions of your pattern.

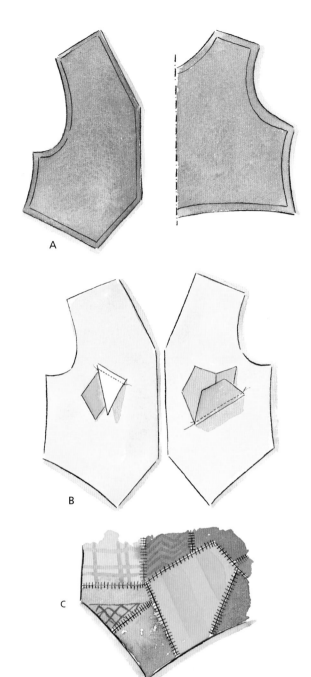

A

B

C

MATERIALS
27in (0.7m) of 35in (90cm) wide medium-weight iron-on interfacing
54in (1.4m) of 45in (115cm) lining fabric
Selection of old silk ties and other silky scraps
Pattern for a lined vest
Rotary cutter (*see pp. 212-3*)
Quilter's ruler
Cutting mat
Matching sewing thread
Steam iron
Vest buckle and buttons (as required)

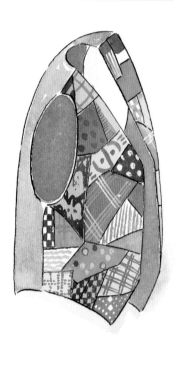

D

CRAZY PATCHWORK VEST

A silk vest instantly adds style to an outfit. If you stitch one in crazy patchwork, you can use all kinds of interesting silky scraps to create a unique and stunning garment. And if your sewing machine is capable of fancy embroidery stitches, then this project will make good use of every one.

The vest illustrated has a crazy patchwork front and a plain back made from lining fabric. Old silk ties are a rich source of suitable patches; alternatively, silk remnants or even lightweight furnishing fabrics will provide you with a wonderful selection of colors and patterns. Check how many silk scraps you will need against the size of paper pattern you are using to make up the vest.

DOROTHY BAG

Named after the bag carried by Dorothy down the Yellow Brick Road in *The Wizard of Oz*, this style of drawstring bag is both attractive and useful. The glamorous version illustrated is ideal for evening use and is made from crazy patchwork using scraps of decorative, shiny fabrics such as old silk ties, brocades, taffetas, and satins. If you want to make a more practical, everyday bag, choose from a selection of pretty, washable, printed cotton fabrics instead.

1 From interfacing and lining fabrics, cut two 12in (30cm) squares. From the interfacing cut one 7in (18cm) diameter circle, and from the lining cut two matching circles.

2 From fabric scraps, cut a few crazy patches, about 2in (5cm) wide in each direction. Sew onto adhesive side of interfacing squares with ¼in (6mm) seams (*see p. 216*). Continue, adding contrasting patches (*Fig. A*), until interfacing squares and seam allowances are covered. Press with warm iron to bond the patches with the interfacing. Decorate all the edges of the crazy patches with some embroidery stitches. Trim patchwork to same size as interfacing.

3 Mark large and small dots on wrong side of the two crazy patchwork pieces. With right sides together, join side seams up to large dots, taking a ⅝in (1.5cm) seam (*Fig. B*). Reinforce stitching at large dots and clip seams. Press seams open. Stay-stitch ⅝in (1.5cm) around lower edge and clip up to stitches (*Fig. B*). Mark halfway points between side seams. Repeat with two lining pieces.

A

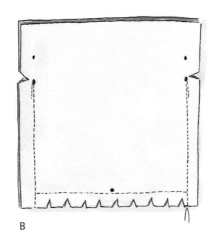

B

C

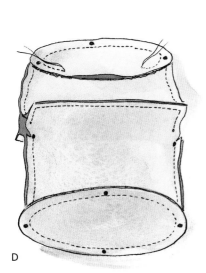

D

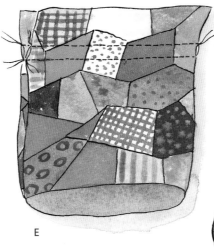

E

F

4 Iron the interfacing circle to the wrong side of one lining circle. Mark the quarter points of the circle (*Fig. C*). With crazy patchwork bag wrong sides out, place on base with the right sides together, matching quarter marks with the side seams and the halfway marks. Stitch the bag to the base just inside the stay-stitching and press well. Sew bag lining to base in same way, but with a 3in (8cm) opening (*Fig. D*).

5 With the bag and the lining inside out, place the flaps of the bag right sides together with lining flaps. Face the flaps by sewing around the three sides of the top as far as the small dots, taking a ⅝in (1.5cm) seam (*Fig. D*). Trim the seams and clip corners. Pull crazy patchwork bag through the opening in lining base and press flaps. Sew up lining opening. With a water-erasable pen, mark stitching lines for channels for the pull-ties on each side of the gaps in the side seams (*Fig. E*). Stitch carefully along the marked lines.

6 To make the drawstrings, cut two pieces from the lining or silky fabric 2in (5cm) wide and 24in (60cm) long. Fold the strips in half lengthwise, then open out and press raw edges up to the pressed line. Fold the strip in half again with the raw edges enclosed, fold in the ends and machine down both sides. With the bodkin, feed ends of one tie through both channels of the bag (*Fig. F*). Feed the ends of the other tie through both channels from other side. Tie together.

MATERIALS

finished size: about 11in (28cm) high

Selection of fabric scraps

12in (0.3m) of 35in (90cm) wide mediumweight iron-on interfacing

12in (0.5m) of 60in (152cm) wide matching polyester lining fabric

Rotary cutter (*see pp. 212-3*)

Quilter's ruler

Cutting mat

Matching sewing thread

Iron

Water-erasable pen

Bodkin

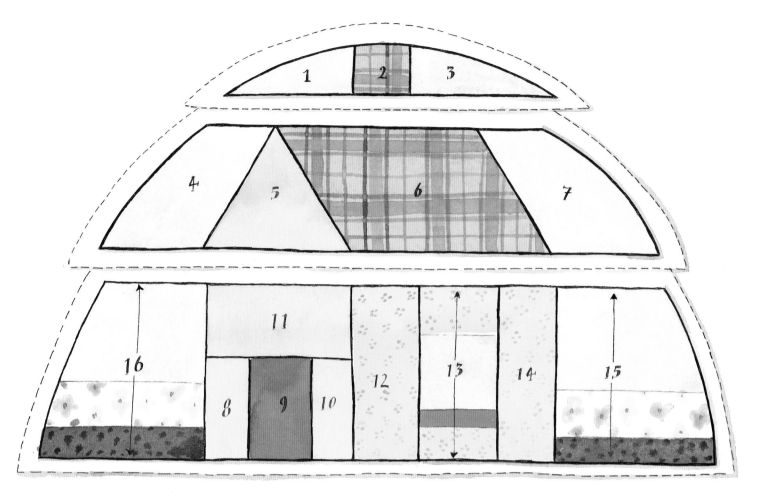

MATERIALS

**finished size: 7in x 13½in
(18cm x 34cm)**

Cotton scraps for "cottage" foundation block: blue for sky and window; light-yellow and mid-yellow prints for walls; red print for door and windowsill; dark-green print for grass; floral print for garden; lace for curtain

1 fat quarter (*see p. 210*) of brown plaid cotton fabric for roof and cozy back, 1 fat quarter of lining fabric (in a toning color)

Photocopied design, greaseproof paper for foundation, scissors, clear adhesive tape, matching sewing thread, steam iron

15in x 24in (40cm x 60cm) piece of 4oz (100g) padding, 1yd (0.9m) of 1in (2.5cm) gray bias binding, button for doorknob

1 Scale up above pattern to 182% onto white paper or enlarge it on a photocopier. This design fits a standard four-cup teapot. If your teapot needs a bigger cozy, just draw or photocopy the "dome" shape to the required size and scale up the cottage to fit. Trace the design from your photocopy onto waxed paper. Be sure to number each area and make a note of which color fabric will cover it. Cut your photocopy into template pieces on the heavy lines, cutting Pieces 13, 15 and 16 as one piece. Cut the waxed foundation into three parts on the dotted lines.

2 Using rolled-up adhesive tape, stick the back of the templates to the right sides of the appropriate fabrics. Cut out fabric around the

templates, leaving a margin of ½in (1.3cm) all around. Leave templates in place until you need the pieces. (Stick on the templates of Pieces 13, 15 and 16 at Steps 4 and 5.)

3 Sew together the three pieces of Part I and then the four pieces of Part II following the instructions for Foundation Piecing on pages 216-7. Press pieces in place with a steam iron and sew around the perimeter, but do not remove the paper foundations yet.

4 Part III is more complicated because you need to pre-piece Areas 13, 15 and 16 before they are pieced to the foundation paper. (All pre-pieced bits are sewn together with ¼in [6mm] seams.) To make Area 13 (the window), cut a 2in (5cm) square

of light blue. Sew a tiny ¾in (2cm) wide strip of red print fabric to one side and press. Pin a lace scrap to the window. Sew a 1½in (4cm) wide strip of mid-yellow to the top of the window to hold lace in place. Sew another strip of mid-yellow 1in (2.5cm) wide to below the windowsill. Press. Stick template 13 to the back of the whole piece. Now sew Area 13 to Area 12 in the usual way. Sew on Area 14.

5 To make Areas 15 and 16, cut three strips about 8in (20cm) long: light blue 2¼in (6cm) wide; light floral print 1½in (4cm) wide; and dark-green print 1¼in (3.5cm) wide. Sew together to make a strip-set. Cut in half, stick on appropriate template 15 or 16 and sew remaining pieces to the

foundation. Stitch around the whole of Part III to hold the pieces in place and then press. Sew Parts I, II and III together on the sewing lines, taking care that you match up the roof's corners accurately with the sides of the house.

6 Cut a strip of dark-green print fabric that is about 14in (35cm) long and 2in (5cm) wide. Sew the strip below the house and press well. Tear away all of the paper foundation, dampening it first with water.

7 To make the loop for the "chimney," cut out a square of roof fabric that is about 3½in (9cm) x 3½in (9cm). Fold in the raw edges to make a strip about 1in (2.5cm) wide. Stitch along the edges on both sides.

8 From the brown plaid fabric, cut a back to the same size as the cozy front (be sure to include the seam allowance). Cut two pieces for lining, and two pieces of padding to match. Fold the chimney in half and pin in position upside down on the cottage roof. Lay the cottage block and the back wrong side down on the pieces of padding and zig-zag around the edges. Place front and back right sides together and sew around dome shape, using a ½in (1.3cm) seam. Sew the two lining pieces together in the same way. Press.

9 Put the lining inside the cozy and then bind around the lower edge with the bias binding to finish. Tack the lining to the inside of the roof and sew on a tiny button for a door handle.

COTTAGE TEA COZY

If you enjoy creating pictures with patchwork, you can have fun making this useful kitchen accessory, which is filled with a thick layer of padding to keep your tea hot in the pot. The same design could be repeated in square blocks to make a delightful crib quilt. Use the foundation piecing method (*see pp. 216-7*), working on a paper foundation, such as waxed paper, which can easily be removed when the patchwork design is complete.

263

DRIED FLOWERS

*MATERIALS AND
TECHNIQUES*

MATERIALS AND TECHNIQUES

At the start of each project there is a list of materials used in that arrangement, including such things as moss, raffia, and various types of dried flowers. Flower names given are, generally, those most commonly used by florists.

Dried flowers normally come in bunches of 10 stems, but this does vary depending on the supplier. As a guide, when making an arrangement you need just one bunch of each flower type, but this does depend on the container size you are using. Before starting, make certain you have sufficient flowers for your intended arrangement and also check that additional flowers can be readily obtained if necessary.

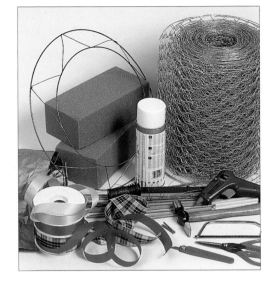

WIRING LOTUS SEED HEADS

Lotus seed heads are often used in arrangements. Take a stub wire and pierce the side of a seed head. Push the wire all the way through and check that an even amount protrudes from either side. Bring both legs down to the pointed end of the seed head and twist the ends of the wire together. The seed head is now ready to be used in an arrangement (*see box opposite*).

GENERAL EQUIPMENT

- Florist's foam for securing flowers
- Mesh wire for making shapes
- Ribbons for bows and decorations
- Canes and wires for fixing and supports
- Hammer, saw, scissors, and knife for cutting and fixing
- Ready-made frames for wreaths
- Spray paints for special effects

USING A GLUE GUN

You will find a glue gun invaluable, and one has been used in most of the projects in this book, mainly to stick flower heads into position. Stub wires can be used for this purpose, but it takes longer and is very fussy. When a wire is essential, this is indicated in the text. Take care when using a glue gun since the glue does become very hot. Wipe any off your skin immediately with a damp cloth. Children using one should always be supervised. Threads of glue from the gun may trail over your arrangement. If so, wait for them to dry and carefully pick them off. A hobby glue gun costs about as much to buy as a bunch of dried flowers.

COLOR HARMONY AND CONTRAST

Choice of flower and foliage color is crucial in setting the right mood. You can be bold here, opting for strong color contrasts or go for subtle shadings within a more restricted color range, such as the blue of the larkspur and lavender graduating into the blue-pink of the statice. This color combination forms a link in the flowers seen here (*right*), allowing the vibrant yellow of the thistles to sit in close proximity to the strong red and peach of the roses. After cutting the flower stems to the right size for an arrangement, don't discard the stems. The foliage can often be used as an integral part of a design, providing a strong green that is difficult to find without having to purchase expensive dried or stabilized foliage.

MATERIALS FOR TEXTURE AND STRUCTURE

In many of the arrangements you will see in this chapter, flowers have been used only as one element of the design. Other materials commonly used, principally for their textural qualities, are pictured here (*right*). Mosses of different types, for example, natural-fiber sackcloth and natural raffia all seem to have a close affinity with dried flowers, and so they are often used to provide those important finishing touches that help both to show off the flowers to best advantage as well as to disguise the underlying florist's foam, stub wires and so on. Cinnamon sticks are also sometimes used, as are the contorted shapes of willow and strips of bark, and these are all invaluable in giving extra form and structure.

TIPS FOR WIRING

● Wrap a stub wire around the middle of the stems of a bunch of flowers, such as lavender, and twist the ends together making sure to leave them long enough to attach to an arrangement.

● Take care not to crack a lotus seed head when twisting the wire together.

● To wire a pine cone, wrap a long stub wire right around the gap in between the lower tiers of seeds, bring the ends of the wire down and twist them together securely. Make sure to leave the ends of the wire long enough to act as a fixing. The pine cone is now ready to be used in an arrangement.

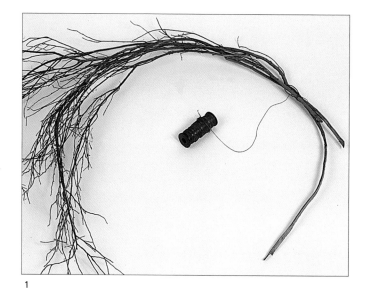

1

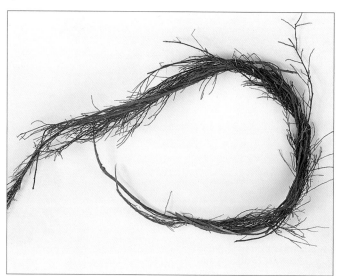

2

3

PREPARING A TWIG WREATH

MATERIALS

Chinese willow branches
(other twig wreaths in this
chapter are made from birch)

Reel wire

Scissors

1 Soak your chosen branches in water overnight, or longer if they are really dry. Take a thin branch and gently bend it into a curve. Use only naturally supple branches for wreath making. Wire another curved branch a little way down from the end of the first. Use lengths of thin, strong wire, known as reel wire, to bind the branches together.

2 Bind more and more branches together, elongating the overall curve until you have sufficient to form the size circle you require for your wreath. Don't always think too big, a wreath can be quite small.

3 Hold the ends of the branches together to form the required size of circle and bind the ends together with reel wire. Tuck the ends underneath into the circle and wind them around the other branches. Form more lengths of branches in the same way and wind them around the circle of branches you have already made. Repeat this until you attain the required thickness for your wreath. Bind all around the wreath with reel wire, securing all the ends, to form a smooth outline. Eventually you can attach the wreath to a wall by making a wire loop secured to the twigs.

WIRE AND MOSS WREATHS OR SHAPES

MATERIALS

Mesh wire

Sphagnum moss

Reel wire

Scissors

1 Making a wreath base to work on out of mesh wire and moss is not difficult, and by using the same technique you can make any base shape you wish. First, cut a length of mesh wire to size. You can cut the width down, too, if necessary, or join widths of mesh wire together if required. Stitch the pieces of mesh wire together with reel wire. Take your mesh wire and start to fill it with handfuls of sphagnum moss.

2 Fill the desired area with sphagnum moss and then roll or bend the mesh wire over to form an outer skin containing the moss inside. Mold the mesh wire into the shape and size you require by firmly squeezing it with both hands.

3 To make a wreath, roll the mesh wire into a log shape and then bring the two ends up to meet each other. Stitch the ends together using reel wire. You will need to leave the moss to dry out for about a week (depending on the weather conditions). When the moss has completely dried out, you can fix the wreath to a wall with a wire loop attached to the mesh wire.

1

2

3

TIPS

● For a twig wreath, choose your materials carefully. Branches that are too thick will not happily form a tight curve.

● Branches become pliable if soaked in warm water.

● For a wire wreath or shape, cut away excess mesh wire before shaping.

● Wear thick gloves when shaping mesh wire.

PREPARING A WIRE FRAME WREATH

MATERIALS
Wreath frame
Reel wire
Sphagnum moss
Wire cutters

1 Wire frame wreaths are readily available from dried flower specialists as well as many ordinary florists. To start preparing one for use, secure some reel wire to one of the supporting struts, wrap the wire around the strut and then twist the two ends firmly together.

2 Take handfuls of sphagnum moss and bind them securely on to the wreath frame, again using lengths of reel wire. Methodically work your way around the wreath in this fashion.

3 Once you have covered the frame, you will probably need to go over the shape again, filling in places that look a bit thin with more moss. Don't overfill the frame with moss, however, or bind it too tightly on to the frame, or you may find it impossible to push the stems of your flowers into position. Once you are satisfied with the shape of your wreath, finish by securing the wire to the frame and snip off any exposed ends with the cutters. When the moss has dried out, which may take a week or more, decorate the wreath with your chosen flowers. Attach a wire loop to the frame to act as a hanger.

TIPS

● You can obtain wreath frames from florists in many different sizes and shapes.

● If you don't allow the moss to dry out thoroughly, which may take a week or more, trapped moisture will rapidly cause the dried flowers to rot.

● If necessary, heat moss in a barely warm oven to speed up the drying process.

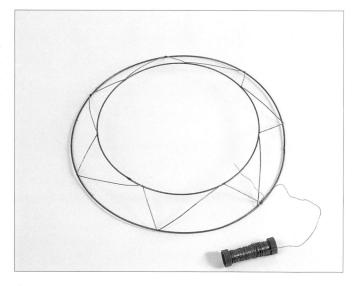

1

2

3

PREPARING A FOAM BLOCK FOR A WALL-MOUNTED ARRANGEMENT

MATERIALS
Florist's foam block
Mesh wire
Reel wire
Wire cutters

1 Take a block of florist's foam and a length of mesh wire, cut so that it is just long enough to wrap around the block. To gauge how long it should be, bend the mesh wire into lengths that correspond to the dimensions of the four sides of the block. Now you will be able to fashion the shape out of mesh wire without actually wrapping it around the foam. If you do wrap the wire around the block to make the shape, you are likely to cut it to pieces. Next, open up the mesh-wire shape and simply slot your block of florist's foam into position.

2 Once you have wrapped the prefolded mesh wire around the block, secure it together with the ends of the cut wire. Lace these over with a pair of cutters or scissors to save your fingers.

3 Now fold in the ends neatly as if wrapping a parcel. Make a wire loop out of reel wire and attach it to the mesh wire ready for hanging on a wall.

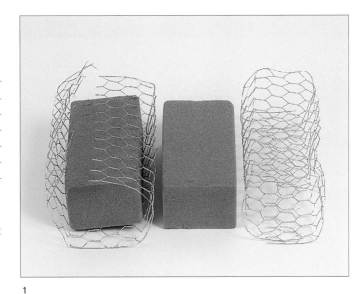

1

2

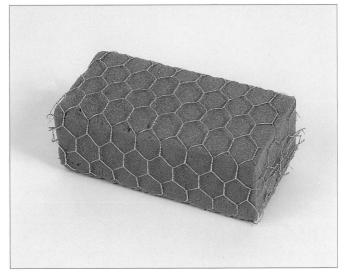

3

PREPARING A TRUNK AND CONTAINER

MATERIALS

Tree trunk

Container

Plastic bag

Mesh wire

Quick-drying cement

Bucket and water

Stirring stick

Scissors

Moss

Glue and glue gun

1

2

1 Take your diminutive trunk and place it in a container. Hold it upright with one hand and squash in mesh wire until it stands by itself. Level the trunk by eye not with a bubble level, since it will look false if perfectly straight.

2 Make up some quick-drying cement with water in a container, such as a bucket. Mix it thoroughly with a stick. Once the mixture is ready, pour it into the prepared container with its tree trunk. Be careful not to splash the cement on to the trunk or dribble it on the rim or outside of the container. If your container is, for example, a terra cotta flowerpot as pictured here, cover the drainage hole in the bottom with a piece of plastic bag. This will prevent the cement running out before it has had time to harden. The mesh wire will bond with and reinforce the cement. Wait for the cement to dry hard—overnight is preferable— and then glue on moss to cover the surface of the cement.

PREPARING A BASKET

MATERIALS

Basket

Florist's foam

Strong knife

Scissors

Stub wire

Glue and glue gun or other strong adhesive

Moss

1

2

1 Fill a basket with foam cut to size. Take stub wires, bend them to form hairpin shapes and push them through the weave to secure the foam in place. You may sometimes have to glue the foam to the bottom of the basket for extra strength. For some arrangements the foam will need to stand just above the rim of the basket so that you can arrange flowers horizontally. Other arrangements will require the surface of the florist's foam to be level with the rim of the basket or container or even a little lower than the rim to leave some room for the addition of moss on top.

2 Now the foam is in place, choose moss to coordinate with your arrangement, and sprinkle it over the foam. Bend stub wires into hairpin shapes and push them into the foam to hold the moss in position. Use only the minimum of stub wires to do this; bear in mind that the flower stems of your arrangement piercing the moss will also help to hold it securely. Make sure the moss is not too damp to use for flower arranging. Leave it to dry out a little. Some moss, such as lichen and reindeer moss, will dry to a hard, stiff texture. Use these mosses damp but never wet.

MAKING A BOW

MATERIALS
Ribbon

Scissors

To make a bow, take a length of ribbon in one hand. Your free hand should be your dominant hand. Hold the ribbon with its shiny side toward you between your thumb and first finger. Leave a tail of ribbon that is a little longer than the desired loops of the bow hanging down. Take the ribbon above your thumb and first finger and twist it so the dull side is now facing you. Loop the ribbon around and back into the grip of your thumb and first finger. Ensure that the shiny side of the ribbon comes back over to face you. Gather the ribbon together and twist again so that the tail has its dull side to you. Bring the tail in a loop up to meet your thumb and first finger. Bring the shiny side around to face you again and, as you do this, make a loop the same size as the first loop. Imagine a horizontal line crossing between the loops at the point of your finger and thumb. Every even number of loops should stay below this line and every odd number above it. Carry on making loops until the bow is the size you wish. Now cut off the last tail, a little longer than the loops. Tie a length of ribbon along the imaginary horizontal line. Now, using this length of ribbon, secure the bow to the pot, basket, or other container you are working on. If you wish, cut "V" shapes into the tails to finish them off. If texture is your most important consideration, you can make a far simpler bow from strands of raffia, as shown here.

TIPS

● When preparing a basket, use just sufficient moss to cover the foam, not so much that you can't easily push the flower stems through it once it has dried out.

● When making a bow, you can tie a ribbon around an object, leaving the ties long. Place a pre-made bow between the ties and secure it with a knot.

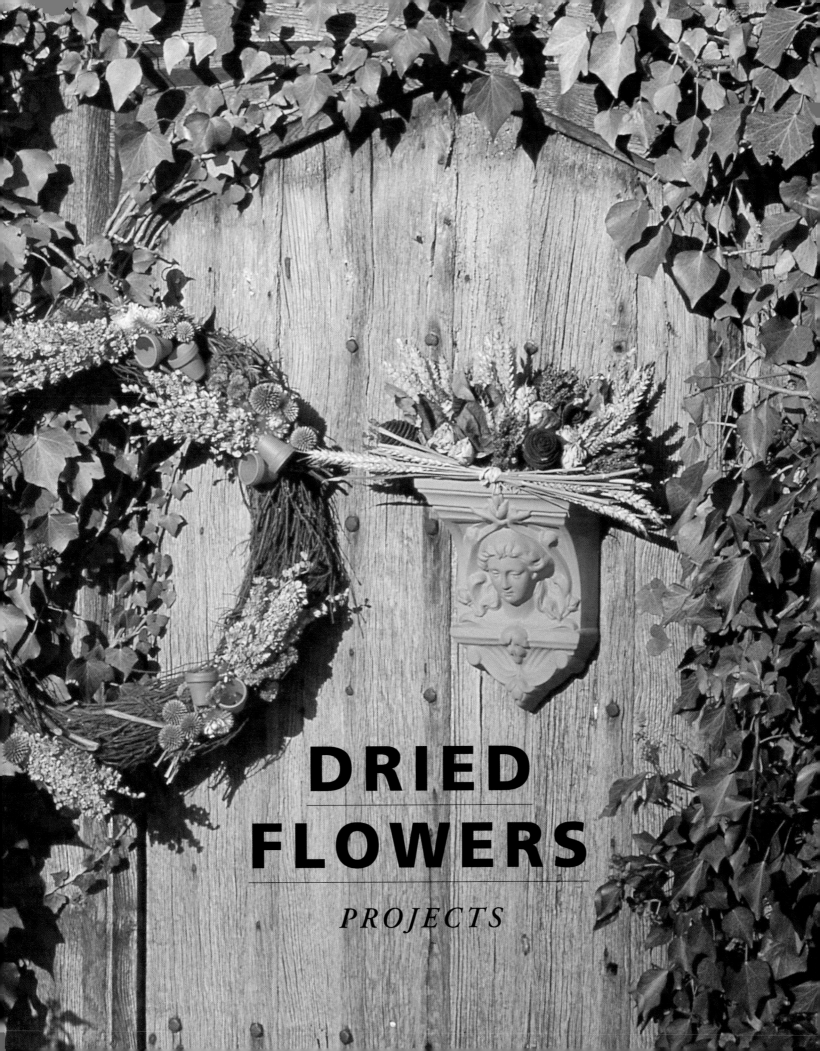

DRIED
FLOWERS

PROJECTS

1 Take a prepared twig wreath (*see pp. 266-73*). Then select five bunches of pink larkspur, cutting the stems short, up to about 9in (23cm), and strip away any excess flower heads. Attach the bunches to the wreath using stub wires.

2 Using the glue gun, secure the miniature flowerpots to the larkspur. Arrange them in groups so that they cover the stub wires around the flower stems.

3 Carefully cut the pink helichrysum heads from their stems and glue just the flowers all around the flowerpots.

4 As the finishing touches, add the flower heads of the pale-blue statice (limonium sinuata) and the eryngium, using the glue gun to attach them securely to the twigs of the wreath.

1

2

3

4

MATERIALS
Prepared wreath
Stub wire
Glue and glue gun
Miniature flowerpots
Pink larkspur
Pink helichrysum
Blue statice
Eryngium

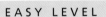

EASY LEVEL

TWIG WREATH

Making wreaths from twigs can be far easier than you would imagine. You need to use supple branches, such as birch or, as used here, Chinese willow (*see also pp. 266-73*).

A wreath such as this can look very eye-catching and most fetching when left in its natural state. However, you can turn it into something really special with the addition of dried flowers, either wired into the weave or glued on to the twigs. Simplicity is the key to this project's success, so keep the design uncluttered and let as much of the branches show through as possible.

This wreath has been decorated with flowers in the pinks and blues of summer. The bright pinks of larkspur and helichrysum against the blue of the eryngium heads and statice encapsulate the essence of a hot summer's day. The flowers have been arranged in five main groupings, each in a different array, to create a random, almost haphazard collection around the wreath. The miniature flowerpots strewn among the flowers help to bring the piece to a visual culmination.

1

2

3

4

1 Take a block of florist's foam and cut it to a size and shape that will fit inside the the vase. Spread glue on the edges of the foam and slide it firmly into the vase. Hold it tightly for a few moments while the glue sets. Take some gray reindeer moss or lichen moss and cover the foam. There is no need to pin the moss, since the flower stems will secure it in place.

2 Hold up the protea to the prepared container to judge the stem length required. Arrange the heads in a staggered formation.

3 Next, make up bundles of wheat. Cut them down to size and wire them with stub wire. Leave the ends of the wire pointing downward and use them to secure the bunches in the foam. You can also gather the stems in your hand, cut them to size and push them into the foam without wiring them. Now make the horizontal double-ended bunch for the front. This must be wired in place. Use raffia to hide the wire.

4 Arrange the Gerdo roses, utilizing the natural foliage of the stems. Place the roses in small groups throughout the wheat and protea, and then take some small bunches of lavender and finish off the arrangement by filling in any empty spaces.

MATERIALS
Terra cotta vase
Florist's foam
Glue and glue gun
Reindeer moss or lichen moss
Stub wires
Natural raffia
Protea
Wheat
Gerdo roses
Lavender

EASY LEVEL

WALL VASE

This terra cotta replica of an old-fashioned wall molding lends itself beautifully to an arrangement of dried flowers. You may be able to find a similar vase in a garden depot, since this one was designed originally as a wall planter. The wheat featured in this project is symbolic of good fortune and plenty, and it is reminiscent of the times when the harvest meant food-filled days. Tailor your selection of flowers to include a variety of textures and colors. Notice how the protea used in this arrangement contrasts with the wheat, while the lavender echoes its shape and texture.

There are many suitable containers for this project, but ones made of natural materials always seem to work well with dried flowers.

1 Take a piece of rigid backing board and mirrored glass cut to a slightly smaller to size. Using large mirror clips, secure the mirror to the board. Screw two large-headed screws into the back of the backing board and secure a wire around the screws to make a firm hanger. Don't wait to do this until after the flowers have already been arranged, since you are then bound to cause some damage to the blooms.

2 Now cut strips of florist's foam to fit right around the outside of the glass. Glue the foam securely to the backing board, making sure that the foam is higher than the glass surface of the mirror and that it is amply thick enough to accommodate the flower stems.

3 Proceed by arranging the hydrangea heads in a massed formation around the mirror to create the frame. Cover all of the foam and ensure that the edges of the frame are also well covered so that no backing board is visible. Look from every angle from time to time to check that coverage is even. Use the glue gun to secure the stems in the foam. When you have covered all of the mirror frame and edges in this fashion, take your roses and position them among the hydrangea heads, pushing and gluing the stems securely into the foam. Arrange them in small groups around the mirror, as you see illustrated in the main picture opposite.

1

2

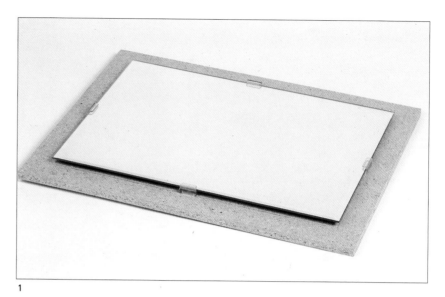

3

EASY LEVEL

HYDRANGEA MIRROR

The deep, rich, heady notes of this design are reminiscent of the full-blooded qualities of a good Burgundy. These regal tones predominate in the hydrangea, blending into lighter, softer pinks and grayish greens.

The collection of red roses and hydrangeas is a perfect foil for the cool stillness of the mirror. Hydrangea blooms are available from most florists, and when in season they can be bought fresh for home drying. Or if you have a large hydrangea bush in the garden, you could save some of the expense of this project. If you want to do it yourself, pick the hydrangeas just after the blooms have reached their prime, and hang them upside down in a dry, cool, well-ventilated room. To ensure a good circulation of air, avoid bunching too many together.

An alternative method of drying is to place them in a vase so that the air can circulate all around their heads. Leave them in the vase with their stems in just a little water—when the water has evaporated, leave the hydrangeas to dry out completely.

MATERIALS
Rigid backing board
Mirrored glass
Mirror clips
Screws and screwdriver
Reel wire
Glue and glue gun
Florist's foam
Hydrangea heads
Paso Doble roses
Jaguar roses

1 Take two plastic containers, sized so that one will fit easily inside the other. You can choose between square tubs (as shown here) or cylindrical ones. This concept works equally well with any shape of container.

2 Cover the outside of the larger of the two containers with green reindeer moss. Glue the moss on to the plastic with a glue gun or any strong adhesive. Cover the container all the way up to the top edge, overlapping it slightly. This will ensure that when the fresh flowers are arranged in the inner container none of the base material will be visible.

3 Now, using bright yellow helichrysum, start to decorate the moss. Group the heads around the container in a random fashion, gluing them into position as you did the moss.

4 Place the smaller container inside the outer one. Fill the inner container with water, leaving enough room for the stems of your fresh-flower arrangement without the water overflowing and wetting the dried flowers.

MATERIALS

Two plastic containers—one large, one smaller

Glue and glue gun

Green reindeer moss

Yellow helichrysum heads

1

2

3

4

EASY LEVEL

CONTAINER FOR FRESH FLOWERS

This container for fresh flowers has been designed with the participation of children in mind. With very little preparation or adult supervision, a young child could be involved right from the start in making this attractive and practical container. You may want to use the technique described here yourself as a springboard for your own ideas.

This container consists of two plastic tubs. These need to be of different sizes so that one easily fits inside the other. Make sure there is enough room for you to be able to get your fingers between the two and then to lift the smaller one out at any time.

It is this smaller tub that will eventually become the receptacle for the fresh flowers and water, and you will have to lift and clean it whenever the fresh flowers have gone past their best and have been thrown away. It is important to include this inner tub, otherwise the dried flowers used on the outer one would soon spoil due to the continued handling and cleaning.

283

1 Plant the amaryllis bulb in a suitable terra cotta flowerpot, or any container of your choice. Cover the compost completely with bun moss. Break up some bark into interesting shapes and glue it to the sides of the pot. Position the bark a little higher than the rim of the flowerpot. Then proceed to cover the sides of the pot completely with broken pieces of bark.

2 Bind the bark with lengths of natural raffia. Knot the raffia securely, leaving the ties quite long. When you cut the raffia ends, cut each strand to a different length to give an interesting and varied finish. Now take more bun moss and glue in on to any parts of the terra cotta container that are still visible between the pieces of bark. Next, start to build the support structure. Place four lengths of pussy willow deep into the compost. Make sure that the supports are all the same length. If your amaryllis is showing just a small shoot, you will have to use your judgment regarding its mature height and perhaps make adjustments as it grows.

3 Finish off the structure with horizontal struts of willow. Wire them together and bind them with raffia at the joins. Decorate the base with poppy seed heads, attaching them with a glue gun or any strong adhesive.

1

EASY LEVEL

AMARYLLIS BULB HOLDER

An amaryllis in bloom is breathtaking. Before it flowers, however, its allure is less evident. This uninteresting stage in the growth can't be totally disguised, since concealing the growing shoot from sight would mean depriving it of the light it needs to develop. It seems distraction is the answer.

First you need to plant your bulb in a terra cotta pot with its growing shoot showing. The decorative moss used here is bun moss. It is important to use a container with adequate drainage to stop the bulb becoming waterlogged. The structure around the amaryllis is intended both to protect and guide the shoot as it grows, but once the plant is heavy with blooms it will also act as a very effective support.

2

3

MATERIALS

Amaryllis bulb
Potting compost
Terra cotta flowerpot
Bun boss
Bark
Glue and glue gun
Natural raffia
Reel wire
Pussy willow
Poppy seed heads

1 Take a prepared basket in the shape of a heart (*see pp. 266-73*). This basket has been pulled into a better shape with reel wire. Cut the florist's foam to the shape of the basket and gently push it on to the reel wire. This will leave an indentation showing where you have to cut the cross. It would be wasteful to cover the foam with moss, since the rose heads will be so close together you should not be able to see any of the foam between them.

2 Take some red Mercedes roses and cut down the stems. Push the shortened stems of the roses into the foam and form the outline of the heart with the flower heads arranged very close together.

3 Fill in the middle of the heart with more rose heads. Make sure that you keep them all level with each other.

4 Once the basket is full with roses, tuck some reindeer or lichen moss under the heads of the outer roses. You can glue the moss securely into position if necessary with a glue gun.

1

2

3

4

MATERIALS
Basket
Reel wire
Glue and glue gun
Florist's foam
Mercedes roses
Natural reindeer moss or lichen moss

EASY LEVEL

VALENTINE BASKET

As St. Valentine's Day becomes increasingly popular, it gets harder and harder to find fresh gift ideas to exchange as love tokens on February 14. But what could be more romantic than to give somebody your very own heart?

This project is simple to construct and, once you have obtained all the materials required, it is also quick to make. The basket itself was no trouble to find, but its shape needed defining a little. This was done with reel wire, threaded through the weave of the basket and attached at the opposite side. The edges were then pulled closer together at certain points to create a much stronger heart-shaped outline.

Massed flower heads have been incorporated into many of the designs featured in this book. And here it is the Mercedes roses that bring the heart-shaped basket to life with color.

You could give this basket as a present to your Valentine, or you could just as easily use it as a table centerpiece for an intimate, candle-lit dinner on this most romantic of all days.

1

2

3

4

MATERIALS
Prepared basket
Stub wires
Natural raffia
Green carpet moss
Lavender
Yellow thistles
Sunflowers
Yellow helichrysum
Achillea

1 Prepare a flat, open trug basket (*see pp. 266-73*). Take a bunch of long-stemmed lavender, bind it with natural raffia and tie it in a knot. Leave the ties long. Ensure that the lavender is long enough to overhang the basket in both directions. Secure the horizontal bunch in position with a few stub wires pushed deep into the florist's foam.

2 Take some yellow thistles and cut their stems in half. Take the flowering halves and position them in a pleasing configuration close to the lavender. Arrange the other half of the stems at a corresponding angle in the other side of the foam. To the eye, it should seem that they are lying in one continuous piece. Now repeat this process with the sunflowers. Cut off the thick leaves from the bottom of the stems and use them to surround the sunflower heads.

3 Now take a bunch of bright yellow helichrysum and tie it with a small raffia bow. Take the bunch and secure it with a stub wire into the foam. Position the bunch next to the stem ends of the lavender, allowing the handle to make a natural division through the lavender and helichrysum, separating them and the basket into two different sections.

4 In the remaining part of the basket, arrange the achillea to look as if they, too, are lying sideways. Fill out this last portion of the basket with the large heads of the achillea overhanging the edges.

GROUPED BASKET

At first glance, this basket looks as though somebody has been walking in a beautiful garden at the height of summer, picked bunches of their favorite flowers and laid them in a basket to dry. This is exactly the effect you want to achieve.

In fact, only the lavender and yellow helichrysum are tied in bunches—the others are set in foam to look like bunches. Setting the bottom of the stems into the other side of the foam gives the impression that the stems are continuous. By doing this, you can arrange the flower heads in exactly the position you want—and they will stay put. It also enables you to leave some space around the heads, making the basket seem more abundant than it really is. Use the foliage from the sunflowers by placing the leaves in the foam around the sunflower heads.

The yellow and blue work together extremely well and the green of the carpet moss enhances the foliage of the flowers. A rustic basket has been used to give a rural look to the design.

1

2

3

4

1 Prepare a frame with moss (*see pp. 266-73*). Take strips of natural-fiber sackcloth and secure them to the frame with stub wires. Distribute the hessian evenly around the ring in three sections. Make soft folds in the material to give it shape and presence.

2 Concentrate the heads of achillea into five main areas, pushing their strong stems firmly into the moss. Next, take lotus seed heads and wire them as shown here. Take a thick stub wire and push it through the soft sides of the head. Once the wire is halfway through, carefully bend it, bringing both ends of the wire downward at the same time. Keep the legs of the stub wire straight. Hold the lotus head in one hand and, with your other, twist the wire together. Now push the wire through the mossed frame, bringing it out the back of the frame. Pull the wire through from the other side so that the lotus head is pulled into position. Now bend the wires back into the moss and attach them to the frame. Group more of the lotus heads around the wreath using this same technique. Position them at various different angles to show them off to their best advantage.

3 Mass poppy seed heads into the wreath. They have strong stems and so don't need wires. Form them into three principal groups, arranging them closely together, covering the moss in a rough bend that takes them from the outside of the wreath to the inside. This is similar to the way the achillea has been arranged.

4 In between the poppy seed heads you will find just enough room for the odd carthamus head. Fill in with the green buds throughout the wreath in other sections, too. Group the yellow roses close together in any areas that require a little more in terms of a color highlight. Then, bunch lavender up into little sprigs and wire them together. Bind them with natural raffia to hide the thick stub wires and tie the raffia off in a knot. Wire the lavender into the wreath as you did the lotus heads. Be sure to keep the lavender flat against the wreath, as shown opposite.

RUSTIC WREATH

This rustic wreath with its massed poppy heads and lotus seed heads has a feeling of abundance, due to the layering of flower upon flower. The natural-fiber texture of the sacking adds yet a further dimension and compliments the other natural tones.

The foundation of this arrangement is a mossed wire-wreath frame, easily obtainable from any good florist. You can see how easy it is to make by referring to pages 266-73.

It is important to note, however, that once you have made your wreath you must leave it for at least a week to allow the moss right down at the middle to dry out thoroughly. If you don't, the materials used to decorate the wreath will trap the moisture and rot. This applies to any mossed frame or mesh wire shape.

Finding the perfect spot to display your wreath will not be difficult. You might want to hang it on your front door as a sign of hospitality or on the kitchen door at the heart of your home—you could also prop it casually against the display shelf of a dresser.

MATERIALS
Prepared wreath
Natural-fiber sackcloth
Stub wire
Achillea
Lotus seed heads
Poppy seed heads
Carthamus
Golden Times rose
Lavender
Natural raffia

1

2

3

4

1 Prepare a block of florist's foam for a wall-mounted arrangement (*see pp. 266-73*). You can work on the spray attached to the wall in place. If this is not possible, lean a board against a convenient surface and fix the block to it with a temporary, but firm, fixing. If you find you can't work using either of these methods, use a tabletop to work on. Occasionally lift the spray up to a wall. This will enable you to correct any errors in overall shape as you proceed. Start your spray off by defining an outline with foliage. Eucalyptus spiralus

has been used here. Take two long stems and determine the width of the spray. Next, cut two shorter pieces to size for the top and bottom center stems. This gives you a grid within which to work. After you have filled in with the rest of the eucalyptus, soften the cross shape by realigning the top and bottom stems slightly.

2 Arrange the dock in blocks. The stems should look as though they are radiating out from a central point, splaying out to give an uneven edge to the arrangement. Next, build up the

textures using sea lavender, again placed in drifts through the spray. Arrange them closely to the dock to create an obvious association.

3 Now use the hydrangeas deep within the arrangement, making sure that they cover the florist's foam. Push their short stems firmly into the foam.

4 Wire sprigs of lavender together and fill in the shape of the spray to make it full and dense. Leave the stems longer than those of the other flowers to create definition and movement.

Next, take two leggy pieces of gnarled branch and push them firmly into the foam. You may find that these pieces are too thick to fit in between the mesh wire. If so, cut strands of wire and open out the shape, giving a larger surface of foam. Place the branches to form a broken diagonal through the spray. Now take five wired lotus seed heads (*see pp. 266-73*). Arrange them in the foam, pushing the wires securely in. Follow the diagonal running through the middle of the spray from top to bottom to create a visual division and provide a focal point.

MATERIALS

Prepared florist's foam

Stub wires

Eucalyptus spiralus

Dock

Lavender

Sea lavender

Gnarled branch or driftwood

Lotus seed heads

Cockscomb (celosia)

Sunflowers

Hydrangeas

White peonies

Pink peonies

Orange carthamus

White Success roses

INTERMEDIATE LEVEL

FREESTYLE SPRAY

This project uses nothing more complicated than a block of florist's foam wrapped in mesh wire and a wire loop to act as a hanger. You can see how to make the basic structure in the chapter on materials and techniques (*see pp. 266-73*).

The materials used here are very textural, and the choice of eucalyptus, lavender, sea lavender, and dock is important for their close color relationship, as well as adding movement and interest. The muted hues of these flowers are united in the tones of the hydrangeas, and they also blend well with the driftwood and lotus seed heads.

The spray has been arranged in a freestyle fashion, using the flowers in blocks of color radiating out from the middle to leave an irregular edge. The lotus seed heads and the branches bind the flowers through the center of the arrangement to give a visual climax.

Throughout the construction of the freestyle spray, hold the work up to the wall from time to time to make certain that its shape is evolving correctly when it is viewed from all angles.

MOSSED TREE
AND
TOPIARY TREE

Many people find it immensely satisfying to emulate the beauty of nature by creating the image and structure of a tree. In the section dealing with materials and techniques (*see pp. 266-73*) you will see how to secure a tree "trunk" in a container. Avoid an unnatural look by setting your trunk slightly off the vertical. Don't discount a branch that is bent—it may produce a more natural appearance in the end.

These likenesses of trees have some obvious advantages over the real thing. Seeing that they don't need light or water, you can use them in a dark position that would kill a living plant.

The moss tree is unashamedly a fantasy creation while, at the same time, being quite visually similar to a conventional tree. If you want, you can travel farther from nature by using combinations of dried flowers or massing a single type of dried flower, such as rose heads.

The topiary tree is made up of box (buxus) foliage, which you can use freshly cut. Box dries well but it takes on a dull yellow color. Enjoy its naturalness as long as it lasts, and then why not cheat by restoring its color with spray paint? Alternatively, you could use a stabilized foliage, although this would be more expensive.

MOSSED TREE

MATERIALS
Prepared trunk and container
Florist's foam ball
Glue and glue gun
Bun moss
Carpet moss
Stub wires

1 Take a prepared tree trunk in a container (*see pp. 266-73*). Push a florist's foam ball on to the top of the trunk. You can buy foam balls ready to use or cut your own from a block of foam. Push the trunk slowly into the foam—this will take quite a bit of pressure. Once it is in place, however, you will find it will easily lift off the trunk. To remedy this, spread glue from a glue gun on top of the trunk and replace the foam ball. Leave it until the foam and wood have securely bonded. Carpet moss has been used here to hide the cement around the trunk and to give the pot a natural finish. Glue the moss into position.

2 Next, take some stub wires and cut them into lengths. Bend the wires to make hairpin shapes and use them to secure pieces of bun moss to the florist's foam ball.

3 Continue to cover the ball with moss using this technique. Slowly build up the shape you require.

4 Ensure that you cover all of the foam, paying particular attention to the area where the trunk enters the foam. Check from all angles that the foam has been completely covered.

1

2

3

4

TOPIARY TREE

MATERIALS
Prepared trunk and container
Florist's foam block
Glue and glue gun
Carpet moss
Box foliage
Spray paint (moss green)

1 Take a prepared trunk in a container (*see pp. 266-73*). Make sure that the trunk is long enough to take the size of the box foliage ball you will be making and still protrude from the bottom. Take a block of florist's foam and cut it in half, creating a rough cube shape. Round off the corners and secure it on top of the trunk. Apply downward pressure until the trunk sinks into the foam. Leave enough foam above the trunk to accommodate the stems of the foliage. Remove the foam, spread glue on top of the trunk, replace the foam and allow the glue to harden. A little carpet moss glued into place has been used to cover the cement.

2 Create a circle with the fresh box, allowing the foliage to radiate out from the foam shape. Keep the box in line to ensure a good circle to work on. This circle divides the foam into two halves.

3 Now repeat this process, this time dividing the foam shape into quarters. Don't worry how rough the outline of the circle is looking, just make sure that it is good and thick.

4 Fill in each quarter of foam with more box. Mass it into the foam, filling the shape out. Keep it in line with the box foliage circles you have already created. You should have a very shaggy looking tree at this stage.

1

2

3

4

297

5 Cut the rough edges of foliage to form a head with a crisp, round outline. Once you start cutting the foliage, continue around and around the tree, angling your scissors accordingly.

6 Initially, cut your shape to a larger size than you require. Once you have a good outline, trim the foliage back until the head is the right size.

7 The tree is in fact finished at this stage. However, you will find that within about a week or two the fresh green color of the foliage will start to take on more of a dull yellow look.

8 To restore the foliage's original dark-green color, hold the tree by its trunk and spray the foliage liberally with a moss-green-colored spray paint. Hold the tree upside down as well to make sure the paint also reaches the undersides of the leaves.

5

6

7

8

TWIG-CAGED BALL

This construction of sticks and branches, enclosing a massed sphere of vibrant dried flowers has a distinctly architectural feel to it. This is somewhat of a departure from conventional floristry, since the framework is built as opposed to arranged. This creates an entirely new look, one that is innovative and certainly worthy of consideration. Creative florists are continually evolving new forms, some startlingly different in design and style, and hopefully this will challenge many preconceptions about flower arranging

The three structures used in this project are designed to provide a contrast in both size and color. Each globe is covered in a different material, two of which are enhanced by a special dyeing process to provide an intensely vivid color that is not normally available in dried flowers. The natural color of the achillea brings its own richness to the trio, one that is superbly bold and dominant.

MATERIALS

Florist's foam ball
Purple botao branco (dyed)
Yellow achillea
Red achillea (dyed)
Long, thick twigs
Panel pins and hammer
Thin twigs
Glue and glue gun

1

2

3

4

1 Take a florist's foam ball—these are available in different sizes and the one you choose depends on the size you want the final construction to be. Choose the dried flower material with which you want to cover the ball. This selection is most important, since the heads of the flower must be small enough to cover the ball evenly while still leaving a distinct ball shape when they are massed closely together. Botao branco has been used here, dyed to a vivid purple color. As an alternative, you could also use moss to cover the foam ball.

2 Cut the stems to about 1in (2.5cm) and carefully cover the ball with the flower heads. Gently push the stems into the ball until the heads themselves rest on the surface of the foam. Continue to cover the ball until no foam is visible. You may need to arrange a second layer in some places to complete the coverage. If so, push the stems in between the heads already in place. These stems may need to be longer.

3 Measure the height of the foam ball, complete with its massed flower heads. Call this measurement A. Take the long thick twigs, which should all be the same thickness, and cut four of them to this length. Now measure the width of the twigs—they should be roughly the same size. Call this measurement B. Multiply B by two to obtain measurement C. Subtract C from A to give measurement D. Now cut eight twigs to measurement D. These eight twigs will be two widths shorter than the four twigs cut to measurement A. Take two long and two short twigs. Nail a pin half the length of measurement B from each end of one of the long twigs.

5

6

7

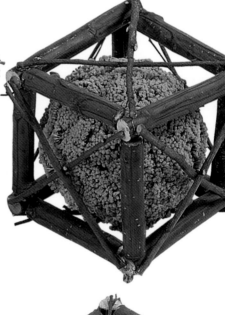

Ensure that the panel pins are at right angles to the twig. Center a short twig end-on to the panel pin and hammer it into place. Repeat this with the other short twig. Nail two more panel pins into the other long twig. Center up the points of the pins to the two shorter lengths attached to the other twig, and hammer them securely in.

4 Hammer pins into the four corners of the square. Position one of the short twigs on the point of one pin and hammer the other end into place. Repeat at each corner.

5 Place the prepared ball into the cage structure, taking care not to disturb the flower heads.

6 Make the top of the structure as you did the base. Secure the twig square with panel pins, enclosing the ball.

7 Cut lengths of thin twigs to size and glue them to the cage, taking a diagonal line from corner to corner. Repeat this to form an "X" shape on each side of the cage construction.

Make other structures and flower balls in varying sizes and colors. Achillea has been used for the balls here. The naturally yellow achillea heads have been cut down into small portions. The red achillea has been dyed to give it a dazzling color. These small heads are ideal for covering the foam without marring the ball's underlying shape.

WHEAT AND ALCHEMILLA

This design encapsulates the very essence of the rural landscape, with its golden fields of wheat edged with wild flowers. And here the effect has been wonderfully offset by the choice of a handsomely weathered flowerpot to contain the whole arrangement.

This project brings together two contrasting styles. First, notice the meticulous manner with which the wheat has been arranged to give the impression of control and uniformity; second, the roses, poppy seed heads, and alchemilla (commonly known as ladies' mantle) have a rambling, informal quality.

The design is divided into three equally important parts – the wheat, the flowers and, finally, the pot itself. This flowerpot isn't just the container for the arrangement, it is also an integral part of the concept. It reiterates artfully the outline of the sheaf head – narrow at the bottom and splaying out toward the top. The flowerpot also echoes the cool restraint of the wheat, rounding off the composition to perfection. As a container, it also lends the important ingredient of height, giving the whole arrangement elegant dimensions and a subtle sophistication.

You could, in fact, finish the arrangement by step 5 (*see overleaf*) if you wished. By that stage the structure is almost an arrangement in itself. However, if you do finish there, you will need to tidy the arrangement by concealing the stub wires with some form of binding, such as natural raffia or sacking.

MATERIALS

Flowerpot
Florist's foam
Glue and glue gun
Stub wires
Natural gray reindeer moss or lichen moss
Wheat
Alchemilla mollis (ladies' mantle)
Poppy seed heads
Gerdo roses

1 Take a suitable flowerpot, quite large in size, and about 10in (25cm) high. Fill the pot with florist's foam, leaving a level top. Now take two full blocks of foam and secure them together with hot glue and stub wires bent into large hairpin shapes. Fasten them on to the flat surface of the florist's foam in the container. Cover with lichen moss or gray reindeer moss.

2 Divide the wheat into equal bunches—about 16 in all. Cut them down to suitable lengths and either wire them together or just hold them in your hand and push them securely into the foam around the edge of the blocks.

3 Keeping the tops of the ears of wheat level with each other, fill in the rest of the foam. Arrange them in rows of four along the top of the foam.

4 Now measure the distance between the top of the wheat to the base of the foam blocks. Cut lengths of wheat to this length, again keeping the ears level. Wire them into thin bunches. Next, place them up against the sides of the foam and pin them securely into place with the stub wires. The bottoms of the stems don't penetrate the foam in the container itself; they are only supported by the wires.

1

2

3

4

5

6

7

8

5 Continue to surround the foam with bunches of wheat until it is completely covered and no foam can be seen when viewed from any angle. In some places you may have to add a second layer of wheat in order to achieve complete coverage.

6 Next, start to mass the alchemilla mollis around the wheat. Push the graceful stems firmly into the florist's foam in the container. Arrange the stems as though they are growing naturally out of the pot, angling them to give a sense of movement and fluidity. As you move around the wheat, make sure that the alchemilla is higher than the line of stub wires.

7 Now arrange some of the poppy seed heads in a random fashion, as if they, too, were growing naturally. Use different heights and sizes of poppies. Push some heads deep into the alchemilla mollis near the stems of wheat. Continue to do this right around the arrangement.

8 To finish off, you need to incorporate the peach-colored Gerdo roses—but use restraint here. Arrange the roses through the alchemilla mollis in much the same way you did the poppy seed heads in step 7—in a random and natural fashion.

FLOWER POT MAN

Children and adults alike will have tremendous fun making this flower pot figure. You will readily find suitable terra cotta flower pots of all sizes at garden depots and hardware stores. The smallest terra cotta pots are ideal for creating the hands and feet.

When you choose the flower pots for your figure, set them up roughly in a body shape, using the picture here as a guide. Keep the terra cotta pots spaced out in a proper relationship to the different parts of the body they are representing, and also try to keep all the body parts in realistic proportions, no matter how small your figure is.

A child will need some supervision while making this project. An adult will, for example, have to make the holes in the sides of the flower pots with an electric drill. You should also take some basic precautions when using long lengths of reel wire. Using lengths suitable to connect all the pots can be hazardous. The wire has a tendency to curl up at the cut end and take on a life of its own, so wear some form of eye protection.

1

2

3

4

MATERIALS
28 flower pots
Reel wire
Drill
Twigs
Florist's foam
Bamboo cane
Glue and glue gun
Natural raffia
Stub wires
Sphagnum moss
Scissors
Eye goggles

1 Take the terra cotta flower pot you have selected to be the lower part of the torso and drill a small hole in each side, approximately where the hip joint will be. Drill a hole in one of the pots selected for the legs. Thread a length of reel wire through these holes. Double the wire into two thicknesses to provide extra strength. Now wrap the wire at a suitable point around a twig just to hold the wire in place.

2 The wire should be long enough to go through all of the flower pots you have selected

for the legs and the lower torso. Take some dry sphagnum moss and half fill the small flowerpot. Stuff it firmly in.

3 Thread another of the leg flower pots along the wire and then half fill it with sphagnum moss as well.

4 Repeat this with a third flower pot and pull them all together so they make one continuous piece. Now thread on another flower pot, this time the other way around. Cup the two flower pots together facing each other to form

the knee joint. Fill the new flower pot with moss and a little more between the two facing pots to make a knee cap. Place a second flower pot up to the other one, facing the same direction. Half fill this flower pot with moss.

5 Take a small flower pot you have selected to become a foot. Face it end-on to the previous pot and thread the remainder of the reel wire through. Take another twig. Wrap the end of the reel wire around the twig and roll it down until it is flush with the bottom of the pot.

5

6

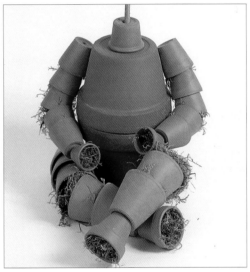

7

8

6 Fill this foot with sphagnum moss. Now repeat the process of building up the flower pots to create the second leg. Pull the reel wire tight when fixing the first flower pot with the twig at the hip, securing both legs into place. Follow the steps through again until the flower pot man has two complete legs. Wedge some florist's foam, cut to size, in place to accommodate a bamboo cane "spine." Alternatively, you could fill the flower pot with quick-drying cement for a really secure fixing. This, however, will make your flower pot man very heavy.

7 Once this is done, start work on the top half of the torso, preparing the arms using exactly the same technique you employed for the legs. Follow the stages all the way through to step 6, stopping once you have filled the hands with moss. Now carefully spread a little hot glue along the rim of the lower torso flower pot. Thread the bamboo cane through the small drainage hole at the top of the upturned flower pot. Gently lower the flower pot down until it joins, rim to rim, the bottom half of the torso. Quickly wipe away any excess glue with a damp cloth.

Slip the flower pot you have selected for the neck over the bamboo cane. Using the glue gun, fix this pot into position. If your flowe rpot is so small that the hole in the top is not large enough for the bamboo cane, use a closed pair of scissors to widen the hole a little by gently wearing away the edges of the terra cotta.

8 Take the last flower pot, the one you have selected to be the head, and fill it with florist's foam, leaving about a ¼in (1cm) gap at the top. To form the flower pot man's hair, first wire one end

of a length of natural raffia into the pot and cut it to length. Rewire the new end of raffia and continue in this way until the flower pot is full. Take a pair of scissors and trim and shape the raffia to give your flower pot man a hair cut. You could make a flower pot woman with long braids or pigtails. (Dried flowers could also be used in place of raffia.) Finally, secure the head to the bamboo cane and glue it into position.

311

MATERIALS

Prepared block
of florist's foam

Wheat

Stub wires

Natural raffia

Dried fall leaves
in various colors

Dried chile peppers

Dried baby corn in the husk

Dried fruit slices

Glue and glue gun

1

2

3

4

ADVANCED LEVEL

HARVEST SHEAF

Harvest is a celebration of nature—a rejoicing in the goodness of the sun ripening the fruits and crops of the countryside. This wheat sheaf is presented in traditional fashion and is evocative of the close of summer, when the long hot months mellow into cooler days and early dusks.

The red, rust, brown, and orange hues of the dried leaves caught up in the raffia binding, alongside the sliced dried fruit, corn and, bright red chile peppers, produce a symphony in honor of the fall. The technique involved in making this piece is not easy, and you should tackle it only after practicing on some of the easier projects in this chapter. For example, in the wheat and alchemilla arrangement (*see pp. 304-7*) a similar method of using bunched wheat is used. The illusion of an intact stem that is, in reality, two separate halves, is explored in the grouped basket project (*see pp. 288-9*).

Tackling these two projects first will help to build up your skill and confidence and ensure that when you attempt this sheaf you will succeed in making a first-class job of it.

1 Take a block of prepared florist's foam for a wall-mounted arrangement (*see pp. 266-73*). Gather some wheat into bunches, keeping the ears level. Wire their stems together with stub wires and twist the ends together. With this wire holding the lower section and your hand the upper, cut the top to the required size and secure it with another stub wire. Put the lower section to one side for later use. Take a prepared upper section and place it centrally in the top of the foam. Continue working from here, arranging more bunches into a fan. Position the bunches horizontally out of the foam about a third of the way down.

2 Arrange a shorter-stemmed fan close against the first. Leave enough space for a third fan, as shown.

3 Build up the third fan. Reduce the length of the stems, as you did the second fan. Fill in with bunches until the top is domed. Take some bottom sections and arrange them flat against the block. Start about 2in (5cm) lower than the dome. Continue until you reach the middle. Cut some shorter lengths, rewire them, and push them into the base of the block, filling it completely. Now continue around the block with the longer stems until it is covered.

4 Form a second layer of long-stemmed bunches on top of the first. This time, arrange the stub wires in the 2in (5cm) of foam left free beneath the dome. Bend stub wires and push them through both bunches. Tie a thick bunch of raffia around the sheaf. Glue fall leaves under the raffia. Wire dried chile peppers and baby corn to the sheaf, and glue on slices of dried fruits.

INDEX

A

Achillea; *DRIED FLOWERS* 300-303
Acrylic gesso; *PAPIER MACHE* 112
Acrylic paints, uses; *PAPIER MACHE* 113
Adhesive, soaking paper in; *PAPIER MACHE* 107
   see also PVA; papier mâché
African bangle; *PAPIER MACHE* 138-139
African bead necklace; *PAPIER MACHE* 148-149
Aging techniques; *DECOUPAGE* 24-25, 48
Aida fabric; *CROSS-STITCH* 154
   black 200
   inserts on bought items 181
   needles for 159
Air bubbles, removing; *DECOUPAGE* 17
Air-drying; *DOUGHCRAFT* 82-83, 91, 103
   flour types 60
   technique 65
Alchemilla, with wheat; *DRIED FLOWERS* 304-307
Alphabet examples; *CROSS-STITCH* 204-205
Aluminum foil; *DOUGHCRAFT* 54, 76-77, 80-81, 82-83, 88-89, 96-97
Amaryllis bulb holder; *DRIED FLOWERS* 284-285
Amish cushions; *PATCHWORK* 234-235
Antiquing paint; *DECOUPAGE* 45, 52, 56-57
Antiquing technique; *DECOUPAGE* 18
Antiquing wax; *DECOUPAGE* 25, 30-31, 48
Aztec patterns; *PAPIER MACHE* 131

B

Baby's: changing mat; *PATCHWORK* 228-229
Back stitch; *CROSS-STITCH* 158
Background, long stitch; *CROSS-STITCH* 158
Background; *DECOUPAGE*:
   applying to glass plate 44-45
   coordinating 50
   masking 56, 68
   natural paint pigment 24
   painted 23, 35

two-color 48-49
   sanding to reveal wood grain 40
   self-colored 39
Backing fabrics; *CROSS-STITCH* 162
Backings: cork, felt; *DOUGHCRAFT* 67
   techniques 67
Bag, cactus motif; *CROSS-STITCH* 178-179
Bags; *PATCHWORK*:
   Dorothy 260-262
   silk clutch bag 238-239
Baking and browning; *DOUGHCRAFT* 64-65, 88
Band designs; *PATCHWORK* 255
Bangle; *PAPIER MACHE* 138-139
Barge ware; *DECOUPAGE* 28
Bark; *DRIED FLOWERS*:
   as container covering 284
   for texture and structure 267
Baseball caps; *CROSS-STITCH* 181
Baskets; *DRIED FLOWERS*:
   for Valentine's Day 286-87
   grouped 288-289
   preparation 272
   reshaping technique 286
   rustic 288-289
   summer flower collection 288-289
Beading; *CROSS-STITCH* 156
   fixing beads 159
Beads; *DOUGHCRAFT*:
   applying 63, 91
   as decoration 75
   as eyes 101
   dough 63
   metal 102
   on wires 67
Beads; *PAPIER MACHE* 113
Beadwork designs, geometric; *PATCHWORK* 255
Bells, on wires; *DOUGHCRAFT* 67
Billfold, Fair Isle; *CROSS-STITCH* 200-201
Binca blockweave fabric; *CROSS-STITCH* 154
Binding; *PATCHWORK* 222
Birch twigs; *DRIED FLOWERS* 276
Birthday card; *PAPIER MACHE* 125
Blanket box; *DECOUPAGE* 54-57
Blanks; *CROSS-STITCH* 163
   home made 194
Blocking patchwork 220
Blockweave fabrics;

CROSS-STITCH 154
   cross-stitch on 158
Border, cushion; *CROSS-STITCH* 171
   perle thread for 156
Borders, decoratively quilted; *PATCHWORK* 231
Borders, scoring 84
Bowl, scallop-edged; *DOUGHCRAFT* 80-81
   see also Candlesticks
Bowls; *PAPIER MACHE*:
   appliquéd shapes 127
   for fruit 116-117
   relief technique 135
Bows, making; *DRIED FLOWERS* 273
Box foliage; *DRIED FLOWERS* 295
   restoring color 295, 298
Boxes:
   DECOUPAGE:
      crackle varnish 48-49
      for blankets 54-57
      sealing inside 48
      Shaker-style 24-25
   PAPIER MACHE:
      relief technique 135
      storage 142-143
Braid, adding to; *CROSS-STITCH*:
   cushion cover 162
   throw 172
Branches, choosing for trees; *DRIED FLOWERS* 295
Bread rolls, dough container for; *DOUGHCRAFT* 88-89
Brooch, string-layered; *PAPIER MACHE* 134-135
Brown paper tape, for card; *PAPIER MACHE* 107
Brush, varnishing; *DECOUPAGE* 18
Bulb holder; *DRIED FLOWERS* 284-285
Bun moss; *DRIED FLOWERS* 284
Bunches; *DRIED FLOWERS*:
   faking 289, 312-313
   wiring lavender 267
Butterflies; *DECOUPAGE* 24-25, 52

C

Candlesticks; *DOUGHCRAFT* 90-93
Canvas; *CROSS-STITCH* 155
   cross-stitch on 155
   needle sizes 159
   preparing 160
   soft embroidery thread 156
Cardboard as mold; *PAPIER MACHE* 111

Cardboard, reducing thickness of; *DECOUPAGE* 62
Cards: birth, wedding; *CROSS-STITCH* 194-195
Cartoon characters; *DECOUPAGE* 46, 99
Cat, marmalade; *PATCHWORK* 248-249
Cement, quick-drying; *DRIED FLOWERS* 272, 83
Center of work, marking; *CROSS-STITCH* 160
Centerpieces; *DOUGHCRAFT* 88-89
Chair, child's; *DECOUPAGE* 32-33
Character plaque; *DOUGHCRAFT* 76-77
Charts, using; *CROSS-STITCH* 163
Cherubs/cupids; *DECOUPAGE* 40-41, 46
Child's room; *DOUGHCRAFT*:
   plaques for 76-77
   white rabbit 98-101
Children, party tray; *PAPIER MACHE* 127
Children; *DECOUPAGE*:
   chair for 32-33
   gifts for 35, 37
   headboard for 46
Chile peppers; *DRIED FLOWERS* 312
Chopsticks holder; *DOUGHCRAFT* 96-97
Christmas star; *PAPIER MACHE* 122-123
Chunky earrings; *PAPIER MACHE* 136-137
Cinnamon sticks; *DRIED FLOWERS* 267
Circus prints; *DECOUPAGE* 34-35
Clock, sun and moon; *CROSS-STITCH* 198-199
Clothing, Seminole strips; *PATCHWORK* 255
Clutch bag, silk; *PATCHWORK* 238-239
Coat and hat rack; *DECOUPAGE* 30-31
Coat hangers; *DECOUPAGE* 36-37
Cockle shells; *DOUGHCRAFT* 62
Coil pot; *PAPIER MACHE* 130-131
Collage; *PAPIER MACHE* 140
Colors:
   CROSS-STITCH:
      conversion chart 206-207
      flower thread 156
      for 3-D effect 190

in metallic thread 156
stranded thread 156
working 2 in same stitch
163
DECOUPAGE:
choosing 15
effects of waxing on 19
pencils 14, 36
tinting 14
DOUGHCRAFT:
blending 66
complementing room 75
contrasting 84
effect of varnishing 67
experimenting with 66, 81
marine shades 84, 88
varying base color 88
DRIED FLOWERS:
contrasting 267, 300-303
harmonizing 267
pink and blue 276-277
yellow and blue 288-289
Color harmony and contrast;
DRIED FLOWERS 267
Colored pencils; DECOUPAGE
14, 36
Coloring and tinting; DECOUPAGE
14-15
see also Photocopies; DECOUPAGE
Containers; DRIED FLOWERS:
clay 279
covering:
with moss 282
with moss and bark 284
for flowerpot man 308
for fresh flowers 282-283
plastic tubs 282
preparing:
for trees 272
to take a tree trunk 272
terra cotta 272, 279, 284
wreathed flowerpot 304
see also Baskets; DRIED FLOWERS
Containers, found; DECOUPAGE
10, 35
Containers, heart-shaped;
DOUGHCRAFT 96-97
Cord, adding to cushion;
CROSS-STITCH 162
Corners, mitring; CROSS-STITCH 182
Corn in the husk; DRIED FLOWERS
312
Cosmetic bag; PATCHWORK 238
Coton à broder; CROSS-STITCH 156
Cottage tea cozy; PATCHWORK
262-263
Cotton evenweave; CROSS-STITCH
154

Count, blockweave; CROSS-STITCH
154
Cow jumped over the moon;
DOUGHCRAFT 78-79
Crackle varnish; DECOUPAGE 48-49
Cracks in dough, mending;
DOUGHCRAFT 63
Craft knife/scalpel, tip; DECOUPAGE
16
Craft supply stores; DECOUPAGE 10
Crazy patchwork 216
vest 258-259
Crewel needles; CROSS-STITCH 159
Crib quilt; PATCHWORK 219,
240-241
Cross stitch 158
tips for working 163
Cups and saucers; DECOUPAGE
42-43
Cushions:
CROSS-STITCH:
making up 162
playing card 188-189
tile 170-171
piped edging 162
PATCHWORK:
Amish 234-235
quilt-as-you-go 232-233
Seminole 254-255
water lily 256-257
Cut-outs:
CROSS-STITCH 185
DOUGHCRAFT:
as relief work 87
freehand 87
technique 63
threaded dough 75
Cutting technique; DECOUPAGE 16
Cutting tools; PAPIER MACHE 106
Cutting; PATCHWORK 212-213
angled pieces 213
tips 213

D

Darning foot; PATCHWORK 211,
219
Decorations; PAPIER MACHE
112-113
appliquéd shapes 127
glass beads 137
postage stamps 140
shells 143
tools 112
Decorative finishes; DOUGHCRAFT
67
see also Texture; DOUGHCRAFT
Designs; CROSS-STITCH:
adapting for knits 155

for blanks 163
sizing 159
Designs; PAPIER MACHE, see also
Patterns/designs
Detailing; DOUGHCRAFT 98
Details; CROSS-STITCH:
back stitch for 158
three-quarter stitch for 158
Diamond block; PATCHWORK
242, 234
Diamond earrings; PAPIER MACHE
120-121
Dicing; PATCHWORK 242
Dinner plate, large; PAPIER MACHE
132-133
Dishes:
fish; PAPIER MACHE 144-147
fish-shaped; DOUGHCRAFT
88-89
Displaying work; CROSS-STITCH 163
Distressed paint effect; PAPIER
MACHE 112, 137, 143
Dock; DRIED FLOWERS 293
Door decorations; DRIED FLOWERS
290-291
Dorothy bag; PATCHWORK 260-262
Double canvas; CROSS-STITCH 155
Dough paste; DOUGHCRAFT:
filling and repairing with 65
making 60, 63
Drawing inks; PAPIER MACHE 112
Driftwood; DRIED FLOWERS 293
Drying process:
accelerating; PAPIER MACHE 111
DRIED FLOWERS:
box foliage 295
hydrangeas 281
moss 269, 270, 291
Duck; DECOUPAGE 30-31
Dutch folk art; DECOUPAGE 54
Dyed flowers; DRIED FLOWERS
300-303

E

Earrings; PAPIER MACHE:
chunky 136-137
diamond 120-121
Edges:
smoothing; DOUGHCRAFT 63
PAPIER MACHE:
smoothing 112
trimming 131
PATCHWORK:
binding 222
securing raw 221
Egg white glaze; DOUGHCRAFT 67
Emulsion paint, household; PAPIER
MACHE 112

Equipment:
PAPIER MACHE 106
PATCHWORK 210
for pressing and blocking
220
for quilting 211, 218, 219
measuring and cutting
212
Eryngium; DRIED FLOWERS 276
Ethnic designs; CROSS-STITCH
172-173, 182-183
Eucalyptus; DRIED FLOWERS 293
Evenweave fabrics; CROSS-STITCH
154-155
CROSS-STITCH on 158
flower thread on 156

F

Fabrics:
CROSS-STITCH:
coordinate with design
188
for starry throw 172
furnishing 172
preparing 160
washing before using 172
DRIED FLOWERS:
as decoration/surface
covering; 291
PATCHWORK 210
amount for cushions
223
cutting, and tips 213
ethnic prints 237
for foundation piecing
216
for pounce bag 218
furnishing weight 258
joining odd shapes 216
metallic prints 237
pressing before cutting
220
scraps 216, 250
silk 210, 237, 238, 258
old ties 258, 260
piecing 216
wool 246
Fancy machine quilting;
PATCHWORK 219
Fat eighths/quarters; PATCHWORK
210
Filling and repairing; DOUGHCRAFT
63
Finishing work; CROSS-STITCH 159,
161
backing aida patches 181
tip for 163
Fish dish; PAPIER MACHE 144-147

Fish; DOUGHCRAFT:
  dish 88-89
  tile 84-85
Fishes; DECOUPAGE 48-49
Flexi-hoop; CROSS-STITCH 160-161
Flour, type to use; DOUGHCRAFT 60
Flower greeting card; PAPIER
  MACHE 124-125
Flower pot man; DRIED FLOWERS
  308-311
Flowerpots:
  DECOUPAGE 26-27
    preparing terra cotta 11
  DRIED FLOWERS
    drilling 308
    miniature, as decoration
    276
Flowers:
  DECOUPAGE 26-27, 50-51
    containers for:
      dried 26-27
      fresh 28-29
    see also specific flowers;
      DECOUPAGE
  dried: holder for; DOUGHCRAFT
  96-97
Flying geese:
  DOUGHCRAFT 77
  PATCHWORK 219, 230-231
Foam balls; DRIED FLOWERS:
  enclosing in twigs 300-303
  fixing and covering 296
  tip for covering evenly 302
  using different sizes 300-303
Foam blocks; DRIED FLOWERS:
  arrangement 271, 293
  fake bunches 288-289, 313
  preparation for wall
Foil paper; PAPIER MACHE 113, 132
Foliage; DRIED FLOWERS:
  as design feature 267
  color sprayed on 295
  using left-over 267, 289
Folk art; DECOUPAGE 54
Foundation piecing; PATCHWORK
  216
  cushion 256-257
  method of working 217
Frames:
  ethnic; CROSS-STITCH 182-183
  see also Hoops and frames;
    CROSS-STITCH
  DOUGHCRAFT:
    dough-coil 82-83
    drying 65
    metal-coil 94-95
    moon-shaped 102-103
    scoring 84

Fraying, preventing; CROSS-STITCH
  160
Free-hand quilting; PATCHWORK
  219
Free-motion quilting; PATCHWORK:
  exercises to practice 219
Freestyle spray; DRIED FLOWERS
  292-293
French knot; CROSS-STITCH 158
Fresh flowers, container for;
  DRIED FLOWERS 282-283
Fridge magnet, snake; PAPIER MACHE
  150-151
Fringing, with tassel; CROSS-STITCH
  172
Fruit:
  sliced dried; DRIED FLOWERS 312
  DECOUPAGE 44-45, 50-51

G
Galvanized metal primer;
  DECOUPAGE 28, 51
  preparing new and old 11
Gesso, acrylic; PAPIER MACHE 112
  applying 112
  as undercoat 112
  for smooth surface 144
Gift wrapping; DECOUPAGE:
  motifs from 12, 24, 32-33,
    39, 42-43, 50-51
Gilt cream; DECOUPAGE 31
Glass beads; PAPIER MACHE 137
Glass, colored; DOUGHCRAFT 95
Glass surfaces, working on;
  DECOUPAGE 44-45
Glazing technique; DOUGHCRAFT
  67
Glue gun, using; DRIED FLOWERS 266
Gluing:
  on to twigs; DRIED FLOWERS 276
  DECOUPAGE 16-17
    techniques and tips 17
Gold paint, highlighting with;
  DOUGHCRAFT 66
  see also Techniques; DOUGHCRAFT
Good luck card; PAPIER MACHE 125
Graph paper; CROSS-STITCH 198
Greeting cards; PAPIER MACHE 125
Grouped basket; DRIED FLOWERS
  288-289
Gypsy style jug; DECOUPAGE 28-29

H
Hair dryer, uses; PAPIER MACHE 111
Half cross-stitch; CROSS-STITCH 158
  fixing beads with 159
Half-baking technique;
  DOUGHCRAFT 64

Hand quilting; PATCHWORK 218,
  219
  method 218, 219
Hand-sewing; PATCHWORK 211
Hangings; PATCHWORK, see Wall
  Garden hanging; PATCHWORK
Hardanger fabric; CROSS-STITCH 155
Harvest sheaf; DRIED FLOWERS
  312-313
Hat and coat rack; DECOUPAGE
  30-31
Headboard; DECOUPAGE 46-47
Hearts; DOUGHCRAFT:
  container 96-97
  hanging 62
Heatproofing; DECOUPAGE 42-43
Helichrysum; DRIED FLOWERS 276
  yellow 289
Hessian sacking; DRIED FLOWERS
  267, 291
Hexagons, hand sewing;
  PATCHWORK 211
Highlighting paint finish;
  PAPIER MACHE 135, 137
Highlights, adding; DOUGHCRAFT
  66
Hoops and frames; CROSS-STITCH
  160
Horseshoe card; PAPIER MACHE 125
Hydrangea heads, drying
  methods; DRIED FLOWERS 281
Hydrangea mirror; DRIED FLOWERS
  280-281
Hydrangeas; DRIED FLOWERS 293

I
Indelible pen; DECOUPAGE 17
Indentations, care with;
  DOUGHCRAFT 84
Initials:
  adding; CROSS-STITCH 185, 200
  DECOUPAGE 23
Interlining, with knits; CROSS
  STITCH 155
Ironing tip; CROSS-STITCH 161

J
Jacob's Ladder, crib quilt;
  PATCHWORK 219, 240-241
Jersey, adding motif; CROSS-STITCH
  155
Jugs; DECOUPAGE:
  cutting technique 16
  enamel 52-53
  gypsy style 28-29

K
Key cabinet; DECOUPAGE 23

Key fobs:
  DECOUPAGE 22-23
  CROSS-STITCH 174-175
Kitchen decorations; DRIED FLOWERS
  290-291
Kitchen; DOUGHCRAFT:
  dish for 88-89
  implements holder 96-97
Kitchenware, uses as molds;
  PAPIER MACHE 109
Kneading dough; DOUGHCRAFT 61
Knitted fabrics; CROSS-STITCH 155
Knitting wool; CROSS-STITCH 156

L
Lacing finished work; CROSS-STITCH
  161
Lacquer effect paint; PAPIER MACHE 112
Larkspur; DRIED FLOWERS 276
Lavender; DRIED FLOWERS 267, 289,
  279, 293
  see also Sea lavender;
    DRIED FLOWERS
Layered method; PAPIER MACHE 107
  applying to a mold 110
  bowl 116-117
  earrings 120-121, 134-135
  equipment 106
  fish dish 144-147
  ingredients 107
  plate 118-119
  storage box 142-143
  tray 126-127
Leaf mobile; PAPIER MACHE 128-129
Leaves:
  DOUGHCRAFT:
    color schemes 66
    modeling technique 62
  PAPIER MACHE:
    applied 117
    as molds 129
Legs; DOUGHCRAFT 75-77
Letter rack; PAPIER MACHE 140-141
Lichen; DRIED FLOWERS 272
Lids, cutting; DOUGHCRAFT 87
Linen; CROSS-STITCH:
  blockweave 154
  crewel wool on 156
  evenweave 154
  flower thread on 156
Lines, painting; DECOUPAGE 56
Lino printing roller; DECOUPAGE 17
Long stitch; CROSS-STITCH 158
Looping technique; DOUGHCRAFT
  63
Lotus seed heads; DRIED FLOWERS
  291, 293
  wiring 266, 267

M

Machine quilting; *PATCHWORK* 211, 218, 219
  fancy 219
  preparation for 218
  securing the edges 221
  straight-line 219
  using sticky padding 221
Machine sewing; *PATCHWORK*:
  crazy patchwork 216
Man's wool vest; *PATCHWORK* 246-247
Markers, quilting; *PATCHWORK* 218
Marlitt; *CROSS-STITCH* 156
Marmalade cat; *PATCHWORK* 248-249
Materials:
  CROSS-STITCH 154-156, 159-161
  DECOUPAGE 10-15
    basic kit 19
  DOUGHCRAFT 60-61
    assembling and arranging before starting 75
    molding 96-97
  DRIED FLOWERS 266-273
MDF, hat and coat rack; *DECOUPAGE* 30-31
Measuring strips and squares; *PATCHWORK* 213
Mediumweight padding; *PATCHWORK* 210
Meshed wire foundations; *DRIED FLOWERS*:
  wreath 269
Metal primer; *DECOUPAGE* 11
Metallic paints; *PAPIER MACHE* 112-113
Metallic pens; *PAPIER MACHE* 112-113
Metallic thread; *CROSS-STITCH* 156, 194
Mirror frames; *DOUGHCRAFT* 82-83, 102-103
Mirror images; *DECOUPAGE* 54-57
Mirrors:
  DOUGHCRAFT
    baking rule; 64, 83
    judging dough thickness 83
  DRIED FLOWERS:
    hydrangea 280-281
Mirror surround; *CROSS-STITCH* 183
Mobiles; *PAPIER MACHE*:
  leaves 128-129

Modeling by hand; *DOUGHCRAFT* 62-63
  cochlea 62
  cockle shells 62
  leaves 63
Modeling clay; *PAPIER MACHE*:
  mobile counterbalances 129
  molds 109, 146, 122
  preparation 110
Mono canvas; *CROSS-STITCH* 155
Monochrome painting; *DECOUPAGE* 14-15
Moon; *DOUGHCRAFT* 78-79
  mirror 102-103
Moss; *DRIED FLOWERS*:
  attaching to container 282
  carpet 289
  drying tips 269, 270, 291
  fixing to foam balls 296
  reindeer 272
  sphagnum:
    tip for using 273
  wreath 269
Mossed tree; *DRIED FLOWERS* 295, 296
Mother Goose; *DOUGHCRAFT* 76-77
Mother's Day present; *DECOUPAGE* 37
Motifs
  CROSS-STITCH:
    cactus 178
    Fair Isle pattern 200
    farmyard faces 181
    letters & numbers 167-169
    pineapple 192
    playing cards 188
    positioning 172
    stars 172
    stegosaurus 202
    substituting 185
    sun & moon 198
    traditional sampler 192
    tumbling blocks pattern 190
    using individual 185
  DECOUPAGE:
    arranging & gluing 16-17
    cutting technique 16
    marking positions before pasting 42
    sticking to glass 44-45
Molding materials: aluminum foil; *DOUGHCRAFT* 96-97
  see also Aluminum; DOUGHCRAFT
Molds:
  DOUGHCRAFT:
    baking 64
    removing when baking 64

    template shape over 88-89
    using 81, 87
  PAPIER MACHE:
    choosing 109
    different types 109
    easing stuck papier mâché 111
    modeling clay, see Modeling clay sources 109, 110
    using 110
Mottled paint effects; *PAPIER MACHE* 112
Moving house card; *PAPIER MACHE* 125

N

Natural fabrics, crewel wool; *CROSS-STITCH* 156
Natural history motifs; *DECOUPAGE* 22-23
Natural paint color range; *DECOUPAGE* 41
Necklace; *PAPIER MACHE* 148-149
Needles:
  CROSS-STITCH 159
  PATCHWORK:
    hand quilting 219
    sizes 211
New baby card; *PAPIER MACHE* 125
New England folk art tradition; *DECOUPAGE* 54
Newspaper; *PAPIER MACHE*:
  best type to use 108
  tearing:
    for layered method 107
    for pulped method 108
Nine-patch block quilts; *PATCHWORK* 240-241
Non-contact glue; *DECOUPAGE* 17

O

Ohio Star; *PATCHWORK* 214-13, 250
Outlining, stitch for; *CROSS-STITCH* 158
Oven glove; *CROSS-STITCH* 192-193

P

Padding sandwich; *PATCHWORK* 211, 219
  practicing on 219
Padding; *PATCHWORK*:
  buying and using 210
  preparing for quilting 220-221
  sticky 221
  traditional 210

Paintbrushes:
  DOUGHCRAFT 66
  PAPIER MACHE:
    for decorating 112
    for varnishing 113
Painting techniques:
  DOUGHCRAFT 66
  PAPIER MACHE 112
    accentuating colors 121
    striped beads 149
    toning down colors 119
Painting, before applying motifs; *DECOUPAGE* 15
Paints; *DOUGHCRAFT* 66
Pansies; *DECOUPAGE* 38-39
Paper, foundation piecing; *PATCHWORK*
  background 216, 263
Paper; *DECOUPAGE*:
  cutting 16
  sealing 15
Party food, container for; *DOUGHCRAFT* 88-89
Paste brushes; *DOUGHCRAFT* 66
Paste; *DECOUPAGE* 17
Patchwork 210
  finishing 220
Patchwork: tea cozy; *CROSS-STITCH* 190
Patterns/designs, practicing; *PAPIER MACHE* 131
  see also Relief modeling; PAPIER MACHE
Pearlized paints ; *PAPIER MACHE* 112-113, 144
Pears ; *DECOUPAGE* 44-45
Pencil holder; *DECOUPAGE* 34-35
Penelope canvas; *CROSS-STITCH* 155
Pens, metallic; *PAPIER MACHE* 112-113
Perle thread; *CROSS-STITCH* 156
Personal organizer cover; *CROSS-STITCH* 200
Petals, modeling technique; *DOUGHCRAFT* 62
Petroleum jelly, as releasing agent; *PAPIER MACHE* 107
Phone number, adding; *CROSS-STITCH* 200
Photocopies; *DECOUPAGE* 36
  colored pencil 36
  coloring 53
  enlarging/reducing 69
  from books 24
  ready colored 54-57
  tea-bag stain 40-41
  tinting 24
  tips 15
Picture, quilted Amish; *PATCHWORK* 219

Piecing, machine sewn; *PATCHWORK* 211

   see also Foundation Piecing;
     PATCHWORK

Pine cones, wiring; *DRIED FLOWERS* 267

Piping:

   on cushions; *PATCHWORK* 223

   adding; *CROSS-STITCH* 162

Plaid tray; *PAPIER MACHE* 126-127

Plastic canvas, preparing; *CROSS-STITCH* 160

Plates: appliquéd shapes; *PAPIER MACHE* 127

   large dinner 132-133

   side plate 118-119

Polyurethane varnish:

   DECOUPAGE 43

   PAPIER MACHE 113

Poppy seed heads; *DRIED FLOWERS* 291, 304

Poster paints; *PAPIER MACHE* 113

Pot, star-shaped, with lid; *DOUGHCRAFT* 82-83

Pounce bag, making; *PATCHWORK* 218

Preserving work; *DOUGHCRAFT* 67

Presser foot; *PATCHWORK* 211

Pressing *PATCHWORK* 220

   wool fabrics 246

Priming and preparing surfaces; *DECOUPAGE* 10-11

Proteas; *DRIED FLOWERS* 279

Pulp tips; *PAPIER MACHE* 10

Pulped method; *PAPIER MACHE* 107-108

   applying to a mold 111

   creating a smooth surface 138

   dinner plate 132-133

   earrings 136-137

   equipment 106

   mobile 128-129

   necklace 148-149

   pot 130-131

   stars 122-123

PVA glue:

   DECOUPAGE 17, 44-45

   PAPIER MACHE:

     using as varnish 121, 138

     ways of using 107

Q

Quarter stitch; *CROSS-STITCH* 158

Quilt-as-you-go cushion; *PATCHWORK* 232-233

Quilting hoop; *PATCHWORK* 219

Quilting; *PATCHWORK* 218-219

   designs for 218

fancy 219

finishing 220-222

marking the middle 221

practicing 211, 219

putting together the layers 220-221

transferring the design 218

   see also Equipment; PATCHWORK;
     Hand & Machine quilting

Quilt sandwich, method; *PATCHWORK* 220-221

Quilts; *PATCHWORK:*

   doll's 257

   edges: binding 222

   nine-patch 240-241

   securing raw 22

R

R.I.T. Squares; *PATCHWORK* 229, 241, 250, 234

   cutting tip 213

   how to make 214-15

   machine patchwork with 214-215

   sewing accurately 211

Raffia, natural; *DRIED FLOWERS* 267, 304

Rayon evenweave; *CROSS-STITCH* 154

Reel wire, working with long lengths; *DRIED FLOWERS* 308

Releasing agent; *PAPIER MACHE:*

   applying 110

   removing residue 111

Relief modeling; *PAPIER MACHE* 135

Relief work; *DOUGHCRAFT* 87

   method for attaching 63

Ribbons:

   and bows; *DECOUPAGE* 36-37

   DOUGHCRAFT 67

   PAPIER MACHE 113

Rose heads; *DRIED FLOWERS* 295

Roses:

   DECOUPAGE 28-29, 52-53

     cutting 46

     wreaths 46-47

   DRIED FLOWERS 281, 304

Rotary cutters; *PATCHWORK:*

   practicing with 212

Rug, tile design; *CROSS-STITCH* 171

Rulers; *PATCHWORK* 212

Rustic wreath; *DRIED FLOWERS* 290-291

Rustproofing; *DECOUPAGE* 11, 52

S

Sacking; *DRIED FLOWERS* 267, 291, 304

Safety tips; *DOUGHCRAFT* 66

Sailing boat changing mat; *PATCHWORK* 228-229

Salt dough; *DOUGHCRAFT:*

   baking techniques 64-65

   balls as texture 63

   basic recipe 60-61

   displaying your work 67

   ingredients 60

   longevity 67

   mixing 60

   storage 61

Salt, type to use; *DOUGHCRAFT* 60

Samplers; *CROSS-STITCH:*

   festival 196-197

   kitchen 185

   numbers and letters 167-169

Sashing; *PATCHWORK* 231

Scissors, tip for using; *DECOUPAGE* 16

Scoring; *DOUGHCRAFT* 84

   practicing 81

   technique 63

Scraped paint effect; *PAPIER MACHE* 119

Screwshells; *DOUGHCRAFT* 62

Sea lavender; *DRIED FLOWERS* 293

Sealing techniques; *DECOUPAGE* 15

Seams; *PATCHWORK:*

   on wool fabrics 246

   pressing 220

Seashell storage box; *PAPIER MACHE* 142-143

Self-healing mats; *PATCHWORK* 212

Self-rising flour; *DOUGHCRAFT* 60

Seminole cushion; *PATCHWORK* 254-255

Sequins; *DOUGHCRAFT* 95

Sewing box; *DECOUPAGE* 24

Sewing machines; *PATCHWORK* 211, 219

Shading, stitch for; *CROSS-STITCH* 158

Shadow, effect for; *CROSS-STITCH* 156

Shaker box; *DECOUPAGE* 24-25

Shell collection, box for; *DECOUPAGE* 39

Shellac, sealer; *DECOUPAGE* 10-11, 56

Shells:

   DOUGHCRAFT:

     modeling technique 62

   DECOUPAGE 38-39, 48-49

   PAPIER MACHE 113, 142-143

Silk fabric, working motif on; *CROSS-STITCH* 155

Silk, stranded; *CROSS-STITCH* 156

Single canvas; *CROSS-STITCH* 155

Snail shells; *DOUGHCRAFT* 62

Soap container; *DECOUPAGE* 49

Source material; *DECOUPAGE* 12

   books 12, 24

   magazines 43

   see also Gift wrapping

Spaces, as part of design; *DECOUPAGE* 28

Spillproofing; *DECOUPAGE* 42-43

Spiral plate; *PAPIER MACHE* 118-119

Sponging paint technique; *PAPIER MACHE* 112

Spraying; *DRIED FLOWERS:*

   foliage 295, 298

Squares, measuring/cutting; *PATCHWORK* 213

Star block; *PATCHWORK* 234

Star pot and lid; *DOUGHCRAFT* 82-83

Starfish; *DOUGHCRAFT* 62

Starting work; *CROSS-STITCH* 159

Statice: *DRIED FLOWERS* 276

Stencils:

   PAPIER MACHE 112

   PATCHWORK 218

Sticky padding; *PATCHWORK* 221

Stippling technique; *DOUGHCRAFT* 66

Stitch-in-the-ditch; *PATCHWORK* 219

Stitches/stitching; *PATCHWORK* 211, 219

   holding quilt layers together 18, 221

   zigzagging edges 221

Stitches: all-over technique; *CROSS-STITCH* 187

   see also specific stitches

Storage tips; *DOUGHCRAFT* 61

String-layered brooch; *PAPIER MACHE* 134-135

Strip quilts; *PATCHWORK* 231

Strip sets; *PATCHWORK* 255

Strippy *PATCHWORK:*

   cat 248-249

   silk clutch bag 238-239

   silk vest 236-237

Strips; *PATCHWORK*, measuring and cutting 213

Stub wires 266

Summer bowl; *PAPIER MACHE* 116-117

Sunflowers:

   DRIED FLOWERS: 289

   DECOUPAGE 50-51

Sun, frowning; *DOUGHCRAFT* 74-75

plaque color scheme 66
Surface decoration; *DOUGHCRAFT* 61
see also Texture
Surfaces, golden sheen; *DOUGHCRAFT* 84
Swags; *DECOUPAGE* 47
Sweet tin; *DECOUPAGE* 39

T

T-shirt, dinosaur ; *CROSS-STITCH* 202-203
Table center for Valentine's Day; *DRIED FLOWERS* 286-287
Table mats:
    DECOUPAGE 42-43
    tile pattern; *CROSS-STITCH* 171
Tableware, as molds; *PAPIER MACHE* 109
Tapestry frame; *CROSS-STITCH* 160
Tapestry needles; *CROSS-STITCH* 159
Tapestry wool; *CROSS-STITCH* 156
Tap test; *DOUGHCRAFT* 65
Tartan fabrics; *CROSS-STITCH* 172
Tea cozy:
    PATCHWORK 262-263
    CROSS-STITCH 54-55
Techniques:
    CROSS-STITCH 158-159, 161-163
    DECOUPAGE 15-19
    DOUGHCRAFT 60-67
        paint:
        gold 84
        pockets 96-97
        varying effects 75
    DRIED FLOWERS 266-273
    PAPIER MACHE 107-108
Teddy bear card; *PAPIER MACHE* 125
Templates:
    DECOUPAGE 56
    DOUGHCRAFT 60, 68-71
    PATCHWORK 224-225
Tension, frame and; *CROSS-STITCH* 160
    tip for 163
Terra cotta, preparing; *DECOUPAGE* 11
Texture:
    contrasting; *DRIED FLOWERS* 267
    DOUGHCRAFT:
        flaws and accidents 60
        highlighting 66, 88
Thimbles, for quilting; *PATCHWORK* 219
Thread organizer; *CROSS-STITCH* 160
Thread:
    CROSS-STITCH:
        conversion chart 206-207

length to use 160
    soft embroidery 156
    stranded 156
    using 160
    see also specific threads
    quilting; *PATCHWORK* 219
Threading technique; *DOUGHCRAFT* 63, 75
Three-dimensional effect;
    CROSS-STITCH:
        festival sampler 197
        fruit bowl 187
        see also Motifs; CROSS-STITCH, tumbling blocks pattern
Three-quarter stitch; *CROSS-STITCH* 158
    quarter stitch with 158
Throw, starry; *CROSS-STITCH* 172-173
Tiles; *DOUGHCRAFT*:
    fish 84-85
    for color experiments 81
Tin, small hinged; *DECOUPAGE* 38-39
Tinting; *DECOUPAGE, see Coloring and tinting*
Tissue paper; *PAPIER MACHE* 113
    plaid effect 127
Tools:
    DOUGHCRAFT:
        assembling before working 75
        basic 61
        for baking 64
        for painting 66
        for varnishing 67
    PAPIER MACHE:
        for cutting 106
        for decorating 112-113
        for varnishing 113
Topiary tree; *DRIED FLOWERS* 295, 297
Towel, baby's; *CROSS-STITCH* 180-181
Toy motifs; *DECOUPAGE* 32-33
Tray, plaid; *PAPIER MACHE* 126-127
Trees; *DRIED FLOWERS*:
    mossed 295, 296
    positioning 295
    preparing the trunk and container 272, 295
    topiary 295, 297
Trinkets, as decoration; *DOUGHCRAFT* 75
Trip-around-the-world throw; *PATCHWORK* 242-245
Tripod, wire; *DOUGHCRAFT* 75-77
Trompe l'oeil effect; *DECOUPAGE* 54

Trug; *DRIED FLOWERS* 288
Tulips; *DECOUPAGE* 54-57
Twigs; *DRIED FLOWERS*:
    caged ball 300-303
    preparation 268
    tips 269
    wreaths 276-277, 290-291
Tying; *PATCHWORK* 218

U V

Undercoat; *PAPIER MACHE* 112
Unworked areas, tip for; *CROSS-STITCH* 163
Valentine basket; *DRIED FLOWERS* 286-87
Varnish:
    DECOUPAGE:
        aging 48
        effects of waxing 19
        matt 18, 32, 40, 57
        number of coats 18
        sanding next-to-last coat 18, 28, 38, 40, 51
        satin finish 18, 26, 28, 35
        see also Crackle varnish
        tips 18
    DOUGHCRAFT 67
    PAPIER MACHE 113
        tools 113
        with adhesive *see PVA medium; PAPIER MACHE*
Vegetables; *DECOUPAGE* 50-51
Vest; *PATCHWORK*:
    crazy patchwork 258-259
    man's 246-247
    silk 236-237
Victorian motifs; *DECOUPAGE* 12, 34-35

W

Walking foot; *PATCHWORK* 211, 219
Wall sconce; *DECOUPAGE* 40-41
Wall-mounted arrangement, preparation; *DRIED FLOWERS* 271
Walled garden hanging; *PATCHWORK* 250-253
Wallpaper paste:
    DOUGHCRAFT 60
    PAPIER MACHE 108
Wall vase; *DRIED FLOWERS* 279-280
Washing work; *CROSS-STITCH* 160-161
Waste canvas technique; *CROSS-STITCH* 155, 172, 192, 202
Water lily foundation cushions; *PATCHWORK* 256-257

Watercolors, applying; *DOUGHCRAFT* 66
Watercolors; *DECOUPAGE* 14-15
Watering can; *DECOUPAGE* 50-51
Water, uses; *PAPIER MACHE* 107
Waxing; *DECOUPAGE* 57
    technique 19
Wax resist technique; *DECOUPAGE* 32-33
Wheat; *DRIED FLOWERS* 279
    arrangement with alchemilla 304-307
    sheaf 312-313
White rabbit; *DOUGHCRAFT* 98-101
Wholewheat flour; *DOUGHCRAFT* 60
Willow; *DRIED FLOWERS*:
    Chinese 276
    contorted 267
Wire cutters; *DRIED FLOWERS* 266
Wire frame, wreath; *DRIED FLOWERS* 270
Wire supports; *PAPIER MACHE* 109
    cutting wire 110
    knitted 109, 138
Wire, for jewelry; *PAPIER MACHE* 113
Wire, metal-coil frame; *DOUGHCRAFT* 94-95
Wiring techniques; *DRIED FLOWERS* 266-267
Wood, prime and prepare; *DECOUPAGE* 10-11
Wool fabric; *PATCHWORK* 210
Wool thread; *CROSS-STITCH*:
    length to use 160
Woven strips; *PATCHWORK* 233
Wreaths; *DRIED FLOWERS*:
    around flowerpot 304
    country style 290-291
    preparation:
        finishing 276-277
        heart-shaped 270
        meshed wire/moss 269
        twigs 268
        wire frame 270
Wristband, child's; *CROSS-STITCH* 176-177

Z

Zigzags ; *DOUGHCRAFT* 102
Zippered, cushion; *CROSS-STITCH* 162
Zipper, inserting in cushions; *PATCHWORK* 223

ACKNOWLEDGMENTS

THE PUBLISHERS WOULD LIKE TO THANK THE AUTHORS AND CREATIVE TEAM RESPONSIBLE FOR THE PRODUCTION
OF THE **HAMLYN DISCOVER SERIES**

DECOUPAGE	**MAGGIE PHILO**	SERIES EDITORS	**JONATHAN HILTON** AND **MARY LAMBERT**
DOUGHCRAFT	**SOPHIE-JANE PRIOR** AND **SUSAN WELBY**	SERIES ART EDITOR	**PRUE BUCKNELL**
PATCHWORK	**TINA EALOVEGA**	ART EDITOR	**ALISON SHACKLETON**
CROSS-STITCH	**STEVEN JENKINS** AND **JANE FRANKLIN**	EXECUTIVE EDITOR	**JUDITH MOORE**
DRIED FLOWERS	**CHRISTOPHER HAMMOND**	ART DIRECTOR	**JACQUI SMALL**
		PHOTOGRAPHER	**LUCY MASON**

THANKS ALSO TO THE FOLLOWING PEOPLE AND ORGANIZATIONS FOR THEIR GENEROUS HELP AND SUPPORT IN THE PRODUCTION OF THIS BOOK:

SUPPLIERS OF ACCESSORIES AND PROPS

ANCHOR
(COATS PATONS CRAFTS)

CASPARI LTD AND DANWAY DESIGNS LTD
(*Donation of papers*)

THE DINING ROOM SHOP
(*Loan of props*)

FRAMECRAFT MINIATURES LTD

JOHN KALDOR
THE MANUFACTURERS OF FABRIC DESIGNED BY AMERICAN TEXTILE DESIGNER NANCY CROW
(*Supplied fabric for Trip-around-the World Throw pp. 242-245*)

MAMELOCK PRESS
(*Donation of scraps*)

SCUMBLE GOOSIE
(*Donation of items, pp. 30-31*)

TEXAS HOMECARE LTD
(*Donation of furniture, pp. 46-47 and 54-57*)

PATCHWORK DESIGNERS

KARIN ROUND WHO DESIGNED THE STRIPPY SILK VEST AND STRIPPY CLUTCH BAG
(*pp. 236–237, 238-239*)
SHARON DARGE WHO DESIGNED THE CRAZY PATCHWORK VEST AND THE DOROTHY BAG
(*pp. 258–259, 260–261*)

CROSS-STITCHERS

KATIE BARON, KATHERINE BROWN, GEORGINA BRYAN, CORINNE DAVEY, MARION DAWSON, AMELIA FRANKLIN,
DAWN HILL, DIANA JONES, SARAH JONES, LUCY MACLAREN, TRACY MEDWAY, CAROL NEVILL, LOUISE NEWMAN, DEBRA PAGE,
SHANI PHETHEAN-HUBBLE, SHEILA WHEELER, JACKIE WILSON

AND

SANDRA AND PETER, NICK AND CAROLINE, JENNY AND STEWART, GARY AND HEATHER, GARY HOPKINS,
ELIZABETH AND CYRIL JENKINS, AND KEN AND PRUE, FOR THE USE OF THEIR HOMES FOR PHOTOGRAPHY